Linking the Americas

SUNY series in Latin American and
Iberian Thought and Culture

Jorge J. E. Gracia/Rosemary Geisdorfer Feal, editors

Linking the Americas

Race, Hybrid Discourses, and the Reformulation of Feminine Identity

Lesley Feracho

State University of New York Press

*55700362

Published by
State University of New York Press, Albany

For information, address the State University of New York Press,
90 State Street, Suite 700, Albany, NY 12207

Production by Marilyn P. Semerad
Marketing by Anne M. Valentine

Library of Congress Cataloging-in-Publication Data

Feracho, Lesley, 1968–
    Linking the Americas : race, hybrid discourses, and the reformulation of
feminine identity / Lesley Feracho.
        p. cm. — (SUNY series in Latin American and Iberian thought and culture)
    Includes bibliographical references and index.
    ISBN 0-7914-6403-2
    1. Latin American literature—Women authors—History and criticism.
2. America—Literatures—Women authors.   3. Autobiography—Women
authors.   4. Women in literature.   5. Self in literature.   6. Race in
literature.   7. Jesus, Carolina Maria de. Quarto de despejo.   8. Campos,
Julieta. Tiene los cabellos rojizos y se llama Sabina.   9. Lispector, Clarice.
Hora da estrela.   10. Hurston, Zora Neale. Dust tracks on a road.   I. Title.
II. Series.

PQ7081.5.F47 2005
860.9'9287'098—dc22   2004052138

10   9   8   7   6   5   4   3   2   1

Contents

Acknowledgments

While the authorship of a book is attributed to one person, it is never truly an individual act. This book would not have been possible without the guidance and support of many people. Two of the most important that I would like to thank are my parents, Desmond and Lorna Feracho, for all their love, encouragement and care throughout.

Such an endeavor was not possible without the professors who provided both professional advice and much needed perspective on my research. Many thanks to Debra Castillo for her inspiration and invaluable input in making this book a reality. I would also like to thank my colleagues at the University of Georgia: in particular, Susan Quinlan, for her constant, untiring help in ways too numerous to count, from the very beginning of this process to the end; Barbara McCaskill, for continually providing encouragement to embrace every challenge that presented itself, and Department Chair Noel Fallows, for his support of the completion of this project. In addition, I would like to acknowledge the professors on my dissertation committee at Duke University whose guidance at the inception of this project helped lay its foundation.

In order to nurture the seeds of any intellectual spark, an idea is only the beginning. One needs time to see it grow. I am grateful to the people and departments that provided me with that time and support to focus on my research and development. Many thanks to the Director, James Jackson, and the professors of the Center for Afroamerican and African Studies at the University of Michigan. Because of the DuBois-Mandela-Rodney Postdoctoral Fellowship of 2001 and 2002, not only was I provided with financial aid for my research but most importantly, a vibrant intellectual space in which to dialogue. I also thank Marvin Lewis, Director of the Afro-Romance Institute for Languages and Literatures of the African Diaspora at the University of Missouri-Columbia for the example of his scholarship, the opportunity the Institute gave me to make important progress, and his insights into my work.

I would also like to extend heartfelt thanks to friends whose encouragement has been an important contribution to this book's completion. Special thanks to Arnetta and Ifeoma who have inspired me to constantly challenge myself and have provided important feedback for my ideas.

This work, while nurtured by many, could not be finished without an outlet for its expression. I owe gratitude to all those at SUNY Press: in particular, Rosemary Feal, Jorge Gracia, Michael Rinella and Marilyn Semerad. Their enthusiasm and input provided the outlet that saw this project to fruition.

Finally, I thank God for health, strength and for placing all the people in my path that have contributed in so many ways to the realization of this dream.

Introduction

Women and Individual and Communal Identities

An understanding of any socially and historically gendered subject must take into account definitions of the individual along with the complex interactions of peoples that form a collective. It is the interaction of the two that defines us and against which we define ourselves. In the end, one consequence of this process of mutual influences of individual and community is a greater understanding of the ways in which identity is formed and redefined.

In defining the representation of identity there are issues that are an integral part of the approaches to each self-definition—whether subjective or objective. Among these are questions of power and its effect on the development of individual agency. This inquiry in its various forms has centered on themes of entitlement to power and its uses, abuses, and levels of engagement. Because it is at the root of human interaction the dynamics of power is displayed in a wide range of arenas, among them social relations, economics, politics, science, history, and literature.

In particular, the ability to exercise power in the construction or reconstruction of identity (whether individual or communal) has been sought after throughout history, since before the written word. As critics like Debra Castillo and Trinh Minh-ha have explored in their works, who has the power to write, and consequently, who is excluded from this activity, are two important questions to be considered in studying the history of writing as a tool of yielding power.[1] Their studies have shown that the answers to these questions are different when exploring men's access to writing versus women's because of women's disenfranchisement and restricted access to instruments of empowerment. In addition, a complex web of factors ranging from race and class to historical context, sexuality, and religion mediates each woman's access to these tools. These factors when considered together contribute to a subject who is defined not only as an individual entity but also in relation to a collective—be it as part of a majority or belonging to a marginalized group. For the marginalized in particular, the process of self-definition includes a search for tools of empowerment. Among the

1

tools at their disposal, writing serves as a means of reconstructing an identity in which women are subjects, navigating sociocultural and economic forces that objectify them.

In analyzing women's literature of the Americas and especially self-representational and autobiographical texts it is important to recognize not just the sociocultural and historical differences that distinguish the experiences represented textually, but also the commonalities that can be used as a bridge between them. This book will explore how four specific works by writers Carolina Maria de Jesus, Clarice Lispector, Julieta Campos, and Zora Neale Hurston demonstrate common methodology that women of the Americas use in exploring and exercising their power of self-definition through writing.

The category "women of the Americas" in itself is an all encompassing term that is not only made up of commonalities of regional histories and social categories but is also importantly separated by specific political systems, different paths of sociocultural development, and histories of migration that in turn affect the conditions under which each woman lives—from North America to the Caribbean to the Southern Cone. An understanding of these differences and similarities is key to a greater awareness of the ways in which autobiographical and self-representational texts in particular have been used to reconstruct identities where women are subjects. For women of African descent this process has included the reevaluation of the concepts of race, diaspora, and dominant versus marginal subject positions. As an African American scholar and second-generation Caribbean woman, these issues of migration and the navigation of different cultural and historical codes have influenced the formation of my personal and professional identity. As I navigate the spaces that constitute my subjectivity, the lens through which I reconstruct an identity linked to the communities to which I belong are consequently in a constant state of adjustment and readjustment. The definition of "community" in itself is as multiple as the identities which can be used to define me. The communities of the Caribbean and African Americans and the discourses of representation at work in each context are as important factors in my self-definition as any biological familial unit.

Similarly, in this book each subject's navigation of subjectivity and community extends far beyond the family to encompass the complex historical, social, and political contexts of each region, ranging from the United States in the 1940s through Brazil of the 1960s and 1970s to Cuba of the 1980s. In an age that some define using the terms "global," "post modern," "syncretic," or "diasporic" in specific cases, the impact of hybridity and cross-cultural connections in particular is critical in understanding current redefinitions of the self. For this reason, I have chosen contemporary texts from three countries—Brazil, Cuba, and the United States—whose sociocultural and historic contexts embody notions of hybridity, especially in terms of the postcolonial racial history of Cuba and Brazil compared to the United States. As Michael Dash observes in *The Other America: Caribbean Literature in a New World Context* (1998), the migrations and intersections of social, political, and historical factors that affect this process can especially be examined in the literature of the "heteroglossic" Americas, a region uniting sometimes complementary, sometimes originally antagonistic forces. Consequently, in a region with a history as complex as the Americas these dialogues are necessarily fluid and exemplary of the concept of hybridity that I will discuss here.

One important link between the various feminine voices in this region is the process of what I term the reformulation of identity that each author undertakes in her work. As part of this process each subject (re)creates not a static product but rather a fluid exchange between the author, protagonist, text, and sociocultural factors that influence her. The prefix *re* indicates that a self-definition is already present at the time the subject chooses to express herself in the written medium. However, as a result of social or ontological forces, this individual exercises agency in redefining herself in a way that promotes empowerment. As Neuman observes, this project is especially important for people who have been prohibited from exercising full subjectivity:

> At the same time they have refused to relinquish the possibility of a unified self: why give up a visibility and a position from which to act, a visibility and a position only just beginning to become available in either social praxis or literary theory to those who are not Euro-American, white, middle-class and male. Moreover, for women, people of colour, colonial peoples, the poor, and non-heterosexuals . . . the understanding of the material as well as the discursive circumstances of their oppression is a primary step towards freedom from that oppression through self-possession. (217)

By rejecting the universal self as a model this theorization opens up spaces for marginalized identities to assert their subjectivity.

While the concept of a unified subject is one strategic site of social and literary empowerment, my analysis of the four texts from the United States, Cuba, and Brazil will center on three key questions about women's redefinition of selfhood that challenge this representation as the only source of power from which to contest oppressive discourses:

How is the reformulation of identity a hybrid process that connects social, historical, political, and discursive or textual factors?

How is hybridity represented in contemporary women's texts
across the multilingual Americas that specifically deal with
the ramifications of writing and self-representation?

What do these different representations of hybridity imply
for future conceptions of feminine writing?

There is ultimately a common link in the reformulative processes of identity experienced in the four texts I will analyze. Despite the markedly
varied consciousness of historical positioning displayed by the protagonists, the differences in their ontological beliefs and the discursive frameworks used, all four authors exhibit three interwoven conditions of
self-reflexivity, displacement, and hybridity.

Autobiography and the Self-Reflexive Text

Regardless of their focus, what these texts share is a varying degree of
self-representation that defines them as autobiography or self-reflexive.
As Laura Marcus notes in her study *Auto/biographical Discourses: Theory,
Criticism, Practice,* studies of autobiography historically began with the
assumption of a unified self that used the genre to represent itself textually—whether it be for confessional purposes or to serve as an exemplary
text for others to follow. As autobiographical criticism developed, the
focus on the self was achieved through the emphasis on categories of
presence/absence, unity/alienation, and self/text that would fall into
one of two possible approaches: (1) the emphasis on subjectivity and the
essential self or, (2) the impossibility of self-representation and the only
certainty being the existence of a self divided between the subject that
writes and the subject that is written (Marcus 183).

As de Man states, there is a mutual influence in the autobiographical text that also breaks boundaries of reality and fiction. As part of each
individual re-creation of identity through writing, the discursive framework chosen to facilitate this reformative process significantly influences
the subject's textual articulation so "that the autobiographical project
may itself produce and determine the life and that whatever the writer
does is in fact governed by the technical demands of self-portraiture"
(69). This cycle of influence is, however, limited by the inevitable instability of the autobiography because of its inability to provide a total

revelation of the author or subject through the textual subject. The gap between the author and second subject is further complicated by the lack of an essentialized, unified being. It is a multifaceted constructed self, created by the interaction of social, political, and ideological factors. Ultimately, therefore, what defines the autobiographical act and, consequently, the autobiographical subject, is the exploration of the possibility of representing the historically positioned subject through language and in accordance with the parameters of the specific discourse used.

In the context of women's autobiographical narratives these questions of the possibility of representing the self through written discourse become even more complex. When women's historical silencing—social, economic, and artistic—is placed alongside these theories of subjectivity, the question of the effect of the possible death of the subject on women's writing as empowerment becomes especially important. Marcus notes that in general, debates about the death of the subject brought about a change in the terms used: "What seems to have emerged from this process is a stronger sense of the plurality and the social construction of subjectivities and, possibly, a shift from concepts of "subjectivity" to those of "identity" and "difference," concepts less philosophically burdened and more overtly attuned to culture and history" (201). I have chosen to include fiction, diaries, journals, letters, memoirs, and testimonials in the genre of autobiographical narrative and in a larger scope, as self-referential texts. The foundation for this framework is based on definitions of metafiction that explore the blurring of boundaries in the literary text and beyond. Linda Hutcheon points out the breaking down of boundaries in metafiction, particularly between the reader and the act itself, leading to its incorporation as "thematized parts of the narrative situation, *acknowledged* as having a co-producing function" (*Narcissistic Narrative* 37). However, as Patricia Waugh points out, the crossing of boundaries goes beyond the reader's relationship with the text and extends into the role between the characters themselves and the concepts of reality and history: "If, as individuals, we now occupy 'roles' rather than 'selves,' then the study of characters in novels may provide a useful model for understanding the construction of subjectivity in the world outside the novels. . . . Literary fiction . . . becomes a useful model for learning about the construction of 'reality' itself" (3). As this wall is broken down, metafictional writing turns on itself and "consistently displays its conventionality, which explicitly and overtly lays bare its condition of artifice, and which thereby explores the problematic relationship between life and fiction (Waugh 4). As such, the very concept of history is challenged, as metafiction serves as "both a response and a contribution to an even more thoroughgoing sense that reality or history are provisional: no longer a world of

eternal verities but a series of constructions, artifices, impermanent structures" (Waugh 7). Hutcheon agrees that such concepts are undone by
metafiction, and by postmodern fiction in particular:

> Historiographic metafiction suggests that truth and falsity may
> indeed not be the right terms in which to discuss fiction. . . . The
> interaction of the historiographic and the metafictional fore-
> grounds the rejection of the claims of both 'authentic' repre-
> sentation and 'inauthentic' copy alike, and the very meaning
> of artistic originality is as forcefully challenged as is the trans-
> parency of historical referentiality. (76–77)

Of particular relevance to my readings of these four women's texts is
Hutcheon's situation of historiographic metafiction in the postmodern
context because of its representation of unstable narrative voices "that
use memory to try to make sense of the past. It both installs and then
subverts traditional concepts of subjectivity; it both asserts and is capable
of shattering 'the unity of man's being" (85).

Based on these designations, I define this discourse that connects all
four writers, as one which attempts some degree of representation of the
reality of the writing subject as the written subject. While I use an umbrella
term of self-referential texts to connect the four writers, all in one sense or
another represent different types and levels of metafiction in accordance
with some of the guidelines I have established. While *Quarto de despejo* and
Dust Tracks on a Road, for example, are autobiographies in the strictest sense
(diary and autobiography or even memoir respectively), *A hora da estrela* and
Tiene los cabellos rojizos y se llama Sabina are more representative of metafiction
because of the incorporation of the author into the text.[2] Both texts exemplify
what Raymond Federman calls 'surfiction' while *Sabina* in particular could
also be seen as a 'self-begetting novel' where the character develops into the
author of the very text being read (Waugh 14).

Subject Position and the Impact of Race

In this study of self-representational texts one significant component of the
approach used to assess each woman's reformulation of identity is a consideration of subject position. In particular I explore the ways in which the
complexities of race (as a historical, social, and political construct) as a
framework for understanding each subject's dialogue with the discourses
of marginality and centrality affect identity development. Two theories in
particular will orient this discussion of the movement between external
and internal structures. The first theory is Barbara Johnson's analysis of

Hurston's textual manipulations of her identity as representative of the movement between inside and outside discourses: "I soon came to see however, not only that the insider becomes an outsider the minute she steps out of the inside but also that Hurston's work itself was constantly dramatizing and undercutting just such inside/outside opposition, transforming the plane geometry of physical space into the complex transactions of discursive exchange" (130). What Johnson highlights is a dialogue (or "discursive exchange") that takes place on the level of the individual's sociohistoric position and the textual plane. When the inside/outside opposition is erased, Hurston, as subject, navigates these levels to the extent that the distinctions are blurred: the discourses operating on each level interact with, sometimes collide with, and ultimately redefine each other and the very meanings of inside/outside as points of origin.

The second theoretical framework for my analysis is based on the internal/external–insider/outsider dialectic as articulated by Nelson Vieira in his study *Jewish Voices in Brazilian Literature*. The foundation for this dialectic is the social marginalization of immigrant Jewish families in Brazil who were redefined as Other yet resident and their attempts to come to terms with such a unique categorization. Vieira's reworking of these terms seeks to understand the workings of a society that tries to impose national unity and homogeneity at the cost of difference:

> Nevertheless, the insider-outsider optic is useful as a starting point because it allows us to see the contrast between Brazil's pervasive nationalist ideology of cultural assimilation or cohesiveness and its muted expression of cultural differences. . . . In addition, we learn to question how writers express themselves when their ethnicity is overshadowed by the dominant culture. (N. Vieira 6, 16)

While Vieira's application of the insider/outsider perspective is used here to represent the sociocultural, political, and economic situation of Jews as a community throughout the Jewish Diaspora, it is a dialogical relationship that can be applied on an individual level within similarly structured sociocultural, political, and economic frameworks.

Displacement and Negotiations of Identity

The insider/outsider perspective as a process brought about in part by migrations of the subject is a significant link in the reformulation of identity of the four protagonists I discuss. As subjects having to experience the destabilization of displacement and marginalization, their navigation of inside/outside subject positions in their new cultural and political contexts is very much influenced by their dislocation. This crossing of experiences through migration, as Boyce Davies points out, is a unifying factor in Black women's experiences: "It is the convergence of multiple places and cultures that renegotiates the terms of Black women's experiences that in turn negotiates and renegotiates their identities" (3). As a result, their experience can be seen as: "a series of boundary crossings and not as a fixed, geographical, ethnically or nationally bound category of writing,"(4). While these boundary crossings are specifically relevant here to Jesus's and Hurston's experience, as a journey marked by dislocation and multiple encounters I contend that this dynamic is relevant in all four women's texts, from Jesus to Lispector and Campos.

Historically, particularly since the 1920s, Brazil has seen large migration patterns of rural citizens of the northeast territories moving to the more industrialized south (especially cities like São Paulo and Rio de Janeiro) in search of work and ultimately a better life. Despite their desires for the Brazilian dream, many faced obstacles of unemployment (in part because of too few jobs for such a great demand), lack of any or adequate housing, and experiences of discrimination. This continuous pattern has been documented by not only historians and sociologists alike but by writers, as seen in texts like Graciliano Ramos's *Vidas secas*, (*Barren Lives*) Gomez Dias' *O pagador de promessas*, (The Payer of Promises) and Clarice Lispector's *A hora da estrela*. By contrast, Jesus's story began in rural Minas Gerais, in the town of Sacramento. She was only able to finish two years of formal schooling, during which time a mysterious illness in her legs forced her to leave home in search of medical attention. This odyssey and the people she met during her travels are documented in her third text, posthumously titled *Diário de Bitita* (*Bitita's Diary*). In a style reminiscent of a Bildungsroman, Jesus learns important lessons about human nature and the impact knowledge can have on other's perception of one's identity. After leaving in order to find work with her mother, she is forced to migrate years later with her own family. This time she moves to São Paulo, becoming one of thousands of Brazilians who have traveled similar routes before her.[3] This journey is marked not just by physical change but also by emotional adaptation. As a result, her diary chronicles her daily routines and incorporates the underlying theme of knowledge and the definitions of the self in her new urban setting. From her early interactions with the residents of Sacramento to her relationships with the other inhabitants of the *favela* (slums) of São Paulo, Jesus had to navigate the dynamics of her education versus societal limitations (Levine and Meihy 18–21).[4] The continuous clashes between these two factors have been especially heightened by the instability of displacement. One effect is that Jesus is compelled to utilize different types of insider/outsider discourses in order to develop an empowering self-definition.

A careful analysis of the insider/outsider interaction as presented by Nelson Vieira clarifies its importance in understanding Lispector's positioning and definition in Brazilian society. As Gotlib records in her biography *Clarice*, Lispector was born to Jewish parents in the Ukraine in December 1920, though she spent no more than two months in that region before finally settling with her parents in February 1921 in Alagoas, Brazil. As a result of a politically motivated exile Lispector had to face her unique position as Other in Brazilian society yet also resident. Vieira's insider/outsider dialectic helps us comprehend the tension that exists between national enforcement of homogeneity and individual difference that is often suppressed, as well as the ways in which cultural assimilation is promoted at the expense of cultural differences. For the writer of ethnic descent like Lispector, this relationship of insider/outsider is often represented on a personal level: "Studying this phenomenon lets us view the Brazilian inside from the Jewish outside and vice versa. . . . In addition, we learn to question how writers express themselves when their ethnicity is overshadowed by the dominant culture" (N. Vieira 16). Equally as important is the sense of displacement that marks Lispector's dual identity and is in turn reflected in her writing. As a writer caught between Judaic heritage (historically and culturally) and a Brazilian tradition (with its Portuguese, African, and indigenous influences), both her nonfictional and fictional texts like *A hora da estrela* (*The Hour of the Star*) chart her navigation of belonging and dislocation in her search for understanding of the self and its relationship to another being. For Lispector, this maneuvering of boundaries is represented in her investigation of the nature of the self, gender, and genre. Because of the influence of her family's migration to Brazil, this process results in the creation of concepts of identity and genre that are marked by displacement and movement between poles of marginal and central positions.

In the case of Julieta Campos, the theme of migration, adaptation, and belonging that are part of the experience of displacement is evident on both a personal and textual level. As a writer who has lived in both the Caribbean as a Cuban citizen and in Latin America as a Mexican resident, Campos's personal identity has been marked by fluid identities of citizenship and Otherness. Her story of departures and arrivals through the Americas is in fact representative of the migrations and interconnections that have historically, socially, and politically characterized the region. Campos's literary works reveal the strong links that exist between her literary vision and her philosophies of life. As Leland Chambers states in his introduction to the English version of *Tiene los cabellos rojizos y se llana Sabina:*

> It is a novel about writing a novel; it is about the subject-object relationship; it is metafictional and intertextual; it is a feminist work that attempts to dislodge the prevailing masculine logocentrism of our culture; it is a Latin American representative of the nouveau roman; it explores one means by which the narrator of the work can be drawn into the narrative and thus it demonstrates that writers cannot truly stand outside their work; it is a triumph of the intellect, aided by the unconscious. (xv–xvi)

The metafictional approach to identity evident here is one that Campos has developed throughout her career. In her three books of criticism—*La imagen en el espejo* (The Image in the Mirror, 1965), *Oficio de leer* (The Role of Reading, 1971), and *Función de la novela* (Function of the Novel 1973) Campos develops a theory of creative production akin to the theories of Natalie Sarraute and Claude Simon (Campos *Sabina* xiii). In *La imagen en el espejo* she summarizes the relationship of the artist with his or her creation and the world which and in which the artist creates by stressing,

> The painter, the writer, is not at the outer margins of the world as a spectator with a singular capacity for establishing other universes within that world. He is one more object within the world, and he can be observed from the outside by a spectator capable of observing his work, observing him creating his work, observing the world that he has created within the world. (98)

These structural and ideological migrations have enabled Campos to create texts that defy strict categorizations as exemplary of Cuban writing or Latin American writing in general, as part of a Modernist tradition or the new Latin American narrative in particular. As such, critics like Chambers consider Campos's blurring of nonfictional and gendered boundaries as postmodernist works because of its questioning and destabilization of ideas of center and periphery:

> This restless narrative continually introduces new elements, some historical, some geographical, and a great many of them literary—for this novelist, Juliet Campos, is quite aware of her position within a sophisticated, post-modern literary tradition

that is fundamentally European in origin. She refers with complete familiarity to many of the most noted exemplars of Modernist Aesthetics—starting with Proust on page 1—and as often as not she rejects their hegemony over Sabina. Campos rejects as firmly the values of the only distinctive voice invented by Sabina, the threatening masculine voice that is so eager to produce hackneyed and sensationalist works intended to become instantaneous Best Sellers. (Campos, *Sabina* 17–18)

Ultimately, the source of the text's structure is the unconscious. Nonetheless, the ordered world of the novel is inscribed within "the chaotic universe of reality" while the fictional and nonfictional stories proceed on parallel paths. In the end, "the extent to which the work 'configures' a new reality capable of being perceived by others allows for this new, more significant and revelatory vision of reality to join with and begin to alter the old" (Campos, *La imagen* 15). These ideological, structural, and visionary movements are what constitute the hybridity of Campos's text as a challenge to the negative ramifications of displacement.

The last text, *Dust Tracks on a Road*, is an autobiography written by the African American anthropologist, novelist, and folklorist Zora Neale Hurston. While *Dust Tracks* stands in contrast to the works of Lispector and Campos that move outside of the markers of historical and sociocultural contexts to define their female protagonists, it also exemplifies the effects of the author's displacment on the structure of the text.

Similar to Jesus, Zora Neale Hurston occupied different subject positions as a result of her travels from Alabama to Florida and later to other countries around the world as anthropologist and writer. As a young girl from Alabama who grew up in Florida and later received her education at Barnard College, Hurston crossed class lines, from the rural, working-class South to the heart of the privilege of academic life. In the process her self-definition also underwent changes, demonstrating the complex interaction of class, race, gender, and religion in the subject's navigation of individual and societal identity. As Johnson's insider/outsider theory attests, Hurston moved between different physical and discursive sites, from outsider to participant and back. These transitions were difficult, leaving her constantly faced with the challenge of balancing multiple discourses, drawing on each to redefine herself in a new sociocultural and political context.

One result was a sense of displacement that manifested itself on an individual, thematic, and discursive level. The stories of *Dust Tracks* trace Hurston's southern roots and northern development, charting the precarious bridging of the distance between the two. The linguistic registers in which Hurston relates her life experiences between the South and the North also exemplify this uneasy tension: at times colloquial and at times formal, implicitly questioning and challenging the concept of belonging for herself and the collectives (Black, female, southern, working class, and academic) which she to a degree represents. Hurston's combination of anthropology and fiction creates a work that demonstrates that esthetic and social concerns are not mutually exlusive and can be present in one work. As she states, "When I began to make up stories I cannot say. Just from one fancy to another, adding more and more detail until they seemed real" (52–53). The result of this hybridity, blending truth and fiction, is a problematization of and displacement from both. This movement between both approaches reveals the spaces where they intersect to create a product which reflects as much on the process of creating a hybrid text to perform a "statue of the self" as on the product itself.

Hybridity and the Feminine Subject

For all four women, one strategic result of and reaction to the projects of self-representation given positions of marginality and conditions of dis-placement is hybridity on various levels. My application of the concept of hybridity is informed by theories of difference, destabilization, mar-gin, and center in a postcolonial and in some cases, specifically postmodern context. In particular, I turn to the work of Ashcroft, Griffiths, and Tiffin in *The Empire Writes Back*, the extension of their argument in the work of Vijay Mishra and Bob Hodge, Stuart Hall's work titled "Cultural Identity and Diaspora," and bell hooks's "Postmodern Blackness."

According to Ashcroft, Griffiths and Tiffin as well as Mishra and Hodge, the unfixed state of discourses in nonsettler colonies leads to an inability to fix meaning: "[M]eaning grows out of a dialectical process of a relationship between the margins and the center (meaning arises out of a discourse of marginality); meanings are not culture-specific" (Mishra and Hodge 286). Consequently, as Ashcroft, Griffith, and Tiffin conclude, the postcolonial representation of such displacement is always character-ized by "a complex and hybridized formation" (10).

Stuart Hall's literary and cinematic interrogation of the cohesive-ness and yet fractured state of cultural identity and its implications for representation and power of the Black subject also reveal important ideas about multiple subject positions. His sense of difference as British and Caribbean subject and his observations of the postcolonial Caribbean illustrate that in one sense: "This second sense of difference challenges the fixed binaries which stabilize meaning and representation and show

how meaning is never finished or completed, but keeps on moving to encompass other, additional or supplementary meanings" (397).

Given these conditions, identity goes beyond permanent positionings of the subject to something " 'strategic' and arbitrary. . . . [M]eaning continues to unfold, so to speak, beyond the arbitrary closure which makes it, at any moment, possible" (Hall 397).

Nonetheless, when speaking of the impact of these theories of difference on postcolonial subjects of color, the ramifications of such a destabilizing process threaten to weaken the acquired social and political power of these groups. As a response to these fears, hooks states that:

> Postmodern culture with its decentered subject can be the space where ties are severed or it can provide the occasion for new and varied forms of bonding. To some extent, ruptures, surfaces, contextuality, and a host of other happenings create gaps that make space for oppositional practices which no longer require intellectuals to be confined by narrow separate spheres with no meaningful connection to the world of the everyday. (427)

My definition of hybridity draws on the theories of difference presented here, incorporating the strategic positionings and relationship between margin and center emphasized as a major characteristic of the postcolonial experience. Nonetheless, it parallels hooks's assessment that such a project does not mean the end of cohesive identities based on race and culture, as in the African American experience and by careful extension, in the experience of other marginalized groups, like women (of color, and so on).

Hybridity as I will use the term is therefore the process whereby authors combine extratextual and textual subjects in a way that highlights the movement between positions of marginality and positions of centrality. This interaction occurs on a metatextual and textual level and encompasses sociocultural, racial, textual, gendered, and linguistic structures. One reason for hybridity in women's texts stems from the sociocultural, economic, and political marginalization that has historically been commonplace. Despite significant advances, on some levels this marginalization continues to occur. When engaging in the project of literary self-representation many writers use all the discursive strategies available and occupy various sites in order to subvert male-centered modes of communication. One strategy employed is the use of marginalized discourses, inspired in part by the condition of Other out of which they have historically had to fight, alongside the deconstruction of male-centered discourses. The result is an expanded definition of what constitutes feminine writing that is chiefly characterized by the dialogic relationship of marginal and central discourses.

My analysis of Jesus, Lispector, Campos, and Hurston's self-representational texts demonstrates how their creation of "statues of the self" is informed by experiences of marginalization, movement inside and outside of sociocultural, historical, and racial discourses, displacement, and desires to redefine their subject positions. All four authors utilize multiple narrative discourses in an interaction of extratextual and textual subjects to explore hybrid representations of the individual. The result is writing that provides a forum for the discussion of women's strategies for obtaining and keeping their agency despite society's attempts to marginalize them while exploring the contributions of these critiques to reshaping and expanding what we define as feminine writing.

Chapter One

The Radicalization of Marginality in Jesus's *Quarto de despejo: Diário de uma favelada*

Autobiographical Writing and Women's Agency

In establishing their subjectivity women have used writing as a means of chronicling personal growth and actively redefining themselves in a society that oftentimes had already established categories of identification for them. This has not proven easy because of societal restrictions, whether it be in North America or Latin America. As Debra Castillo notes, "Women in Latin America are consciously involved in a practice that has long been recognized in their male counterparts. To play on a famous structuralist formulation, to write in Latin America is for them more than a verb, transitive or intransitive—it is a revolutionary act" (20). The principal reason for the revolutionary nature of this act is its transgression of historically traditional established norms governing gender roles, especially in the area of literary production. One of the most important difficulties women writers face is lack of opportunity and agency. For lower-income women in particular, denied access to continued formal education to develop reading and writing skills, as well as women financially unable to pursue a career in writing, the only outlet for their life stories is through the mediation of others. However, by telling their stories to others what is affected and compromised are individual agency and the development of a voice as subject. In cases where women have had to tell their stories to mediators of disparate socioeconomic backgrounds, one challenge has been the navigation of differences of privilege and hierarchy between the subject and the collaborative voice (Castillo 29).

There has been not only limited access to literary production for women but also a difference in the terms used to classify men and women's application of knowledge. Men are oftentimes categorized as lucid beings while women are seen as purely intuitive. As Castillo observes:

> This explains the different status given the representative man's self-reflection which is seen as a self-construction which can represent the terms of identity of his culture and epoch and women's self-writings which are seen as 'merely' autobiographical, subjective and personal, failing to ramify beyond their immediate context, other than to confirm women's narrow self regard for their inchoate natures. (28–29)

Women, however, have found ways of breaking the silence and participating in literary activities that allow for self-expression. Diaries, letters, testimonials, and memoirs proved especially open to personal expression when other forms of writing were prohibited, allowing women, especially in the case of the first two categories, to record private thoughts without fear of public criticism.

The struggle then became the legitimization of these personal writings as important texts in understanding feminine subjects. As Laura Marcus points out in *Auto/biographical Discourses: Theory, Criticism, Practice*, women have historically been situated outside the laws of genre and selfhood within which the 'pacts' of fiction and of history operate (230). However, progressive feminist studies of the autobiographical genre have recognized its ever-expanding parameters and consequently, the importance of these literary categories in tracing the development of the feminine subject in a particular socioeconomic, historical, and political environment, and as texts in their own right that provide more than just biographical knowledge. In *A Poetics of Women's Autobiography*, Sidonie Smith presents an inclusive definition of autobiography that opens up a space for these forms of writing:

> Since all gesture and rhetoric is revealing of the subject, autobiography can be defined as any written or verbal communication. More narrowly it can be defined as written or verbal communication that takes the speaking "I" as the subject of the narrative, rendering the "I" both subject and object. From that operational vantage point, autobiography includes letters, journals, diaries, and oral histories. (19)

The construction of this self is an aspect that is especially exposed in autobiographical writings, represented not only in terms of women's socioeconomic evolution but also in terms of the psychic construction of femininity. On one hand these writings are a vehicle for female self-expression, while on the other hand if read 'symptomatically' they can reveal, as Simone de Beauvoir says (qtd. in Marcus 221), how one becomes a woman.

This subjective process of socialization and its multiple representations in the autobiographical narrative is a necessary element in understanding the reformulation of individual identity. In particular, the diary has been legitimated as a form of autobiographical narrative that has proven especially useful in understanding women's reconstruction of the self. The structure is one that allows the writer to record daily events and emotions that have an impact on her life in a personal forum, usually without the pressures of writing for a specific readership.

Among the emotions the subject is free to explore is the content written solely for the subject's edification. This intimate expression of self-analysis makes the diary very similar to what Raoul defines as the "journal intime." However, the subsequent redirection of the diary to a wider audience bestows Jesus's writing with qualities of an autobiographical narrative. Yet, given these dual incentives of self-reflection and public display, the text serves as an example of and challenge to definitions of diary and autobiography.

According to Raoul part of the diary's attraction for women writers is the self-reflexive textuality that explores the uncertainty of the constructed self as well as its relation to writing. This is achieved by the triple self-projection of author/character/reader characteristic of the journal intime. Through this projection the "I" subject is converted into an "I" object and "I" addressee. Stylistically, Raoul notes the use of suspension to mark hesitation, rhetorical questions, exclamations, parentheses, short meandering sentences, and gaps as examples of this analysis of the subject's tenuous positioning in the text (59–60).

Gilkin also notes that the diary's chief characteristics are "[i]mmediacy, authenticity, accessibility accretion, density, fragmentation and repetition. . . . Written in the moment or about the . . . moments recollected from a day, diaries draw their readers into their moments of being" (5). It is this reliving of the subject's life over a period of weeks, months and years that Gilkin believes "shows us individuals in a process of creating what may be called spontaneous autobiographies, narratives of the self as the self unfolds" (3–4). The use of these stylistic features of the diary to recount important moments from her life in the favela allows Jesus to not just narrate and explore the self, as Raoul and Gilkin propose, but reformulate it in relation to her historical positioning. In this sense, Gilkin's theory of spontaneous autobiography falls short by not accounting for the active reformulation of selfhood.

The act of using writing within a specific discursive model in a self-reflexive way is what makes Jesus's endeavor an autobiographical one. This participation in the autobiographical act allows an examination of the degree to which her diary incorporates the four principles Smith believes are present in women's autobiography (45–46).

While the diary lends itself to a freer structure and unlimited thematic content, it does have thematic characteristics that distinguish it from other forms and provide the reader with a certain sense of constancy each time the diary is read. As Judy Simons notes in her book *Diaries and Journals of Literary Women from Fanny Burney to Virginia Wolf*:

> The format of the diary, with its record of routine personal activity, naturally encourages introspection in its conscious recall of individuals' encounters with others or, more usually, with themselves. Repeatedly, women's diaries document their loneliness, highlighting the lack of comfort and understanding available to them in their daily lives. (8)

These first two chapters highlight the extra- and intratextual elements that work together in Jesus's formulation of her identity through her diary *Quarto de despejo: Diário de uma favelada*, as well as the effects of the autobiographical discourse on the reformulation of the individual subject.

This first chapter focuses on Jesus's redefined identity through the interaction of inner and outer discourses on social, racial, and structural levels. In chapter 2 I apply the principles of Vieira's insider/outsider framework and Johnson's analyses of the inside/outside oppositions in autobiography to Jesus's text in order to demonstrate how she creates a hybrid discourse of individual representation on a thematic level. Ultimately, the text displays a hybridity of marginal and dominant discourses while opening up questions about its applicability as a possible representation of feminine writing and the problematics of the definitions and challenges of such a categorization.

My analysis will focus on the edited, published diary *Quarto de despejo* while also referencing her unedited manuscript and collection of posthumously published poetry *Meu estranho diário*. Given the complicated nature of Dantas' collaboration and intervention, these original manuscripts provide a fuller account of an individual who in the edited diary was:

> . . . a different woman from the one that emerges from the pages of her unedited diaries. The former was docile, wistful, and seemingly reluctant to comment on the gritty realities of Brazilian politics. Dantas presented her through his editing as

a woman who was aware of her miserable condition but who stood at a curious distance from the events she lived through. (Levine 15)

The subject that emerges has a clearer sense of her voice, particularly as a poet, and her relationship to the community of poor and favelados. However, my study will focus on her edited diary as a text, however mediated, that is still able to reveal within the mediated discourses and silences the important aspects of her redefinition as a hybrid process that navigates insider/outsider identity.

As I later discuss in my analysis of Hurston's work, the study of this dynamic between the edited and "non-mediated" voice is a point of comparison between Jesus, Hurston, and other writers still to be explored, that reveals the complex process for subjectivity that Black women writers of the diaspora must navigate.

Jesus: The Early Writer

Jesus was born in Sacramento, Minas Gerais, in Brazil in 1914, in a rural area populated mainly by descendants of slaves. In Sacramento, Jesus was not exposed to the comforts of life but had to struggle with her family to survive. Although not initially interested in attending school, she was convinced to attend by the White woman who ran the school. She was only able, however, to receive two years of formal education before she and her mother were forced to leave because of a new job made available outside of Sacramento. These two years nonetheless were enough to provide her with the basic reading and writing skills that would later result in a writing career.

Jesus was eventually forced to move to one of the *favelas* in Canindé, São Paulo, struggling to support herself and her three children by collecting and selling paper and tin cans. In an attempt to record her life but at the same time escape from the poverty that surrounded her, Jesus started writing fiction (especially short stories) and poetry. In 1955 she decided to concentrate her efforts on writing a diary of her life in the favela. In 1958, while involved in a shouting match with neighbors at the dedication of a new playground, Jesus's threats to record everything in her diary aroused the interest of journalist Audálio Dantas, sent to cover the inauguration ceremony. After contacting Jesus and reading some of her diary, Dantas edited and published segments of it in 1960 under the title *Quarto de despejo: Diário de uma favelada* translated in English as *Child of the Dark: the Diary of Carolina Maria de Jesus*. In general it covers Jesus's life from July 15, 1955, to January 1, 1960, with gaps in between. The recollections she places in the diary can be grouped into five broad categories: (1) Her personal routine; (2) observations and emotions about life in the favela; (3) social commentary (for example, neighbors' behavior, relations between Black and White Brazilians, etc.); (4) future plans for herself and her family; and (5) political commentary. The diary turned out to be an unexpected financial success, outselling the 1960 novel published by best-selling Brazilian author Jorge Amado. Critically however, its impact on discussions of social inequities was recognized but not its possible exemplification of high art.

Quarto de despejo's financial success allowed Jesus and her three children to live the dream they always had, to leave the favela and move to a better neighborhood. For six years they lived in a brick house in Osasco, until the prejudices of her neighbors and the press as well as dwindling finances forced them to move to a more affordable house. It was during her stay in Osasco that Jesus wrote her second diary, the follow up to *Quarto*, entitled *Casa de alvenaria: Diário de uma ex-favelada*. While this text was also a realistic portrayal of Jesus's life, it was a happier one because of her change in fortune. The public's reaction to this second book however was not as good as the first. Despite the cold reception, Jesus continued to write and publish over the next few years. In all she published four books after *Quarto de Despejo*: *Casa de alvenaria* (*I'm going to have a little house*, 1961), *Provérbios de Carolina Maria de Jesus* (*Proverbs of Carolina Maria de Jesus*, 1963), *Pedaços da fome* (*Pieces of Hunger*, 1963), and the posthumously published *Diário de Bitita*. The result of her literary failures and the decline of her celebrity status, however, was poverty, forcing Jesus and family to move back to the poorer sections of São Paulo, although not to the poverty of the favela of years before. Jesus died in February of 1977, seventeen years after the success of her diary, but economically in only a slightly better situation than before its publication.

When studying Jesus's life, critics always focus on two questions: what caused the incredible success of her first diary, and why, given that success did her life end in such poverty? While the answer to the second question is a complex fusion of issues of racial, gender-based, and class prejudices, combined with pressure to conform to particular societal standards and the nature of publications, the first can be answered in part by understanding the historical situation in which she was writing.

In the midst of the national debate on progress, Jesus's voice called attention to its negative consequences. Levine astutely notes that the Jesus of *Quarto de despejo* was a societal product who reflected the distance between rich and poor, the inability to ascend socially, and the perpetuation of poverty in the country (46–47). Her diary was received in part as an indictment of the political and economic system from one of the marginalized most affected by its weakness and least empowered to speak.

Under Kubitschek's presidency the racial, class, and gender inequities became even more apparent, despite his promise for "fifty years of progress in five" (Skidmore 174). Although the newly constructed capital of Brasília served as a monument to this ideal of progress, this symbolic gesture was not able to erase the poverty faced by a great number of Brazilians. Nonetheless, Jesus's challenge to these politics, although not explicitly calling for action, encouraged closer scrutiny of the treatment of the disenfranchised while still in its own way keeping alive the possibility that change was possible. As Meihy and Levine note in *Cinderela negra:*

[The social involvement as such becomes an explicative element for the understanding of the trajectory of *Quarto.* The alliance of civil society and the support of the government corroborate the hypothesis of the transitoriness of the woman from the favela. In this sense the book definitively influenced community action . . .][1]

O envolvimento social portanto passa a ser elemento explicativo para o entendimento da trajetória do *Quarto.* A aliança da sociedade civil e o apoio do governo corroboram a hipótese da transitoriedade favelada. Neste sentido o livro influenciou definitivamente a ação comunitária. (125–126)

Meihy and Levine point out an important aspect of both *Quarto de despejo* and its author: their complexity. Neither Jesus nor her text gave clear, unequivocal answers about the reality of poverty in the favelas and its solutions. In fact, while denouncing those left behind by the "projeto desenvolvimentista," *Quarto de despejo* still reveals a belief in its redemptive power:

[[T]he book became one more emblem. As a filter between the semicolonial world that came from the interior of the country and another, a proof of the future, Carolina's words confirmed the belief in the project of development.]

[O]livro passou a ser um emblema a mais. Como filtro entre o mundo semicolonial que vinha do interior do país e o outro, atestado do futuro, as palavras de Carolina confirmavam a crença no projeto desenvolvimentista. (Meihy and Levine 126)

As both authors note, Jesus's problem was not just declining sales but a lack of acceptance by the middle-class Brazilian society of which she wanted to be a part, as well as by the press that originally hailed her as a star:

Ninguém, contudo, procurava entender os dilemas que expli-
cariam as contradições e apelos de uma migrante, ex-favelada
que, num contexto tão conturbado como o dos anos 60 e 70,
teria dificuldade de ajustamento. (39)

No one, nonetheless, tried to understand the dilemmas that
would explain the contradictions and appeals of a migrant,
ex-slumdweller who, in a context as turbulent as the 60s and
70s, would have difficulty adjusting.

Although the diary as a genre is simple in structure and relatively
free of limitations, Jesus invests her text with the same complexity that is
present in her own character. On one hand she writes for herself, relating
everyday events and encounters in a conversational, idiomatic style while
on the other hand constantly keeping in mind the public (mainly White
Brazilian) to which the diary once published would be marketed. Thus,
inclusion of poetry using metaphors and other symbolic imagery serves as
a stylistic contrast that helps Jesus demonstrate her literary influences to
her readership and in so doing dispel stereotypes about *favelados*.

The Diary and Historical Positioning

It is this complexity that makes *Quarto de despejo* a compelling study not
just of the nature of poverty, nor of the consequences of failed social and
economic systems, but also of the effects of these factors on the individual. Neuman explains that in conjunction with nationality and the
juncture of historical and political forces, "Gender, sexuality, attitudes
about our bodies, and socioeconomic class all figure crucially in the
autobiographer's representation of self" (222).

In *Quarto de despejo* we have an example of an individual affected
by several of these factors, particularly nationality, historical forces, politics, gender, educational patterns, and the psychic and social trauma
suffered by the poor. While Neuman here places the socially constructed
self in direct opposition to an individualistic resistance to social forces, I
contend that the two are not mutually exclusive. She later takes a similar
position when defining the autobiographical self. The "poetics of difference" present in autobiography that Neuman proposes best elucidates
the coexistence in the individual of agency and a constructed self. When
the individual recognizes his or her historical positioning and attempts
to reformulate identity in a specific discourse, working both within and
outside the discursive limits, the result is an identity that draws on yet
questions sociocultural categories for its conceptualization.

Rewriting Race in Brazilian Society

A beginning understanding of the role of historical positioning in Jesus's hybrid redefinition of her identity must start with an examination of the interaction of race, gender, and class as well as their connection to Brazilian society of the 1950s and 1960s. In the Brazilian society of her time (and to a certain degree, today as well) Afro-Brazilians were judged by different standards based on expectations of inferiority. Jesus was not only subject to such racism but also acutely aware of it: "I wrote plays and showed them to directors of circuses. They told me: 'It's a shame you're black.' . . . The black is persecuted because his skin is the color of night" (*Child of the Dark* 61–62, 106). Afro-Brazilians were not seen as equals–and certainly not as writers.

By addressing both racial inequality and her racial pride in her diary Jesus confronted head on the stereotypes and persecution and turned the diary into a weapon of subversion: "They were forgetting that I adore my black skin and my kinky hair. . . . If reincarnation exists I want to come back black" (62). She took the negative stereotypes and turned them inside out, stressing instead the positive aspects and wearing her race as a badge of honor. As further subversion and manipulation of society's discrimination Jesus offered her text as a self-declaration: a diary, to be published, by an Afro-Brazilian woman.

Jesus further asserted her rights as a Brazilian woman of African descent in terms of her sexuality. Throughout her life she insisted on cross-racial relationships instead of the more popular belief in relationships within one race. As Levine and Meihy observe: "One of the reasons that Brazilian society disparaged Carolina's preference for white men was that it violated an unwritten code that judged it entirely unacceptable for a black woman to initiate and control sexual choice. White men could choose dark-skinned sexual partners, especially if the women were unusually attractive" (*Life and Death* 141–142).

Unlike the mores of Brazilian society, Jesus did not believe that her sexuality should be determined by prejudices and sexism but rather that it should be in her hands to decide. As a woman of African descent her insistence on a personal choice of partners allowed her to assume an agency traditionally reserved for Caucasian men.

Subverting Gender Roles

Jesus's process of rewriting her textual and social self could not be complete without addressing her role as a woman in Brazilian society. By confronting her socialization from girlhood to womanhood she could use the diary as a space to challenge the roles she was asked to play. As a gendered subject Jesus's position as a woman and her role as a mother illustrate Smith's first principle of the effect of the autobiographer's gendered status on the text. In addition, her day-to-day performance of these roles exemplifies what according to Béatrice Didier "are two faces of the same process of affirmation of oneself in a society" (*qtd. in Bunkers* 26) by using to its advantages the very tools and concepts employed in its domination.

One of the ways in which Jesus affirms herself is through the reversal of negative gendered stereotypes like the ones that told her as a child that men were brave and the only ones capable of defending their principles and their nation: "When I was a girl my dream was to be a man to defend Brazil, because I read the history of Brazil and became aware that war existed. I read the masculine names of the defenders of the country" (*Child of the Dark,* 53). As such, part of her perception of herself was as girl/not-man and not able to defend her country. This association of weakness and inactivity with femininity and its converse with masculinity stayed with Jesus, to a certain degree, in the present during her writing of the diary: "If I were a man I would not let my children live in this miserable hole" (*Child of the Dark,* 156). In this quote the power associated with masculinity is again of ability—the ability to change one's location and everything associated with it. Because of this misconception and her desire to be an agent of change, in both instances cited, Jesus expresses a desire to switch her gender.

However, as Jesus matured, her writing developed, allowing her to reverse the negative connotations of femininity and demystify to some extent her perception of masculinity. Even though the war that Jesus read about in the history books was an armed one in which men defended their nation, she recognized that, together with all the poor, they were in their own battle: "Here in the favela almost everyone has a difficult fight to live. But I am the only one who writes of what suffering is. I do this for the good of the others" (*Child of the Dark,* 37–38). In this quote Jesus—the woman—chooses an action that makes her a participant in the battle of the favelados, as opposed to a passive bystander. One key difference from the history books she read is Jesus's position in the war. Here she is clearly an army of one, fighting for her compatriots. Jesus's representation of her relationship with her own mother not only is another key to understanding her gendered self but also exemplifies the effect of temporality on her self-definition. Because of its link with social and historic elements (for, as Sartre points out, lineage is part of the proof that we are historical beings) Jesus's representation as a temporal being is important to understanding how she perceives her identity.

When we consider temporality as a factor affecting the development of social constructs (that is, of the individual, of family), it is possible to understand its application as a force linking the present and future, in both linear and nonlinear representations of time as well as more specifically through the impact of memory on Jesus's self-definition. Consequently, we can carry the link of temporality to social constructs into the present, future, or other nonlinear permutations by examining the role of memory in reformulating a contestatory identity against society's limits.

Jesus's mother, for example, not only influenced her past but equally as important, her present identity. The first connection is that of social position and cycles of poverty: "Today I looked in a mirror. . . . My face is almost like my departed mother. A tooth is missing. . . . The fear of dying of hunger!" (*Child of the Dark*, 147). Jesus's mother was someone intimately familiar with poverty and passed this on to her daughter. When Jesus looks in the mirror she not only sees her past through a remembrance of her mother's suffering but also experiences an instant connection with her present, for her face is her mother's face. The cycle of poverty threatens to engulf Jesus as it did her mother. The daughter of a poor woman has become a poor woman herself, possibly carrying that stigma to her grave.

The cycle of poverty and loss of hope is passed on to Jesus's relationship with her daughter yet becomes another space in which her writing subverts the traps that gender and class strictures have laid for her. In one moment of optimism Jesus observes, "[S]he put on the shoes and began to smile. I stood watching my daughter's smile, because I myself don't know how to smile" (*Child of the Dark*, 92). It is interesting to note that here, Jesus's focus is not on her own survival and provision but that of her daughter. When she is a good mother, she feels like a worthwhile being. Her identity is not only tied to her children's but is also, as we saw with her mother, part of a legacy passed and on affecting her children's identity as well. Although Jesus is the principal "utterer" asserting her space in this society, it is her daughter who plays a part in reinforcing that space. The last line shows the psychological effects of Jesus's constant struggle: the unfamiliarity of happiness. However, the mother-daughter relationship provides her with someone—Vera—who can reclaim that emotion and the right to it. It is Vera who smiles—because of her mother's care, and, just as importantly, in her mother's place.

What this demonstrates is an affirmation of the parent-child relationship in an oppressive society and specifically, of the mother-daughter relationship as an important identity in the restrictive "universe" Zilá Bernd refers to. Jesus also stresses the parent-child relationship as a principal responsibility, especially considering her identity as a single mother. "I reflected: I've got to be tolerant with my children. They don't have anyone in the world but me. How sad is the condition of a woman alone without a man at home" (*Child of the Dark* 27).

Nonetheless, if we look at Jesus's refusal to marry, we initially question her awareness of the difficulties of single parenthood while refusing to take the one step that would change that—marriage. One answer can be found in the theory by bell hooks that proposes a positioning of the self in a marginal space that is radical and empowering, continuing the ideas first presented in her text *Feminist Theory: From Margin to Center*. As hooks emphasized, the power of the margin lies in finding and holding to "a site one stays in, clings to even, because it nourishes one's capacity to resist.... I make a definite distinction between that marginality which is imposed by oppressive structures and the marginality one chooses as a site of resistance—as a location of radical openness and possibility" (149–150, 153).

By society's standards, marriage was not only a woman's goal but also a way of being accepted. Consequently, a single mother would be looked upon negatively, as someone outside of society's standards of morality: a marginal. Jesus was completely aware of the extra hardship this added to her and her family's life, but realized a truth expressed decades later by bell hooks: she realized the positive aspect of her marginalized space and saw it as a priority over the acceptable alternative. The marginal space of a single mother afforded her freedom from the restrictions a husband would place upon her writing: "Senhor Manuel showed up saying he wanted to marry me. But I don't want to, because I'm in my maturity. And later a man isn't going to like a woman who can't stop reading and gets out of bed to write and sleeps with paper and pencil under her pillow" (*Child of the Dark* 50).

Jesus knew that according to society's rules a married woman was not to have any interests outside of the home. Therefore, she had to reject the state of marriage in order to keep her freedom. This freedom and the writing ability it allowed her to explore and develop were a part of her resistance. As Levine and Meihy note, Jesus's engagement in temporary love affairs and her unwillingness to commit to one lifetime relationship was in general a point of criticism by many journalists of the time: "But these were liaisons, not marriages.... Carolina's desire to have lovers but not submit to a husband (in a culture rampant with marital violence against poor women) also annoyed her critics" (*Life and Death* 141).

There were the two facets of Jesus's relational identity in which she dared (in society's view) to make her own rules: her relationships with her children's fathers or possible stepfathers, and the consistent choice of White Brazilians as her lovers. What Levine and Meihy add to my contention that Jesus rejected marriage because of its conflict with her desire to write is the sociocultural concern: a concern with the subservient role women had taken on in the domestic sphere throughout Brazil, especially given the noted cases of domestic violence involving poor women:

Yet in other ways, Carolina's environment shaped her. She was submissive when she dealt with men. . . . The lives of females are often seen as more trivial and less important than the lives of males. Women internalize this view, diminishing their self-esteem as a result of social pressure. This was certainly not the case with Carolina Maria de Jesus. She commented succinctly and matter-of-factly on the disadvantages being a woman added to the other obstacles in her path as an indigent, unskilled black migrant. That she was a mother who self-confidently brought up her children amidst squalor, insisting that her children be honest, moral and attend school, was entirely lost on those who judged her. (*Life and Death* 141–142)

These two reasons both demonstrate Jesus's concern to present a model of a strong Afro-Brazilian woman who would not compromise her intellectual integrity (and growth) or her psychological and physical principles and development. However, Levine and Meihy astutely note the complexity of Jesus's decision to assert her sexual preferences. It was not just an assertion of her agency but an example of her submissiveness. Despite her many attempts in various areas of her life to control the effect of the environment on her, her relationships with men were a direct result of sexism that continuously emphasized her unimportance in society. It is another example of Jesus's movement between a marginal approach to relationships where she asserted her will and a vulnerability to dominant discourses of devalorization.

Ultimately Jesus occupied several marginalized spaces that nonetheless contained points of commonality as well as areas of difference. On one hand she is the single mother, but also the writer: a mother who is engaged in a professional activity apart from her job of collecting tin cans and paper. On the other hand there is the added marginalization of color and its further isolation from mainstream Brazilian society when combined with the aforementioned categories. As bell hooks described, Jesus saw these spaces as sites to cling to as means of resistance: a resistance that was a key part of her reformulation of identity. She was not willing to give up any of these sites for the possibility of acceptance. As Jesus stated, "That's why I prefer to live alone, for my ideals" (*Child of the Dark* 50).

Rewriting Class Status

Jesus's awareness of her class position in Brazilian society is another significant step in her identity reformulation and resistance to categorization. The first step is to overturn the codes of behavior associated with her specific class status. As a marginalized member of the Brazilian nation she is all too aware of how society sees her. In one example she declares, "On a rainy day I'm a beggar. . . . I wear the uniform of the unfortunate. And today is Saturday. The *favelados* are considered beggars" (58). Like a soldier in the army she wears the "uniform of the unfortunate," and as a result is marked as indigent/favelada (slumdweller)/beggar. This realization is a clear example of Jesus's movement from individuality to a group coupled with her recognition that different aspects of her identity carry negative connotations.

As the diary's title suggests, Jesus is conscious of how the position of favelada differentiates herself and her family from other more privileged Brazilians. In one entry in the diary she observes:

> I spent a horrible night. I dreamt I lived in a decent house that had a bathroom, kitchen, pantry, and even a maid's room. I was going to celebrate the birthday of my daughter Vera Eunice. I went and bought some small pots that I had wanted for a long time. Because I was able to buy. I sat at the table to eat. . . . When I reached for another steak I woke up. What bitter reality! I don't live in the city. I live in the favela. . . . I don't even have sugar, because yesterday after I went out the children ate what little I had. (*Child of the Dark* 40)

What begins as a dream becomes a terrible reminder of the problems Jesus faces daily. Her dream is to possess the basics—a habitable house with the necessities (bathroom, kitchen) and possibly more (servant's quarters). However, she recognizes that housing alone cannot create a fulfilled life without economic freedom to provide for oneself and her loved ones. This is summed up in the sentence "Because I was able to buy." Within this one declaration of economic stability Jesus also addresses issues of independence and empowerment. In her dream what was most empowering was being able to provide for her children without worry and without assistance from anyone.

Family, nonetheless, is more than an indicator of the responsibilities Jesus has as a mother; they are part of her identity and the lens through which she views her position in society. Friedman's theories explain this duality by pointing out that one common factor women share is their inclusion in a collective. While there are negative connotations, the advantage is the assertion of these collective identities as transformative and empowering (39).

Close study of Jesus's character shows a complex interaction between the individual and the collective that does not limit her self-definition to one or the other. When Jesus states that in her dream she was able to buy things her children requested, this is another affirmation of her elevated class status. As one moves up the economic ladder, belonging is partially predicated on the ability to provide for one's children. Conversely, the inability to provide for them and for oneself is yet further proof of the poverty in which the family and particularly the head of the family are immersed.

The separation of the classes is especially exemplified by one particular trip to São Paulo to collect paper and scrap metal. On one such occasion Jesus goes to an apartment to collect papers and upon leaving, finds herself in an elevator with a gentleman from the upper echelons of society: "On the sixth floor a man got into the elevator and looked at me with disgust. I'm used to these looks, they don't bother me. He wanted to know what I was doing in the elevator. I explained to him that the mother of those two boys had given me some newspapers. And that was the reason for my presence in his elevator. . . . He told me he was a Senator" (*Child of the Dark* 98). Ascending in the elevator is symbolically ascending the social ladder. When Jesus is confronted with a senator from the upper social register he reminds her of her social position and its place: "The man was well dressed. I was barefoot. Not in condition to ride in his elevator" (98). The interaction between the two is telling because it exemplifies the dual aspect of historical positioning and the importance of the gaze in influencing an individual's identity. In a Lacanian analysis of language acquisition this connection is seen in the mirror stage of development when the child sees him- or herself and becomes aware of the fragmented self. At this moment the subject is aware that the "I" watching is different from the "I" being watched. Through the use of fantasy and identification with the mother and with others the subject then tries to integrate this alienated split image. Therefore, the gaze on the whole serves as an identifier of the self through another person or a specific reality (Agüera 532). In Jesus's case there is first a social categorization motivated by the repugnant gaze. When Jesus comments on her inappropriate physical state for such a place she recognizes once more that she is a part of this marginalized social category. She is not repeating for the reader what the senator has told her but is stating what is fact according to society's standards. This conclusion is not drawn from a single event but from several events and several gazes similar to the one she received, resulting in an internalization of this stereotype.

In order to counteract the internalization of certain codes of marginalization that had built up in her over the years, Jesus manipulates the text to change the very purpose of the diary, from a document written by a subject historically denied access to literary discourse to a transformed identity as a writer from the favela. One paradox of Jesus's writing however is that it serves to chronicle and distance her from the common experience of poverty. As Carlos Vogt points out in "Trabalho, pobreza e trabalho intelectual":

> [On one hand, the author belongs to the world she narrates and whose content of hunger and deprivation she shares with the social environment in which she lives. On the other hand, upon transforming the real linguistic experience of misery into the linguistic experience of the diary, she ends up distinguishing herself from herself and presenting the writing as a form of new social experimentation, capable of offering her the hope of breaking the circle of the economy of survival that locks her life into the day-to-day of the money matter.]

> De um lado, a autora pertence ao mundo que narra e cujo conteúdo de fome e privação compartilha com o meio social em que vive. Do outro, ao transformar a experiência linguística real da miséria na experiência linguística do diário, acaba por se distinguir de si mesma e por apresentar a escritura como uma forma de experimentação social nova, capaz de acenar-lhe com a esperança de romper o cerco da economia de sobrevivência que tranca a sua vida ao dia-a-dia do dinheiro coisa. (210)

Vogt's observation points out the dual nature of Jesus's writing: as an economic opportunity and psychological transformation that emphasize the tension and distance that the act of writing provokes. Once Jesus becomes a writer she is both author and subject of her reality and no longer just a favelada.

As Meihy notes in *Meu estranho diário*, "No ordenamento social de Carolina havia hierarquias. Os *iducados* sempre seriam os alfabetizados que, afinal, teriam cultura e esta era a chave para o bem viver" (294). [In Carolina's social order there were hierarchies. The *educated* would always be the literate that, in the end, would be cultured and this was the key for the good life." (Translation mine)] Therefore, for Jesus, being thought of as someone who was "stupid" or "uneducated"(the original Portuguese phrase used is "não tem iducação") implied not only being illiterate or not having social graces but more importantly not having (or being denied) opportunities for success. As a writer Jesus is proof that these labels are not all inclusive. She best demonstrates this when she describes one motivation for her writing: "The *favelados* themselves say the *favelado* is stupid. I thought: I'm going to write." What this quote suggests is that although her love of writing and decision to pursue it began as a result of familial influence (particularly of her grandfather) and some formal education, she was further motivated by a desire to recreate an identity apart from social categories.

The Diary's Framework and
Individual-Community Interactions

Jesus uses the very framework of the diary as part of this separation by working both within and outside of it. One significant feature of its form present in *Quarto de despejo* is the recurring account of daily life, exemplified by the numerous references to Jesus's routine of going to get water for the household duties, collecting cans and paper, and taking care of the children. This underscores for the reader the difficulties in her day-to-day survival and the lack of physical and emotional comfort she feels. One entry early on in the diary gives us an example of her routine, adapting the themes of loneliness and a lack of comfort to the life of a favelada: "I said goodbye and returned home. I made lunch. While the pots boiled, I wrote a little. I gave the children their lunch and went to Klabin paper mill to look for paper. I left the children playing in the yard. . . . I worked fast, thinking that those human beasts are capable of invading my shack and mistreating my children. I worked on, nervous and upset" (*Child of the Dark* 23–24).

The lack of physical comfort available to Jesus is evident by the rigorous routine that leaves her little time for herself and her writing. However, the most noteworthy element is the emotional unease and apprehensiveness Jesus feels, heightened by her sense of isolation. As she later points out, her resulting cautiousness comes from the lack of community and the distrust that exists in the favela between herself and her neighbors. Ultimately, it causes her to fear for the very safety of her children: "They wait for me to leave so they can come to my shack and hurt my children. Always when I'm not at home. When the children are alone they can't defend themselves" (*Child of the Dark* 24).

This lack of solidarity is in sharp contrast to the sense of community exhibited in subsequent statements by Jesus when she speaks of her unity and empathy for the poor. What these seemingly disparate remarks reveal is the complexity of Jesus's own character and of her relationships with others. In describing this interaction María Lugones notes that this relationship is in fact a strategic one defined by the level of awareness of group needs:

> Individuals are transparent with respect to their group if they
> perceive their needs, interests, ways, as those of the group and

if their perceptions become dominant or hegemonical in the group. Individuals are thick if they are aware of their otherness in the group, of their needs, interests, ways, being relegated to the margins in the politics of intragroup contestations. So, as transparent, one becomes unaware of one's own difference from other members of the group. (474)

If we also place Jesus's isolation from other favelados in the context of Friedman's expanded theories of the valorization of community in women's selfhood we have not a contradiction, but a struggle for control over the terms of self-definition. By maintaining a distance from other favelados Jesus is individually striving to maintain and continually reformulate a self-identity not governed by the negative behavior she believes the favelados represent.

As Levine and Meihy note:

From the days of her childhood to her final years in self-exile, Carolina's response was to distance herself from others, in order to maintain control over her life. This trait, in fact, was in many ways the key to her ability to keep her sanity. This helps explain why she was so much of an outcast. She was the one who persisted in reading when others played. She was the one who refused to drink alcohol or to gossip or give in to hopelessness. She decided when to pack up and move on. (*Life and Death* 143–144)

There were days when Jesus was overwhelmed by the despair of her daily life and gave in to negative behavior she usually was able to avoid. In her diary one can find a few examples of such behavior: engaging in gossip with other women from the favela, or taking a drink of *pinga*. However, the greatest difference between her behavior and that of others is that it did not turn into a controlling, habitual act. Jesus knew that allowing this to happen would jeopardize both her and her children's chances for fulfilling their dreams.

When Jesus highlights for her reader her difference from the favelados and the model of behavior she espouses it has double meaning for her representation to and relationship with the reader. While on one hand it stresses her difference and control, it also brings her reader closer, by emphasizing values they both share. As Kimberly Nance observes, it is an example of the political side of Jesus and represents

a considered political and rhetorical stance. [H]er attempt to forge a social connection between herself and her likely readers might be considered as more than an individualistic attempt to separate herself from her own class. This writer's insistent domesticity serves to challenge her readers' comforting notions regarding poor people's differential experience, adaptation, and inurement to their poverty. (43)

As a strategic identity, Jesus in fact alternated between "thickness" and "transparency," to use Lugones's terms. One of the factors that in part determine her level of individual and group interaction is her level of nationalism—an allegiance, not to a class-based community, but rather, to a national one. As Stephen Hunsaker notes, "This narrative is remarkable for its strong sense of national identification despite poverty, hunger, and cynicism toward government. . . . Carolina's 'thickness' is for the most part limited to the *favela*, and she suppresses the 'thickening' facts of race, class, and gender to imagine herself as a Brazilian rather than isolating herself from the surrounding nation" (43, 47). As a collective act opposite to her individualism Jesus also engages in the community's fight for empowerment to counter society's marginalization of them. However, she also engages in "transparency" when asserting an individual identity, even in the midst of collective allegiance. Her attempts at empowerment of the self and collective is an example of the duality of women that Rowbotham describes as "a dual consciousness—the self as culturally defined and the self as different from cultural prescription" that is similar to DuBois' identification of dual consciousness for Blacks living in a dominant White culture (qtd. in Friedman 1988, 39).
As DuBois notes:

[T]he Negro is a sort of seventh son, born with a veil, and gifted with second-sight in this American world,—a world which yields him no true self-consciousness, but only lets him see himself through the revelation of the other world. It is a peculiar sensation, this double-consciousness, this sense of always looking at one's self through the eyes of others, of measuring one's soul by the tape of a world that looks on in amused contempt and pity. One ever feels his twoness, —an American, a Negro; two souls, two thoughts. (3)

For Jesus, her identity as a Black Brazilian woman in a nation known as a racial democracy demonstrates some important parallels with the tension of the African American condition described by DuBois. On one hand, Jesus sees herself as part of Brazilian society, exemplified by her at times euphanistic declarations of love for her country. Yet, in contrast, her accounts of racism and marginalization reveal to her and the reader the limits to her belonging.

As Eva Bueno observes, "As a member of a group or a race continuously threatened into silence through slavery, joblessness, and oppression, Carolina relies not on an idealized concept of kinship, tradition, and community. Her body, a black one, is all she owns" (277). As such, Jesus's voice lets outsiders begin to understand the complexities both of "the subject Carolina Maria de Jesus and of those other women who live at the margins of capitalist society" (Bueno 277). While citizenship supposedly guarantees her certain rights and privileges as an equal partner in Brazilian national identity, the reality of her life as a Black Brazilian woman together with that of other poor is one of alienation and disenfranchisement. In the diary, several references stress the tension between a Brazil of opportunity and the marginalization of poverty: "They say that Brazil used to be good. But I am not living when it was good. . . . I was horrified" (147).

A second aspect of the double consciousness as applied to Jesus sets up a contrast not between the individual ideal of belonging and the isolation of oppression, but between citizenship to a national entity and a racial identity that forms part of the whole. As a Black woman she expresses pride in this identity yet realizes its tension with a Brazilian national image that privileges the European. As a result, throughout the diary Jesus embraces her blackness and Brazilianness yet recognizes the ways in which the two are at times constructed as mutually exclusive. As such, her conflicting emotions vacillate between feelings of isolation and the desire for an independent identity where the marginalization she experiences would have no impact. Such tension is reflected on two levels in her text, in the diary's overall thematic and structural license.

The Diary as Emotional Redefinition

Jesus's multiple use of the diary as it reflects her development of subjecthood is best understood by answering three important questions: 1) For what purposes does Jesus write? 2) How does she use the diary to achieve these goals? and 3) To what extent does she hide, reveal or reinvent the "true" Jesus through the textual Jesus's interactions with cultural codes?

Else Vieira provides a framework in which to answer these questions when she places Jesus's writing in the context of Freire's theories of postliteracy and empowerment for marginalized, oppressed people:

> The investigation of the theme entails the investigation of the way individuals think, which can only be carried out with the individual not as an object but as a subject of his thinking. . . . [B]ut thinking implies more than situatedness: 'os homens são porque estão em situação'; ("Men are because they are situ-

ated") (Vieira 120) they will be even more human if they not only think critically about *situatedness* but also act critically upon that situatedness. . . . This is a pedagogy of the oppressed that Carolina, again, has anticipated in some ways when she critically thinks about and acts upon her situatedness, puts on to paper her words and the words she hears from her world of the *favela*, narrating her story/history, and becoming a witness to a history of which she, in turn, becomes an author. (120–121)

Vieira's application of Freire's theory of subject positioning, or situatedness, as a step towards affirming individual identity is particularly relevant to Jesus's oppression and her resistance to it.

Jesus's constant fight against the sense of uselessness that the favela foments leads her to use writing in three important, connected ways in order to critically combat her situation: (1) as an emotional outlet and escape in an attempt to fight the misery that the life of poverty in the favela had prescribed for her; (2) as an economic escape; and (3) as a reinvention of the self by an exploration and reshaping of the many facets of her self-definition.

In order to fully understand how Jesus uses writing as a means of emotional survival, escape, and assertion of agency it is relevant to know why she chose this tool of expression. What are the external factors that affect how Jesus developed her strategies for self-definition? One such factor is a familial influence whose historical specificity will help us understand her relation to questions of race, class, and the acquisition of power in Latin America and Brazil in particular.

A key figure in Jesus's life was her grandfather, a wise man known as Sócrates Africano who passed on his curiosity for and love of books to his granddaughter. He was considered a wise man not just by blacks but also by the rich and powerful of his region—those who lived in a different world with different standards of judging one's erudition. As a child Carolina spent a lot of time with her grandfather, the only other adult who was around other than her mother. As a result his passions influenced her passions:

> [According to the testimony of Vera, the grandfather was the intellectual mold for Carolina. . . . Vera continues to historicize the life of the writer, stating that "my mother learned to read and write with him, the love of reading came from the curiosity to know more the history of places, the heroes, Tiradentes, Zumbi dos Palmares. . . . She listened, became interested and searched in the books. (Translation mine)]

Segundo o depoimento de Vera, o avô foi a matriz intellectual da Carolina. . . . Vera continua a estoricizar a vida da escritora dizendo que "minha mãe aprendeu a ler e escrever com ele, o gosto pela leitura veio com a curiosidade de saber mais história dos lugares, dos heróis, Tiradentes, Zumbi dos Palmares. . . . Ela ouvia, se interessava e ia procurar nos livros. (139)

In *Cinderela Negra* Meihy and Levine explain further the grandfather's influence on Jesus's future:

[Belonging to the descendants of a Socrates Africano was a symptom of a destiny or vocation that would be refined through culture. Wanting to dominate the written code, aspire to the authorship of books, were pieces of the same system that straightened the rebelliousness of insubordinates to assume a place on the level of White men. In this sense the work of Carolina is the result of an important historic impulse that has a fundamental moment in her.]

Pertencer a descendência de um Sócrates Africano, . . . era sintoma de um destino ou vocação que se refinaria através da cultura. Querer dominar o código da escrita, pretender a autoria de livros, eram peças do mesmo sistema que endereçava a rebeldia dos insubordinados a assumirem lugar no plano dos homens brancos. Nesta linha o trabalho de Carolina é resultado de um impulso histórico importante, que tem nela um momento fundamental. (139–140)

This biographical information is important because of the foundation it lays for Jesus's sense of self and her use of writing to develop it. First is the tradition of knowledge established by the grandfather and passed on to his granddaughter. Her hunger for books and information is not simply a product of two years of schooling, but more importantly of her contact with a family member who shared this hunger. As a component of Jesus's identity this is one part of the explanation of her sense of being part of a world full of knowledge and not just limited to the daily concerns of the favelados. Second, these statements provide early proof of Jesus the writer. Her desire to express herself through words is shown here to begin long before her life in the favela, indicating that this component of her identity cannot simply be linked to her socioeconomic position at the time of her life in São Paulo, but at an earlier historical moment and alongside family traditions.

The family legacy of constantly seeking to acquire more knowledge can also be placed in the context of grammatical and literary assimilation in Latin America in general. According to José Piedra in his article "Literary Whiteness and the Afro-Hispanic Difference" in the Spanish colonial system "Spanish grammar became the colonial pretext for the assimilation of otherness . . ." Linguistic and literary rigor was a way of allowing a safe amount of difference but maintaining a sense of unity and conformity that allowed its participants "official entry into the Hispanic *Text of Otherness*,"—a text that was in actuality "a grammatical contract of servitude." The result was the creation of a system whereby Blacks and other minority groups could attain some power and prestige through linguistic grammatical and literary assimilation (303–304). As Piedra notes, "Grammar constituted the core of a citizen's apprenticeship: it guided the recording and the actual making of history as the official channel of spreading 'the truth.' This constellation of circumstances led to a theoretical welcoming, on paper, of black newcomers under the far-reaching umbrella of a 'Hispanic race' " (306–308). Acceptance was based on the "literary whitening" of the participants: access to some social prestige and power at the expense of the different aspects of one's identity. Nonetheless, those once considered "marginal" were, no matter their title, always marginalized from any meaningful (in a political sense) control over language in print. Although there were in later years more and more Black writers who dared to insert difference into their writing, it was always in direct conflict with a rhetoric that stifled difference: "To this day, language remains the relative dictator of Hispanidad. Nonwhites could write as long as they did not address the issue of difference, a stricture which practically denied them self-conscious literature" (Piedra 312).

For Jesus, the foundation of her family and two years of schooling provided a beginning access to the skills she could later use as an emotional escape from the harsh reality of the favelas. However, the social and cultural limitations that Piedra establishes as a part of a Hispanophone colonial legacy can also be seen to an extent in the Lusophone context. As such, Jesus, like the early Black writers of Spanish America, would have to navigate the possible successes that writing might bring her and the parts of her identity that were prohibited full expression. As part of this navigation Jesus does use her writing to represent her emotional life, in particular as a way to counter the depression of a constant fight to survive: "I left the bed at 3 a.m. because when one is not sleepy he starts to think of the misery around him. I got out of bed to write. . . . I must create this atmosphere of fantasy to forget that I am in a favela" (*Child of the Dark* 57).

Many times the escape is not just from the extreme emotions that the favela evokes but also from the daily feelings of frustration and anxiousness that together lead to despair. Instead of giving in to these emotions and interacting with the favelados in discussions that only serve to highlight their frustration, Jesus separates herself: "I like to stay inside the house with the door locked. I don't like to stay on street corners talking. . . . I like to be alone and read. Or write!" (*Child of the Dark* 29) This act of physical escape to accompany her mental escape is pointed out by Jesus's daughter in her interview with Levine and Meihy: "Acho que os livros foram os únicos companheiros constantes dela, porque eles não escolhem seu leitor. . . . Por isso é que ela aprendeu tanto e acabou sendo escritora: se afogava em livros para fugir da solidão" (67). [I think that books were her only constant companion, because they don't choose their reader. . . . For this reason she learned so much and ended up a writer, she drowned in books to escape the loneliness." (Translation mine)] While Vera Eunice's quote refers to her mother's escape from a negative sense of isolation and solitude from greater society that her mother achieves through books and writing, *Quarto de despejo* also demonstrates a positive use of solitude in order to remove oneself from surroundings and situations that are counterproductive and destructive. Jesus isolates herself in order to escape the negative emotions of the favela and favelados and take part in activities that bring her some sense of happiness—no matter how temporary it may be.

Writing's functions, however, go beyond catharsis. It has historically given men not just emotional release but financial gain as well. For women these opportunities were not as easily available. As Raoul pointed out in her study "Women and Diaries: Gender and Genre," "The implicit rules they were to follow included staying away from business and consequently, the business aspect of writing and not self-indulging in any excessive focus on themselves." As a way around these restrictions, personal writings like letters, journals, and diaries became socially sanctioned emotional outlets that let women begin to commercially present their lives and in a sense, themselves, as a marketable product (58).

Nonetheless, over time as these barriers were slowly but surely broken down, women gained entrance to commercial and public writing which could provide them with greater economic stability. In Jesus's case, even before meeting the journalist Audálio Dantas she was aware of the economic opportunities her writing held—to change her life but more importantly her children's. Once she does meet Audálio Dantas—someone who can make this a reality—we can see more references to the mercantilist nature of her writing: "I am writing a book to sell. I am hoping that with the money I can buy a place and leave the favela" (*Child of the Dark* 31).

The recounting of the change of a family once they moved into the favela is for Jesus proof of its profound effect on its residents: "Sometimes families move into the favela with children. They are diamonds turned to lead. They are transformed from objects that were in the living room to objects banished to the garbage dump" (*Child of the Dark* 39). Conversely, a future opportunity to move out of the favela into the city would cause a change of not only attitude but of social status. Given the scarcity of both the resources around her and the few she possesses, it is only Jesus's writing that can bring this future closer.

The Writer as Poetic Activist

As part of the process that Jesus undergoes to actively redevelop her sense of self, she creates a writing characterized by hybridity: specifically, including within the diary's narrative poetry that serves multiple purposes of reformation and resistance. According to Meihy in *Antologia pessoal*:

> [A contemporary of the Concretists, Carolina was the embodiment of resistance, of the traditionalism and of the memory that fled from the new. . . . It is certain that being a poet evoked a nobility in her and this was all that was necessary to distinguish her from the group of other illiterate Blacks and the forgotten poor in the rural world. . . . the idealized genealogy serves her as an imagined recourse to explain the constant unhappiness. It is as if suffering were vital to her. To be a victim would be, in the end, the fate of the poet as she herself affirmed. (Translation mine)]

> Coetânea dos concretistas, Carolina era a encarnação da resistência, do tradicionalismo e da memória que fugia do novo. . . . É certo que ser poeta lhe evocava nobilidade e nobreza e isto era tudo o que se lhe fazia necessário para se distinguir do grupo de outros negros analfabetos e de pobres esquecidos no mundo rural. . . . A geneologia idealizada lhe serve como recurso imaginado para explicar a infelicidade constante. E como sofrer era-lhe vital. Ser vítima seria, por fim, sina de versejador como ela mesmo afirmava. (17–19)

Three objectives of Jesus's poetry especially stand out: 1) a means of channeling the daily suffering she experienced; 2) a means of acquiring a status that would set her apart form other favelados; and 3) a form of resistance against social and cultural forces that oppressed her. Jesus's act of resistance and distinction from her favelados was especially evident in her use of poetry to develop and express her political voice. She is the poetic (and at times prophetic) voice of a people silenced by politics, poverty, and prejudice. However, her opposition is especially important when one considers, as I have discussed, the public for which the diary is intended—one outside of the favela and therefore, most likely unaware of the effects of political mismanagement on the poor. This readership could include some politicians themselves, curious to read the opinions of an electorate usually ignored except around election time. Jesus's comments on her political strategies show us the contrast between her usual handling of political deceptions and disappointments and the change brought about by her ability to possibly write a commercially visible text. Although still not convinced that direct confrontation with politicians was a viable option for her, her diary and poetry served as a way of registering her opinions and of developing a political identity: "Who must be a leader is he who has the ability. . . . [T]hose who govern our country are those who have money, who don't know what hunger is, or pain or poverty. If the majority revolt, what can the minority do? I am on the side of the poor, who are an arm. An undernourished arm. We must free the country of the profiteering politicians" (*Child of the Dark* 40)."[2]

Here Jesus assesses the problem of injustices committed by the politicians and the distance between them and the people and suggests a possible course of action. Unlike the politicians who rarely see the results of their actions, Jesus expresses her allegiance when she states, "I am on the side of the poor." She reminds the reader of her connection to those on the lowest rungs of Brazil's economic ladder, strengthened by her knowledge of their struggles. Jesus's belief in revolt as a solution ultimately serves as a catharsis for her and for the other favelados that she carries out through her writing.

Alongside Jesus's daily recollections of struggle and survival were poems whose diverse themes showed her many inspirations and interests. While Jesus's poetry usually dealt with more universal themes of love (albeit unrequited), she also touched on themes of national pride, criticisms of politicians, and the worsening economic situation in Brazil. The choice of these themes shows a desire to use her poetry to record the more culturally and politically specific themes of Brazilian politics and in so doing legitimize the socially conscious aspect of her identity. It was one thing to document the conversations about politics that the women drawing water from the well held, and yet another to include political commentary in a diary that would eventually be presented in a public forum. This inclusion made the statement that here was a woman who was capable of critically reflecting on the politics of her country, again contradicting the stereotype that favelados were not concerned about or educationally equipped to understand complex issues like politics. According to Bunkers, this use of political commentary in a diary serves to blur the lines of discourse, as evidenced in the 1845 diary of an American woman named Lucinda: "Lucinda's diary became a place where she recorded her understanding of the relationship between personal circumstances and political views, thereby blurring the artificial distinction between the private and the public realms" (19). By redefining herself as a poet Jesus also blurs these lines by examining the implications of this categorization for her as individual and member of a collective:

> The politicians know that I am a poetess. And that a poet will even face death when he sees his people oppressed. . . . I saw the poor go out crying. The tears of the poor stir the poets. They don't move the poets of the living room, but they do move the poet of the garbage dump, this idealist of the favela, a spectator who sees and notes the tragedies that the politicians inflict on the people. (*Child of the Dark* 40, 52)

Jesus's declaration is another example of the dual consciousness that both Rowbotham and Vogt emphasized. On one hand, as a writer and poet she is distanced from the community (and actively distances herself), yet on the other hand she recognizes that there is a responsibility that comes with the privilege of having a voice that could break society's imposed silence. Her poetic and literary voice was in sharp contrast to the silence that surrounded her: "How horrible it is to hear the poor lament. The voice of the poor has no poetry" (121). As the "poet of the garbage dump," Jesus chooses to embrace this part of her identity and represent her community's suffering. In these quotes it is clear that the poetry she speaks of is a poetry of power that is both social (expression of a community or collective) and political (expression to those outside this community).

Jesus's reformulation of herself as a poet is consequently also part of her reformulation of class strictures, by giving a voice to the silenced: "I was disgusted with that Social Service that had been created to readjust the maladjusted, but took no notice of we marginal people. . . . The marginal people don't have names" (*Child of the Dark* 41). Through her accounts of the daily struggles of the favelados Jesus is able to give them names—as the subjects of their written stories—and change the framework of the poetic discourse itself to respond to their needs and realities.

However, she feels that her destiny is to express a poetry of tragedy. In the collection *The Unedited Diaries of Carolina Maria de Jesus*, which includes previously unpublished excerpts of her diaries, one finds further elaboration on Jesus's feelings about the responsibilities that accompanied her talent. In the section of the 1958 diary entries she elaborates on her reactions to discovering her true vocation:

> I told her: that when I realized that I am a poetess I became sad because the excess of imagination was too much. That I had my brain examined in the Hospital das Clinicas. That the examination results showed that I was calm. That I greatly educated my brain. That I did not let ideas overcome me. That the disrespect that people have for poets made me sad. But now I am in the mature state and don't get affected with the attentions of just anybody That to those who please me, I am pleasing (*Unedited Diary* 58).

As Meihy notes in the conclusion of *Meu estranho diário*, one important reason for Jesus's association of poetry with misery is what she perceives to be the nature of this literary act:

> [The idea of her role in society is a constant determined by her own awareness that she was different. Thinking of herself as a poetess, Carolina assumed the idea that a poet would be synonymous with being sad.]

> A noção de seu papel na sociedade é uma constante determinada pela própria consciência de que era diferenciada. Sentindo-se poetisa, Carolina assumia a noção de que poeta seria sinônimo de ser triste. (294)

Jesus herself gives us two reasons for her sadness that expand on the connotations of poetry's "capacidade crítica" by clearly illustrating the relationship of her community with knowledge. Her initial trepidation is because of what she sees as a connection between education and what she describes as a possible mental instability. The "excess of imagination" that Jesus feels has inspired her poetry leads her to see a doctor in order to assure herself that she is in fact calm or most likely, sane. What this need for assurance demonstrates is a distrust of knowledge that her community holds (as evidenced by their distrust of Jesus's diary and their surprise at her literary aspirations) and that Jesus to a certain extent shares as well. Her comments show the belief that too much "imagination" or creativity can lead to the individual's loss of control over herself.

However, it is precisely Jesus's ability to do what others possibly cannot do that highlights the difference Meihy speaks of, in particular, from other poor Brazilians: "A noção de ser poeta seria um aval para a responsabilidade de escrever e de publicar pois seria sempre um ser amargurado devido sua capacidade crítica" (*Meu estranho diario* 294). [The idea of being a poet would be a target for the responsibility of writing and publishing since she would always be a bitter person due to her critical capacity.] Writing therefore becomes more than an unqualified transmission of thoughts to another medium. It is an act that necessitates critical reflection on the surrounding world. Jesus however seems to vacillate between a resignation to the sadness of a poet and a desire to assert her domination over it. As she boasts, in the end she is in control of the knowledge she acquires and how it affects her. She is calm because she has "educated" her brain to not let the many ideas she takes over dominate her. Unlike the others around her, she can process knowledge and harness her imagination and mold it and her identity as she wills.

Jesus soon after acknowledges that despite all her control, this does not in fact free her from the sense of tragedy she feels poetry brings. There is an added sense of sadness not so much because of the responsibilities or the subject of the poetry but rather from the reaction of the people to this literary endeavor. In both *Quarto de despejo* and *Meu estranho diário* Jesus documents moments of distrust targeted toward her diary's daily accounts of life in the favela, her opinions, and poetry. Nonetheless, Jesus asserts her fundamental difference from others in the community as a way of resolving her vacillation between a fear of poetry's domination over her and her ability to control it: "Não menos significativa é a forma com que ela deixa registrada sua análise da circunstância que lhe foi dada para viver e de como sendo inconformada-poeta ela se esforça para mostrar ao mundo, através do livro, seu sofrimento e experiência" (Meihy and Levine 296). [No less significant is the way in which she registers her analysis of the circumstance that she was given to live and how, being the bitter-poet she forces herself to show the world, through the book, her suffering and experience."] This very sense of tragedy that threatens to engulf her is turned around to supply much of the source of her writing and simultaneously further establish her singularity among the favelados.

Hybrid Discourse: Erasing Poetic Boundaries

Throughout the diary the movement between categories of formal and informal poetic discourse accompanies similarly intersecting lines of the public and private. The result is a conceptualization and representation that questions and ultimately breaks down the hierarchization of marginal (informal) and dominant (formal, highbrow) poetry. Meihy points to one poem in particular that summarizes Jesus's concerns while highlighting the knowledge she possessed and lyrical style she could bring to her poetry. It is the poem "Vidas":

Nem sempre são ditosas	The lives of famous people
Vidas das pessoas famosas	Are not always fortunate
Edgar Allan morre na sarjeta	Edgar Allan dies in the gutter
Na guilhotina Maria Antonieta	Marie Antoinette on the guillotine
Luiz de Camões teve que mendigar	Luiz de Camões had to beg
Gonçalves Dias morre no mar	Gonçalves Dias dies at sea
Casimiro de Abreu morre tuberculoso	Casimiro de Abreu dies of tuberculosis
Tomaz Gonzaga, louco furioso	Tomas Gonzaga, furious crazed man
Getúlio para impedir outra revolução	In order to prevent another revolution
Suicida-se com um tiro no coração	Getúlio shoots himself in the heart
Santos Dumont inventor do avião	Santos Dumont inventor of the plane
Que foi utilizado na revolução	That was used in the revolution
Para ver o Brasil independente	In order to see Brazil independent
Morre na forca nosso Tiradentes	Tiradentes dies on the gallows
Luis XVI, rei incidente	Louis XVI, incidental king
Morre tragicamente	Dies tragically
Sócrates foi condenado a morrer	Socrates was condemned to die
Ciente lhe obrigaram a beber	While conscious they forced him To drink
João Batista repreendia os transviados	John the Baptist reprimanded Those gone astray
Foi preso e decapitado	He was imprisoned and decapitated
Abrão Lincoln abolindo a escravidão	Abraham Lincoln abolishing slavery
Foi morto à traição	Was killed by betrayal
Euclides da Cunha escritor proeminente	Euclides da Cunha, Prominent writer
Sua morte foi cruelmente	His death was cruel
Joana D'Arc vendo a França oprimida	Joan of Arc seeing France oppressed

Defendendo-a pagou com a vida	Defending her paid with her life
Camilo Castelo Branco foi escritor	Camilo Castelo Branco was a writer
Ficou cego, suicidou-se	He ended up blind and committed suicide
Kennedy desejava a integração	Kennedy desired integration
Reprovaria a segregação	He reproved segregation
Foi morto à bala	And was shot in the city of
Na cidade de Dallas	Dallas
Jesus Cristo não foi julgado	Jesus Christ was not judged
Foi chacinado e crucificado	He was slaughtered and crucified
Com requinte de perversidade	With the height of perversity
O pior crime da humanidade	The worst crime of humanity

(234–235)

According to Meihy this poem was written in the last decade of Jesus's literary career (and life) and represents a maturation in her treatment of the topic of marginality while employing a universalist vision that she had developed in her diary and other poems. Jesus represents and identifies with those ultimately persecuted by referring to writers and politicians. In the case of the politicians this persecution was because of their support of unpopular and threatening political ideas. The combination of an alliance with the persecuted along with sympathy for and identification with them, without boundaries, is an important part of Jesus's reformulation of identity. It emphasizes the part of her that does not want to be tied to the expectations of a favelada. While her sympathy for the persecuted can be seen as stemming from her own personal experiences, Jesus crosses boundaries in other ideas expressed in the poem:

> [The identification of Carolina with the persecuted was a type of conclusion of her history. It was also a pole of identification with the misunderstood. Her lack of recognition in life and exclusion closed the circumference that encircled the rejected people who would later be accepted. . . . Along the same line, the universalist vision of Jesus is interesting. In the case of the present poem the thematic of justice goes beyond borders and proposes various approximations].

> A identificação de Carolina com os perseguidos era uma espécie de conclusão de sua história. Era também um pólo de identificação com os não compreendidos. O não reconhecimento

em vida e a exclusão fechavam a circunferência que cercava os refutados que seriam aceitos depois. . . . Na mesma linha, a visão universalista de De Jesus é interessante. No caso do presente poema, a temática da justiça supera fronteiras e propõe aproximações várias. (Meihy, "O Inventário" 23–25)

By referring to famous people whose lives were cruelly cut short, Jesus once again shows the broad range of subjects about which she is knowledgeable as well as her stand on the inequities of the world. This poetic forum gives her an opportunity to give her views on issues of justice and injustice that crosses boundaries, and present a politicized voice that is not linked to a party or government strategy but to human behaviors.

Jesus's poetic treatment of marginality, from either her point of view or that of the poetic voice, is dealt with even more in the collection *Antologia pessoal*. In poems like "O Marginal" (The Marginal) the narrator states, "Vivo, ao relento, sem abrigo / Sem afeto e sem amigo / Sou um marginal" (90) [I live, outdoors, without shelter / Without affection and without a friend / I am a marginal.] In "O colono e o fazendeiro"(The Farmhand and the Farmer) she explores the exploitation and abandonment of the farmer, exposing the myth of 1888 being the official end of any kind of slavery:

Diz o brasileiro	The Brazilian says
Que acabou a escravidão	That slavery ended
Mas o colono sua o ano inteiro	But the farm hand sweats the year round
E nunca tem um tostão	And never has a cent
É espoliado sem lei, sem proteção	He is robbed without law, without protection
Quando o coitado sucumbir	When the unfortunate one succumbs
É sepultado como indigente.	He is buried as a beggar.

(147–149)

In "Atualidades"/("News") Jesus continues her exploration of marginalization with a representation of the suffering of a poor woman who sees no hope in her future, only confinement to the suffering experienced by the lower socioeconomic classes:

Não sei porque estou vivendo	I don't know why I am living
Se me falta até a ilusão	If I don't even have a dream
Não percebem as autoridades	Don't the authorities realize
Que já estou aprisionada	That I am already imprisoned
Com estas dificuldades	That with these difficulties
Que sou uma desgraçada?	That I am disgraced?

Vivo ao léu sem ter morada
O mundo do pobre acabou-se
Luta e sofre por fim se cansa
Igual ao viajante no deserto."
(164–165)

I live without a home
The world of the poor has ended
He fights and suffers and finally tires
Just like the traveller in the desert.

Textual Identity and Reader Reception

Quarto de despejo is a text that serves as one woman's account of a life struggle shared by others in her favela and a single life seeking to stand out. Within this identity of difference is Jesus the writer, an ability that allows her to express the other facets of her self-definition. As an Afro Brazilian woman in the favela her conception and representation of her identity are strongly influenced by the socioeconomic categories used to describe her. For this reason, Jesus reformulates her identity in part in terms of race, gender, and class. However, there is at the same time a tension between her original marginalized position and the more central positioning represented by her access to the dominant discourse. Jesus navigates between adopting certain social standards of how to achieve success and inverting the prejudice and stereotypes she faces in order to create a representation of herself that is positive, and not captive to society's expectations. Nonetheless, Jesus's reformulation of the self is one in progress. Through her writing she conceives of but also actively works to achieve a life and identity different from her present reductive one of favelada.

In a text with a commercial awareness (that is, of a public outside of the favela who would not only be interested in the subject but able and willing to purchase it), Jesus and Audálio Dantas (through his editing of the diary) engage their readers' interest by speaking to them (in ways that at times ask their approval) yet maintaining a fine balance between providing guidance or asking for an involved understanding of aspects of Jesus's life philosophies. Jesus addresses her public in such a way that, while making the reader aware of the critical distance at work in interpreting the text, allows an active interpretation of her identity reformulation. Such engagement in her life leads the reader to feel a personal investment in this process (rather than a somewhat distanced curiosity) that continually seeks to balance the multiplicities of her identity.

Chapter Two

Jesus's *Diário* and the
Hybrid Forms of Textual Agency

Moradia: Figurative Reconstructions of Identity and Language

For Jesus the process of redefining her identity goes beyond the contestation of social limits by the mere act of writing and publishing. Within her text she utilizes language and explores themes that also serve as a subversion of the expected knowledge of a favelada. In *Quarto de despejo* Jesus engages in such textual manipulation by creating a hybrid work in three important areas: (1) the use of marginalized and mainstream discourse that alternates between the figurative and literal; (2) a poetic discourse within a narrative framework whose use of symbolism represents a structural and thematic hybridity; and (3) the grammatical manipulation that reveals her tension between an individual and a collective identity. If we first look at Jesus's language in the diary we see that she does not solely use personal anecdotes and an informal confessional style to represent her historical position but also makes use of different metaphors to illustrate her awareness of her present status in society. The most powerful metaphor used is that of the rooms in a house, as best exemplified in the first half of the title *Quarto de despejo*, which in English literally means "the back room." Through this metaphor of the house Jesus contrasts her present historical positioning with her desired future positioning: "I have the impression that I am in a living room with crystal chandeliers, rugs of velvet, and satin cushions. And when I'm in the favela I have the impression that I'm a useless object, destined to be forever in a garbage dump" (38). Jesus's self-worth as described here is intimately linked to her physical position. When she is in the city her sense of worth is expressed through a self-positioning in a protected, valorized, even luxurious space: in a living room. However, in the favela

49

her lack of worth is expressed through devalorization and vulnerability: as "a useless object." She is stripped of not only her utility in society but also her humanity. As a favelada she is objectified, becoming just another piece of garbage to be discarded.

While the metaphor of the living room is transitory and therefore temporary Jesus uses the metaphor of the *quarto de despejo* for a seemingly permanent, unchangeable state that illustrates what she is. Nonetheless, this devaluation is still predicated on being surrounded by poverty.

In general the place referent *moradía* has two important meanings. While it literally means "dwelling", I use the concept to describe longing for a permanent home that Jesus expresses throughout *Quarto de despejo*. First, it indicates that the subject possesses a home, and consequently, a place of belonging. Second, it is a space one has taken over and can use as a site of resistance. It was this sense of belonging and the opportunity to participate in acts of resistance that Jesus used to redefine herself. As Mervin Arrington Jr. points out, the use of the concept of moradía in defining the self, in resistance to the labels placed upon her, is important to Jesus because of the poverty from which she originated: "The predilection for houses reflected in the titles of her two books and the house metaphors she employs throughout may seem an obsession to those for whom access to adequate shelter is not problematic. The poor, however, cannot take this basic necessity for granted" (9). The metaphor of moradía has a special meaning for Jesus because she has been without permanent shelter most of her life and understands the sense of power it brings. Jesus's fascination is not merely the valorization of what she lacked, as Arrington states, but an awareness of the control this sense of belonging brings, especially in a society that tried to deny her control in other areas of her life (for example, in job opportunities, her self-perception, and her interaction with others.) Jesus also exerts this control in the favela and not just in her journeys (both physical and mental) to the city. As Meihy and Levine observe "E sua casa era seu mundo: nele estavam seu filho e os cadernos onde escrevia" (22). [And her home was her world: in it were her child and the notebooks where she wrote."] Through the possession of books in her home, this site becomes a statement against the stereotype of faveladas as ignorant and illiterate, thus asserting her status as a literate, knowledgeable woman and as a mother.

Jesus's use of moradía in affirming her historical positioning is also part of the reflection of the subject in cultural mirrors that both Friedman and Rowbotham's theories address. While Rowbotham stresses that solidarity with another helps the individual woman assert her identity, Friedman astutely emphasizes that women create a unique sense of self by navigating cultural factors and collective interactions (Friedman 95).

Jesus's use of metaphors of moradia is also significant because through it she demonstrates her ability to use a symbolic discourse and not just rely on a direct, factual narration of her life. The metaphors used to illustrate this concept of moradía change as her views and focus on the contrast between wealth and poverty, city and favela change. In the beginning, as evidenced by the example previously cited, the contrast was based on a physical transportation between the city and the favela that occurred whenever Jesus went to work to earn money for her family. However, moradía is also a place she sets up in her mind to escape: "When I write I think I live in a golden castle that shines in the sunlight. . . . My happy hours are when I am living in my imaginary castles." (*Child of the Dark* 57).

Unlike the dreams of a "casa de alvenaria," which in English literally means "the brick house," the purpose of envisioning a different surrounding is to provide a temporary hope and respite from daily troubles by traveling mentally to a place she may never physically reach.

The contrast of the metaphors of living room and back room throughout the *Diário* connect us with a metaphor of moradia used not only in this diary but also in *Casa de Alvenaria* published in English as *I'm Going to have a Little House*. This is the follow-up to the first diary and continues from the family's departure from the favela to a middle-class area where they fulfill Jesus's dream of living in her own brick house. Living in one's own house was a sign of a certain social status, and therefore, for Jesus and her family, an escape from the stigma of the favela.

The difference in title from the first to the second diary illustrates the link between one's moradía and one's social status. In *Quarto de despejo* the reference in Portuguese to the back room is clarified by the subtitle *diário de uma favelada*/diary of a slumdweller. By contrast, the second diary—*Casa de Alvenaria*, expains the change in Jesus's life and fortune by including the subtitle *diário de uma ex-favelada*/diary of an ex-slumdweller. Nonetheless, despite her ascension to a higher social category, Jesus is defined in relation to her past in the favela. The second diary does not present a new word to define Jesus, nor does it describe her as middle class. She is the woman who was a slum dweller, an "ex-favelada" who has not been accepted as a legitimate member of the middle class and therefore, is an outsider. As Melvin Arrington Jr. notes, this fact does not take Jesus by surprise. She makes the reader aware that she is conscious of this inacceptance, that what he terms "the fundamental reality of her marginalized condition" (8) has not changed despite changes in status.

Ultimately, the concept of moradía links Jesus's historical positioning, expressed in terms of place and consequently class, with her reworking of its implications for her identity. Because she lacks one sole community of belonging, Jesus is displaced within the favela (to a degree as intentional as incidental). The result is a relationship of identification and distance from them. Her displacement as a child in Sacramento is later mirrored in her movement from the favela to her middle-class surroundings. This physical dislocation has a profound effect on her identity. The physical and economic changes cause a shift in her self-definition, yet do not resolve it, as evidenced by the continued use of the favela ("ex-favelada") as the foundation of her identity. When Jesus and her family move to the middle-class area of Osasco in São Paulo this tension is continued, both on her part and on that of a society refusing to allow her to erase her past.

Discursive Dualities of Identities: Favelada versus Letrada

Jesus's redefinition as someone whose voice is both a marker of an individual identity that straddles both poor and educated communities, and a collective identity that posits itself as a representative of the poor is structurally achieved through the inclusion of three related elements that reflect the duality of the writer: nonstandard Portuguese grammar, repetition, and ellipses.

Gilkin's observation on the immediate, yet at times disjointed structure of the diary help demonstrate the relation of structure to life and memory that is evident in Jesus's text: "Diaries, by their very nature, are fragmentary—selective siftings that are not always concerned with the most important events, thoughts, or feelings of a particular day. . . . All of these topics are placed side by side with a disarming discontinuity that imitates the randomness of memory and of life itself" (7). However, this perceived discontinuity of singular events is different from the cumulative effect of a detailed account of the course of a life: "Viewing her own accumulated evidence from a year's perspective, the diarist can accept or can resolve on a pattern-breaking, even a cataclysmic change" (7–8).

In *Quarto de despejo* discontinuity is achieved through an alternation of structures, linguistic registers, and nonstandard grammar that especially highlight the tension of Jesus's identity as favelada yet author who is ever distancing herself from her origins in poverty. This duality is also representative of the collaboration between Jesus and Dantas. For Dantas, Jesus's writing was an important element to be maintained, but in the larger context of the diary's overall success with a predominantly White Brazilian readership. Therefore, there were times when her orthography was corrected and, even more commonplace, when Dantas omitted facts that he deemed repetitious and counterproductive to the diary's message.

One important document is Dantas's own explanation of his role as editor, given in the introduction of the second edition, an Editora-Atica reprint of the text entitled "A atualidade do mundo de Carolina" (The Present Time of Carolina's World): "Li todas aquelas vinte cadernos que continham o dia-a-dia de De Jesus e de seus companheiros de triste viagem. . . . Mexi, também, na pontuação, assim como em algumas palavras cuja grafia poderia levar à incompreensão da leitura."(3). [I read all those twenty notebooks that contained the day-to-day of de Jesus and of her companions on the sad journey. . . . I also worked with the punctuation, as well as some words whose orthography could lead to incomprehension in the reading.]

Dantas confesses to some correction of Jesus's grammar to clarify certain sections for the reader but insists that his orthographic corrections were minimal. While much discussion has revolved around the range of Dantas's corrections and its effect on the published text, I believe that the grammar left unedited was in order to serve his needs and represent Jesus. On one hand, there is the power of the editor consciously leaving the subject's grammar intact in order to reinforce the text's marketability as a realistic document of nonfiction. On the other hand, however, is the subject herself, writing as she does, refusing to edit herself, in order to document faithfully her life at that moment. If we return to my discussion of the metaphors used in the text, combined with selections of poetry, we see a pattern of informal Portuguese carefully broken up by uses of formal metaphoric language. In other words, it is the colloquial, informal language—errors and all—that is predominant throughout the text, allowing me as a reader to speculate on Jesus's intentions in varying her literary style the way she did as a way of asserting a complex identity.

When we view Jesus as an active participant in the writing of *Quarto de despejo* and not an editor's pawn, the issue of nonstandard Portuguese becomes a tool used to maintain some power over her representation. If one looks at the relationship this way, it is Jesus who is using or taking advantage of the opportunity Dantas provides in order to have the forum to present as unmediated and unedited a self-representation, albeit in progress, that the commercial purpose of the text will allow.

Two examples from the text especially illustrate the power and purpose of Jesus's grammar. I include the Portuguese original to highlight this effect:

- Eu cançava e sentava . . . Depois começara a chorar. Mas o povo não deve cançar. Não deve chorar" (48). I got tired and sat down. Afterward I started to cry. But the people must not get tired. They must not cry (*Child of the Dark* 53).

- Alguns homens em São Paulo Andam todos carimbados Traz um letreiro nas costas Dizendo onde é empregado. Some men in Sao Paulo Walk with lettering on their back On them is plainly written Where they're working at (*Child of the Dark* 106).

In the two quotes that I have selected we can identify three categories of errors in Jesus's Portuguese. In the first quote there is an error in orthography: "Cançava" instead of "cansava". The second is an error of verb agreement: "Alguns homens ... traz un letreiro" instead of "Alguns homens ... trazem um letreiro." The last is incorrect verb usage. "onde é empregado" instead of "onde estão empregados."

With these specific examples it is easier to see the effects of the grammar that I previously discussed. In the first quote there is some reference made to the reaction of the poor to their circumstances. The juxtaposition of the ideas expressed with the grammatical mistakes made creates a tension that translates to similar tension in the reader's reaction. It is between the expectations of her social status and the keen insight her observations express. This insight is in part from belonging to the community which she describes and the objectivity that her sense of difference and distance give her. It is precisely this tension that exemplifies the complexity and nonconformity of Jesus and her text, choosing to not let the textual manifestation of her identity fall into her reader's definable categories. The tension serves as her space to emphasize the process that is her identity—a nonstatic identity.

The question remains however how this relates to the aspects of textual interruption found in the text. The interruption is caused by the tension or interaction that I have just discussed. In a text that was edited for coherence, fluidity, and style, the maintenance of nonstandard Portuguese used to express Jesus's insights emerges time and time again to unbalance the reader's perceptions of the text and its author.

While Jesus does not explicitly state her decision to keep her grammar as is in order to make a statement about her identity and its resistance to appropriation, a close reading of her references to the act of writing can lead us to meaningful conclusions in this respect. We begin to see that she was not one to relinquish total control of her product and livelihood to Dantas. The result was a balancing act: trying to write freely and uncensored about themes that were important to her while showing the proof of her intellectual growth and capacity.

In fact in later texts Jesus attempts to document her intellectual and educational advancement through improved grammar and writing style, as Levine and Meihy attest: "We should not be surprised that Carolina made progress in her writing. She always had worked hard to improve herself."[3]

Another element of the diary's structure that was used to emphasize certain truths about Jesus and her life is repetition. Throughout the
text there are various references to her daily routine and responsibilities,
stressing the constant struggles she endured just to survive: "I got up
and . . . I went to get the water. . . . But the poor don't rest. . . . You all
know that I go to get water every morning" (9,10,110). In the favela the
oppressive conditions that remained constant required survival tactics
that as a result remained the same. As Vogt observes:

> Carolina unfolds over time her poverty and that of the
> favelados. But since the days repeat themselves equally and
> monotonously in the ritual of hunger-work-survival, the re-
> sult is, as we said, the construction, throughout the narrative,
> of a type of diametaphor of the every day.
>
> Carolina desdobra no tempo sua pobreza e a dos favelados.
> Mas como os dias se repetem igual e monótonos no ritual de
> fome-trabalho-sobrevivência, o resultado é, como dissemos, a
> construção, ao longo da narrativa, de uma espécie de
> diametáfora de todos os dias. (210)

Jesus uses this common characteristic of any diary to emphasize her
daily rituals and what through time become important parts of what
define her. Nonetheless, as we have seen throughout the diary the individual identity is caught up with a collective representation of the life of
favelados. As Vogt asserts, her personal ritual of hunger-work-survival
becomes a metaphor for the unchanging life of her community.

While the repetition of these activities provides the reader with a
compelling portrait of the physical side of her existence, Jesus also stresses
the emotional consequences by reiterating phrases like "Today I'm sad.
I'm nervous. I don't know if I should start crying or start running until
I fall unconscious" (42) and "Today I'm happy. I'm laughing without any
reason. I'm singing" (106). Arrington notes that repetition plays an important role in the follow-up to *Quarto de despejo* entitled *Casa de Alvenaria*:
"The reader must keep in mind that what may appear to be routine,
mindless activities, such as eating a regular meal and bathing, are special
occasions for Carolina and she treats them accordingly. This perspective
can only be fully appreciated within the context of the first diary, where
her constant, overriding theme was the fight against hunger" (5). In this
respect, the second diary provides a positive ritual of survival to contrast
with the first diary's negative ritual of hunger.

However, by engaging in positive activities like writing the diary,
Jesus is able to experience a release that transcends the emotional roller

coaster of her daily struggles. Through the repeated juxtaposition of daily activities necessary for physical survival with writing that provides an equally important emotional survival, she structurally underscores her difference from the other favelados and ultimately her individuality.

Lastly, by highlighting certain themes while omitting others, Jesus's use in *Quarto de despejo* of ellipses and the spaces left by these omissions are significant factors influencing the reader's interpretation of Jesus's life story and her process of identity reformulation. Once more Dantas's role can help us understand how the issue of agency works here. As is the case with the correction of grammatical errors, Dantas, as editor did exercise some power by omitting phrases and passages he deemed unnecessary. The result, however, is a sharing of agency, albeit problematic, between himself and Jesus as opposed to a complete shift to one person. The reader and critic should always remember that the words and emotions expressed, regardless of their placement, are Jesus's not Dantas's. In that sense her agency is clear. Dantas's mediation was to arrange phrases in a way that would maximize the emotional impact of her words for the targeted white Brazilian reader. Careful study of the spaces and the information surrounding them demonstrates three important functions of the ellipses and their subsequent impact on the reader: (1) to provide concise accounts of Jesus's life; (2) to highlight the transition from an example of her daily life to a commentary on issues of violence, politics, or relationships; and (3) set up a situation of cause and effect that explains her writing.

While providing direct accounts of Jesus's life, the ellipses also provide a concise presentation of daily events and emotions. One such example is when Jesus describes wanting distance from the favelados and repeats the difference between herself and them, namely, her self-control: "What infuriates me is that the parents come to my door to disrupt my rare moments of inner tranquility (. . .) But when they upset me, I write" (*Child of the Dark* 21). The reader is guided straight to the heart of Jesus's desire for separation, at times, from the other favelados yet at the same time must put it in perspective with her daily routine, political positions, and other aspects of her character.

Also interspersed with Jesus's day-to-day life are observations connecting daily issues with social and political commentary. One example is in the entry of May 19, 1958. Starting out with a comparison between the ease of a bird's life and the difficulty of a favelado's life, she extends the metaphor to then President Juscelino Kubitschek and the concern he should have for the suffering of the favelados. Jesus subtly continues her commentary with an example of a woman who, in trying to better her life, ignored the suffering of her children, and moves on to express her own despair and the falseness of politicians who pretend to want to help. Although this diary entry also includes a praise of her country (despite all the suffering she faces in it), by the end of the day there is a repetition of the imagery of Jesus's sense of valorization in the city and sense of devalorization in the favela. The combination of the social, political, and psychological exemplifies her constant critical assessment of what goes on around her and affects her directly instead of a simple retelling of daily events.

The third function of the ellipses is to alternate events and emotions in a way that helps the reader further understand the importance of writing to Jesus. One example can be found after one of the usual fights in the favela: "—Oh, If I could move out of this favela! I feel like I'm in hell!" . . . I sat in the sun to write. Silvia's daughter, a girl of six, passed by and said: "You're writing again, stinking nigger!" (Jesus, *Child of the Dark* 30). One result of such a juxtaposition is the reader's interpretation of the situation as one very similar to cause and effect or, in other words, cause (provocation) and reaction. In both situations Jesus tells of feelings of despair and unhappiness with her surroundings and hostility from other favelados. The effect—or reaction—is given after the ellipses: she writes. While this sequence of events probably did not immediately follow each other in Jesus's original text, their placement this way in the edited Portuguese diary stresses Jesus's writing as an important way of combating her unhappiness and mistreatment by those around her. In these examples especially, the reader is handed a situation and guided to a conclusion of cause and effect.

Throughout this chapter I have raised the issue of how much power over the text Jesus was able to maintain once it left her unedited notebooks and passed on to Dantas's hands. The ellipses that one finds point to areas where Jesus's voice is very much mediated by Dantas and the commercial and editorial concerns he represents. This takes into consideration that Jesus as well was aware of the commercial aspect of her text and of at least some of the implications of this. The grammatical mistakes however, tell a more complicated story. Here, more than in the case of the ellipses one can see more of the collaboration between Jesus and Dantas that I believe was the case. The interaction between Dantas and Jesus can be seen as a tension between the power of the editor consciously leaving the subject's grammar intact, and the subject refusing to edit herself. Her grammar at that moment is part of the identity of favelada and therefore, to change it would be to deny the existence of that part of her. Although Jesus wants to change her social status, she accepts that being a favelada is part of who she is and is not willing (nor educationally equipped) at that time to achieve change at the expense of her agency.

Poetry as Symbolic Hybridity

Despite the obstacles that societal norms and prejudices posed, Jesus attempted to reflect her reality and emotions not only by establishing herself as a poet, as I discussed in chapter 1, but also by rewriting poetry. This revision of the genre included manipulating the figurative elements of the discourse in order to do so. The result is a writing characterized by hybridity: incorporating her poetic voice within a narrative form in order to serve the multiple purposes of reformation and resistance. This hybrid poetic structure unites the subject matter of the favela with the redefinition of individual identity through the use of more traditional Brazilian poetics combined with contemporary experience.

One of the most telling examples in *Quarto de despejo* of the use of metaphorical language is Jesus's reflection on the beauty of her country: "The leaves moved by themselves. I thought: they are applauding my gesture of love to my country. . . . Vera was smiling and I thought of Casimiro de Abreu, the Brazilian poet who said: 'Laugh, child, Life is beautiful.' Life was good in that era. Because now in this era it's necessary to say: 'Cry, child. Life is bitter' " (*Child of the Dark* 37). It is a significant progression for Jesus from the use of poetic imagery to a reference to a well-known Brazilian poet, Casimiro de Abreu. This reference exemplifies the functions of poetry Meihy pointed out: proof of knowledge and an opportunity to subvert it. First, by quoting from a renowned Brazilian poet Jesus is proving that she is not only literate, but also well read, and in doing so is engaging in an act of resistance against the labels placed on her. As Meihy observes, Jesus's poetic lineage can be traced to other Brazilian writers as well:

> [Carolina was by self-definition a poet. She so much as called herself a poetess. . . . Ugly in form, her poems were a kind of poor cousin of consecrated beauty. . . . The rough poems of Carolina were, nevertheless, rich rhymes of the essence of the most miserable aspects of our progress. They were the depravation of pure beauty and the subversion of an order which consisted of Vinícius de Morais, Lygia Fagundes Telles, João Cabral de Mello Netto, Carlos Drummond de Andrade, and so on. Carolina was the navigator of a sea of transformations. It was she who would be the conqueror of the world.]

> Carolina foi e era por autodefinição *poeta*. Sequer dizia-se *poetisa*. . . . Feia na forma, suas poesias eram uma espécie de *primos pobres* da beleza consagrada. . . . Os versos toscos de Carolina eram, contudo, rima rica da essência do que de mais

miserável tinha o nosso progresso. Eram também a depravação da beleza pura e a subversão de uma ordem da qual constavam Vinícius de Morais, Lygia Fagundes Telles, Joâo Cabral de Mello Netto, Carlos Drummond de Andrade et alli. . . . Carolina era navegante de um mar de transformações. Ela é quem ia ser conquistadora do mundo. (*Antologia pessoal* 17–18).

In this quote Meihy emphasizes the relationship that Carolina's poetry has with the more classical styles and with the renowned writers of the time. Although her forms were often considered deformations of the beauty of more aesthetic poetry, what made Jesus special was that her poetry was a subversion of these forms. Her greatest credit was the belief that she could be a poet who transformed instead of merely copied. What this desire therefore created was a poetry that represented the spaces where the refined and the rough could coexist equally.

Second, Jesus is bringing the traditional to the reality of the favela. In this passage she articulates her suffering by using poetic language which bridges the gap between a more traditional poetry read by members of the upper echelons of society and the language and daily life of the favelados. Instead of the pure joy that Casimiro de Abreu encouraged his readers to feel, Jesus contextualizes the poem to the emotions of the favelados: from skepticism to happiness to sadness and cynicism. However, she, as the poet, stands in the middle, never truly claiming the former as her identity (in part because she was never truly accepted by that dominant society) but not able nor wanting to return to the latter.[1]

These themes show Jesus's allegiances as a self-confessed "poet" to be far-reaching and not confined to the favela. In other poems from her body of work she reflects on what writing in the poetic genre implies as a social and political act. One poem in particular that demonstrates Jesus's voice and another classic source of her love of poetry is "O exilado" (The Exiled One):

Eu não esqueço aquele dia:	I will not forget that day:
A vez primeira que li	The first time I read
Era uma linda poesia	It was a beautiful poem
E a emoção que senti	And the emotion I felt
O meu autor predileto	My favorite author
O imortal Gonçalves Dias	The immortal Gonçalves Dias
Eu lia com muito afeto	I read his books of poems
Os seus livros de poesias	with much affection
Pobre poeta exilado	Poor exiled poet
Na terra que não é sua	In the land that was not his own

Sente saudades dos prados	He longs for the plains
Das nossas noites de lua	For our moonlit nights
Minha terra tem brilhante	My land has diamonds
Nosso céu é cor de anil	Our sky is the color of indigo
O poeta lá mui distante	The poet over there, so distant
Tem saudades do Brasil.	Longs for Brazil.
(160)	

Whereas before, Jesus observed the unfortunate circumstance of continuing to create one's poetry in exile, here she questions if the poetry itself is not the cause of the distance or exile. She thus opens up a space to examine the transgressive nature of poetry and its possible consequences. Her last question leads the reader to recall her accounts in *Quarto de despejo* of the ridicule and isolation she faced from other favelados because of her ability to write, be it the diary, plays, fiction, or poetry. Jesus's writing disconcerted many of the faveladas around her, causing them to separate from her in order to protect themselves from the perceived invasion of their privacy. This isolation did not bother Jesus but allowed her to care for her family and write, without the disturbance or the temptations and traps she felt association with the other favelados would bring.

The second important aspect of this poem is the relation established in the last stanza between exile or isolation and poetry. Jesus notes that despite the beauty of his verse and the enormity of his talent, Dias was forced to live outside of his country of birth, with only his longing for Brazil to keep him company. Here, the relation is subtly alluded to by the observation that Dias is no longer just the "favored author" or the "immortal" but the "poor exiled poet." His separation becomes part of what identifies him for others along with his ability as a poet—like the narrator of this poem. His poetry then takes on the new dimension of distance, manifesting itself in his verse. In the last stanza Jesus establishes more directly the connection that she had only previously alluded to: "O que fez o Gonçalves Dias/Para ser um exilado?/Será que escrever poesias é pecado?"(160) [What did Gonçalves Dias do/To be exiled?/Could it be that writing poetry/Is a sin?]

Jesus's question to her readers becomes not just about Gonçalves Dias but also about herself. "O exilado" takes on a double meaning as a meditation on personal expression and dislocation by a renowned Brazilian poet and by Jesus (another Brazilian poet, though less renowned), who in a sense fostered this isolation as a means of survival.[2] Just as the metaphor of moradía taken in the context of the prejudices she (and her children) faced in her transition from the community of favelados to the higher socioeconomic community, this work reveals the effects of Jesus's displacement on her relationship with society's norms.

Like her use of structures and themes taken from Casimiro de Abreu, Jesus's use of Gonçalves Dias's work as a template for her own exploration of her marginalization is a challenge to the stereotype of illiterate favelados, and particularly faveladas. She implicitly emphasizes that she was like so many other educated Brazilians who read Dias's poetry and found themselves inspired. By subtly emphasizing such a connection, Jesus stresses this commonality with her readership that bridges class difference.

Discursive Representations of Feminine Writing

The analysis of Jesus's conceptions of language, structure, and discourse as elements in the representation of her historical positioning and reformulated self-definition raises the question of the impact of the author's identity on the discourses chosen to represent it. In the case of women's writing, one way in which this question is framed is in terms of feminine writing, a focus that specifically questions the impact of the gendered component of the subject's self-definition on the discursive framework within which it is reconstituted. Although the argument for *Quarto de despejo* as feminine writing is mainly supported by a socioeconomically based definition represented in its thematic content, the articulation of the woman's condition and the creation of spaces of resistance also help shed light on examples of more linguistically based definitions of *l'écriture féminine*. The combination of the two provides a more comprehensive understanding of the redefinitions of Jesus's sense of self.

One theory that helps determine the extent to which these characteristics qualify as feminine writing are three principles that Smith believes are germane to women's autobiography: (1) the ways in which the autobiographer's status as woman influences the autobiographical project and the four fictions that determine it: memory, the "I," the imagined reader, and the story; (2) the means through which the autobiographer establishes her discursive power; and (3) the relation of this authority to her sexuality. Along with the principles of the structural aspect of Jesus's writing, the theories of the linguistic construction of the feminine are helpful in understanding her writing as falling within or challenging previous models of feminine writing.

The linguistic and psychoanalytic approaches to the representations of the individual provide a particular complementary focus on the problems of the psycholinguistic means of gendering the self. As Julia Kristeva asserted, the social and the symbolic are closely linked: "Sexual difference—which is at once biological, physiological, and relative to reproduction—is translated by and translates a difference in the relationship of subjects to the symbolic contract which is the social contract: a difference, then, in the relationship to power, language, and meaning" (476). In the text this is revealed in an investigation of the impact of language on counterpositions of the feminine to rigid "masculine/authorial" discourse and the areas where there is a subversion of these standards. This corresponds to the second school of thought that Maggie Humm describes as "developing a specifically female discourse . . . a language that allows the eruption of the semiotic into the symbolic in a rich new form. . . . [T]here must be a difference between men's libidinal expression (as valorized by our culture) and the libidinal expressions of women (as repressed in our culture) which incurs a necessary difference in language" (47). An equally significant definition of feminine writing that I will return to because of its applicability to Jesus's text is Bernd's assertion that feminine writing is born of societal oppression and therefore uses the discourse to reclaim women's stolen, repressed space.

Jesus's diary exemplifies one strategic recuperation of a silenced voice through textual disruption that is both an interruption of language and the use of themes oriented around a woman's experience. In this linguistic and thematic interruption Jesus exhibits once more the hybridity that I have emphasized in other areas of her writing and self-definition. In the following examples she uses a more lyrical style than what is used to recount her routine in the favela:

> The night is warm. The sky is peppered with stars. I have the crazy desire to cut a piece of the sky to make a dress. (*Child of the Dark* 35)

> Don't you ever think you're going to get
> My love again.
> No, my hate will grow,
> Put in roots and bear fruit.
> (*Child of the Dark* 135)

The first aspect of these quotes that stands out is the use of certain adjectives, personification, and metaphors that distinguish these passages from the others. When Jesus refers to the sky as" peppered with stars" [salpicado de estrelas], and to a possible romance or friendship turned sour—"my hate will grow, Put in roots and bear fruit" [o meu odio vai evoluir, criar raizes e dar semente] the effect of these symbolic elements is similar to the tension discussed before between her standard and nonstandard grammar. The routine life of the favelada that the reader is lured into envisioning is at once upset by a style seemingly foreign to both the life and the poet.

The second salient element of these quotes is the theme: aspects of a woman's life, nature, and love. Again, the thematics can be seen as an example of Jesus's assertion of the gendered (and specifically non-masculine) component of her identity, particularly because these themes point to an emphasis on concerns and elements not usually considered as ruled by reason and logic—and therefore not considered masculine according to convention.

The specific themes found in these quotes serve as a way of returning to the question posed at the beginning of this section: Can *Quarto de despejo* be seen as an example of feminine writing? If we define it according to the emphasis on nonmasculine themes, then there is evidence that seemingly supports its categorization as such, but not without highlighting Jesus's expansion of what are considered masculine themes by her many social commentaries. When she states, "Oh, São Paulo! A queen that vainly shows her skyscrapers that are her crown of gold. All dressed up in velvet and silk but with cheap stockings underneath—the favela" (*Child of the Dark* 42), Jesus uses feminized images of a queen and her clothing to make a social commentary on the hypocrisy and inequality of the extreme dichotomy of vast wealth and vast poverty. What is interesting about this comment is that she broaches difficult political problems—engaging in an activity often thought to be masculine—in a language that is poetic and linked to the feminine. The result is a questioning of these labels while actively subverting them. Jesus also questions the labels of "feminine" as emotional and "masculine" as dominated by reason by the combination of poetry dealing solely with love and nature and explicit political commentary. The production of both types of poetry demonstrates her reluctance to be relegated to one form of expression.

If we look at the French feminist assertion that the feminine can be represented as a linguistic interruption then we see the limitations of an attempt to superimpose French feminist theory on this Latin American, and specifically Brazilian, text. This problematic is evident when we consider once more the societal emphasis on dominating the written code (which in the end I also relate to Piedra's explication of "literary whitening") and its effects on Jesus. Here was a woman who in part believed in the benefits of education, not only in terms of knowledge of history and literature, but also of grammar. Although throughout the text we see many examples of her questioning of social roles, politics, and racial stereotypes, her search never completely reaches the level of doubting the authority of language. For this reason the disruptions I pointed to in her text are more orthographic and representative of her current position, both educationally and socially. Given her socioeconomic positioning at the time of writing the diary, a distrust of language on a linguistic level was not a part of Jesus's view of herself. In fact, as her daughter later recounts, her mother believed so much in education as part of the process of reformulating identity that she continuously tried to apply the lessons of the texts she read to her own writing style:

> She preferred to spend her time reading and writing. . . . In a short number of years, my mother ended up learning a good deal, both through me and on her own. Her Portuguese style improved significantly in comparison to her early writing. I actually heard from her mouth that she was ashamed of all of the grammatical errors in *Quarto de Despejo*, her first book. In Parelheiros she even read encyclopedias. (qtd. in Levine and Meihy 111).

This is confirmed by the authors of *Cinderela negra* when they emphasize that Jesus studied writing as one studies a craft: constantly finding resources to improve, such as her purchases of "a dictionary, desk encyclopedia, thesaurus, and daily newspapers." (Levine and Meihy 89).[3]

Another key to answering this query is found in the effects of Jesus's nonstandard grammar. The doubling of Jesus's voice into both an individual and collective tool opens up her text beyond the strict gender specific categorization that feminine writing usually denotes. When Jesus's voice is more collective she speaks for either a socioeconomic or racial community that is not always necessarily gender specific. Although there is textual evidence to support the contention that Jesus's gender is always present, whether explicitly or implicitly, the emphasis or point of reference is not always a gendered one. As a result, the categorization of Jesus's writing as an example of feminine writing must be expanded by 1) the continual presence in such works of a gendered subject even when the text's purpose is other, and 2) the stretching of the boundaries of feminine that is especially influenced by her movement between marginal and dominant positions.

If we return to Bernd's determination that feminine writing at its heart is characterized by the individual's attempts to situate herself as subject counter to society's oppression and claim a position to articulate identity, Jesus's text demonstrates this process. It is, however, a complicated act for Jesus and must be understood as such. The subject she posits is a hybrid that both challenges dominant labels of race, class, and gender while aligning herself in other ways with national discourses that establish specific relationships between class, education, citizenship, and identity.

As autobiography Jesus uses her writing of the diary to explore yet also justify her individual complexity while at the same time working to reformulate it. In so doing she uses, expands, and exposes the parameters of the autobiographical process, especially in diary form, in which she operates. One of the overall effects of her navigation of marginal and dominant discourses is the creation of a hybrid text that not only pushes its own limits but also challenges the boundaries of feminine writing by proposing a type of writing that is in constant movement like its author.

The process of self-reflexivity in women's literature is not found solely in autobiographical texts. How does a project of identity reformulation work in a fictional text that nonetheless crosses the boundaries of representation? One example that can provide an answer is found in the Brazilian writer Lispector, whose marginalization is different from Jesus's although linked as well to her historical positioning. Like Jesus, she navigates positions of marginality and her engagement with dominant discourse, but on a more structural level as well as social. The reformulation of identity that will be explored in her text is a process that stems from and influences the other important question Lispector asks: from an ontological viewpoint, how do we define the Other, both outside of and within us? As she explores that question Lispector's movement between the margin and center demonstrates how the understanding and reworking of the self is intimately tied to this exploration while exposing the difficulties and limitations in this endeavor.

Chapter Three

Authorial Intervention in
A hora da estrela: Metatextual and
Structural Multiplicity

Self-Representation and the Metatext

Jesus's diary *Quarto de despejo* reformulated the strategies used to define her and contested her social, economic and historical positioning. The result was the manipulation and expansion of this confessional form through the use of centralized, traditional, and marginalized discourses to recreate herself in terms of race, sex, and gender. As a woman coming from a site of marginalization, her reformulation represented a constant movement between society's marginal and central spaces to reform her life and her children's lives economically, socially, materially, and symbolically. Through this continuous hybridity of content and form she was able to change from historical object to subject and use the diary to maintain this privileged position through her implicit dialogue with her readers.

By contrast Lispector studies the interplay between the self and the other in a specific Brazilian historical context of migration, displacement, and difference. In *A hora da estrela* she reformulates representations of selfhood and alterity through the insider/outsider framework of displacement and identity, together with an interplay of the structures of interior/exterior that crosses boundaries of gender and author/narrator/protagonist. Through Lispector's creation and manipulation of a fictional narrator in a discourse with a marginalized protagonist, she produces a text that on an extratextual and structural level reflects a movement between marginal and central discourses. The result is writing that questions phallocentric discourse, gendered definitions, and racialized identities by blurring the lines between them while commenting on the multiplicity of identity brought about by these dislocations of the subject.

A hora da estrela: Self-representation and Authorial Interference

Although *A hora da estrela*, published posthumously in 1977 is categorized as a work of fiction, the interaction between the author, narrator, and character creates a work that reveals elements of a metafictional text in part based on Federman's definition of surfiction. The dynamics between the textual subject and reader is best explained by de Man. In his description of the substitutive element of autobiography, "the autobiographical moment happens as an alignment between the two subjects involved in the process of reading in which they determine each other by mutual reflexive substitution" (70). The "figure of reading" represented in a text occurs when the author identifies him- or herself as subject. In Lispector's text this moment of interiorization occurs with the author and narrator. De Man's theories of autobiography also reveal the inability to totally reveal the self, which therefore leads to a constant search for closure through the hybrid movement of discourses within the text. However, this search is in a state of flux because of the subject's inconsistencies. As a result neither a marginalized nor a centralized position allows a satisfactory and complete representation of the subject. Therefore, it is only through a constantly refigured hybridity that the subject can find the tools necessary to redefine him- or herself. This was demonstrated in *Quarto de despejo* by Jesus's tensions between an individual representation of herself and a collective embodiment of a Black Brazilian favelada. As a subject not willing to be defined solely by her writing and personal philosophies of racial, class-based, and gendered identification, Jesus's diary displayed the continuous use of discourses that represented and challenged her individual and communal identities. By contrast, Lispector's questioning of the boundaries between the representation of the self and the Other is carried out through multiple cross-identifications of authorial and narrative voices entangling and complicating centralized, masculine, and marginalized feminine voices.

Historical Positioning, Displacement, and
Textual Hybridity in the Nonfictional World

A study of Lispector's oeuvre reveals a common theme of tension: always moving between two worlds. The instability and flux of the narrative voices are due to several destabilizing factors found inside and outside of the texts, including the author's geographic and linguistic displacement and the influence of a poststructuralist orientation in her work. Like Jesus, Lispector begins from a position of marginality and engages in a constant dialogue with various sometimes dominant discourses, be it on a social, economic, or structural level. In *A Hora da estrela* the instability of language and subject results in a self-examination through the structural representation of hybridity in three areas: (1) the connection of authorial and narrative voice established in the "Dedicatoria"; (2) the interconnectedness of author/narrator/protagonist embodied in the title's multiple perspectives; and (3) the textual subversion of masculine and feminine discourses as an authorial subversion and postfeminist critique of her own process of self -definition. The first step to understanding the particular dynamics of this dialogue for both the author, Lispector, and the characters in her text is to establish the levels of marginalization and centrality on which they are operating. Vieira cites Fiedler to illustrate that the author's relevance to the understanding of the text cannot be disregarded:

> Leslie Fiedler's study of the relationship between biography and poetry, "Archetype and Signature," . . . provides another defense for the inclusion of ethnic biography within the interpretation of an author's writing. In other words, from a cultural view of ethnic difference and history, it does matter who is doing the writing if we are to close the gap between literature and society. . . . These observations recognize the need to understand the artist within a context of sociocultural difference in artistic and cultural vision as well as alterity in the social and historical experience. (Fiedler qtd. in N. Vieira 47–48)

An understanding of the aspects of the textual representation that express Lispector's alterity must therefore begin with an examination of the sociological, cultural, and psychological considerations Fiedler speaks of—considerations that together constitute her historical positioning. For Jesus, this alterity was rooted in her marginalized social identity as a favelada living in relative poverty until the success of her diary. The social and psychological stigmas and lessons of this imposed identity are part of the foundation for the reader's understanding of her textual attempts to counteract the socioeconomic devalorization of her voice while retaining certain links to the favela community. The starting point for Lispector's alterity is a biographical note, namely, her original nationality as a child born in the Ukraine to Jewish parents who migrated to Rio de Janeiro. While the reasons for the family's departure were many, among the principal motives was the need to escape the persecution (which included pogroms) under which the Jews lived following the Russian Revolution of 1917, and following World War I (Gotlib 58, 62).

According to Nelson Vieira, it is Lispector's biculturalism and particularly her Jewish heritage in a predominantly Catholic country (although there is also the equally strong presence of Afro-Brazilian religions like candomblé and macumba that are not considered official religions) that serve as simultaneous causes and explanations for a sense of alterity, instability, and ultimately, hybridity in her narratives: "Lispector's originality stemmed from a unique style that transmitted a sense of indeterminacy and alterity as well as an eagerness to understand the mysteries of existence. This quest kept her grappling with Derridean feelings of displacement and decenteredness, which are recurring features of Jewish exegetic thought and culture" (101–102).[1] As Vieira notes, part of the Jewish heritage that is reflected in Lispector's texts is the constant refusal to commit to any permanence that encourages concretization. In general, Vieira cites that Jewish writers' resistance of facticity and rigid discourses, together with an incorporation of prophetic thinking "establishes a link between an openness toward indeterminacy and a resistance to closure" (25).

As someone incorporating both, Lispector negotiated the terms of her nationality with a society that defined itself as the opposite of her Jewish origin. On a personal level, feelings of alienation and distance were constant preoccupations for her, as she expresses in this segment of an article she wrote entitled "Belonging":

> I am certain that right from the cradle my first desire was to belong. . . . I must have somehow felt that I did not belong to anything or anyone. That my birth was superfluous. . . . Over the years, especially of late, I have lost the knack of being like other people. I no longer know how it is done. And a whole new kind of "solitude through not belonging" has started to smother me like ivy on a wall. (Lispector, *Discovering the World* 148)

The feelings of isolation Lispector reveals here are ones that accompanied her from birth, despite her ties to family members, particularly her parents. In order to examine and combat the "solitude through not belonging," she uses a tactic that Vieira cited as one of the distinctive aspects of her narratives, also common in Jewish thought—turning difference and isolation into a quest for meaning. This is the stability that Lispector seeks, a lasting sense of belonging and an understanding of the workings of the self that would provide her with a sense of equilibrium:

> Belonging does not simply come from being weak and needing to unite oneself to something or someone stronger. An intense desire to belong often comes from my own inner strength—I wish to belong so that my strength will not be

useless and may serve to strengthen some other person or thing. . . . Life has allowed me to belong now and then, as if to give me the measure of what I am losing by not belonging. And then I discovered that: *to belong is to live*. (*Discovering the World* 148–149)

The equilibrium Lispector seeks to obtain is one of the driving forces behind her desire to belong. By being a part of something larger than herself she has the opportunity to develop her strengths and achieve a balance by passing them on to another and not let them weaken by inactivity. Nonetheless, the state of belonging is not stationary but is rather a process of continuous recalibration of the balance that is always at risk of being lost.

While Nelson Vieira explains this sense of otherness in Lispector's work as representative of a Jewish theoretical and cultural influence, de Sousa points to Lispector's personal experiences as citizen yet Other:

For Lispector, the literary terrain became a quest born of the tension between an effect of deterritorialization and her insertion into a space at the very limits of the language to which she actually desired to belong. In the tension between the clear boundaries of a geographically referentialized space and the search for a potentially unlimited space that could subsume all creative energy lay the fact that she was a foreigner, trying not to be one yet being one at the same time. Her nomadic transit originates, then, in the habitable zone of conflict that language constitutes. (21)

Though Jesus's movement from rural Brazil to the favelas to middle-class São Paulo creates a constant destabilizing force in her identity, the application of the insider/outsider framework to Lispector's identity on an individual and national level within the Brazilian sociocultural and historical context illustrates her negotiation as a displaced migrant finding a place within the dominant culture across even sharper geographical and ethnic lines. Both migrations on one hand result in a tension between marginalization and belonging played out on the battlefields of language and identity. For Jesus and Lispector the individual is caught between her uniqueness and an incorporation into the collective—whether imposed by economic and social factors or sought out by the subject as a marker of national identity. Both subjects experience a sense of dislocation caused by a national reinforcement of their Otherness and a resulting linguistic tension. For Lispector, this results in her occupation of what de Sousa calls the "space in-between," a nomadic space characterized by "heterogeneity, discontinuity and instability" (23). The instability brought about by this constant flux is one significant contributing factor to the hybridity which Lispector's work, and in this case, *A hora da estrela* in particular, exemplifies.

The discontinuity that is part of Lispector's identity is not solely based on geographical Otherness and facts of birth. A close study of works like *A paixão segondo G. H.* *(The Passion According to G.H.), Água viva (Stream of Life), Um maça no escuro* (An Apple in the Dark), *Um sopro de vida* (A Breath of Life), and *A hora da estrela* demonstrate the influence of poststructural theory on her narrative structure, development of characters, and use of language. As Earl Fitz notes, "[H]er narratives are driven by a sense of unfulfilled desire in which her characters develop more as conflicted and fragmented poststructural sites than as stable presences" (*Sexuality and Being* 1). This "poststructural ethos" is played out in "public and private identities" as opposed to solely on the ontological and epistemological level. As such, her work demonstrates themes representative of such an orientation: the struggle with the self-referential fluidity of language and consequently an inability to truly escape from it, a use of figurative language that is both subject and object of analysis, and a blurring of the boundaries between nonliterary and literary genres (6, 11). The subject who then uses language as a tool for self-definition, influenced by such instability, is "splintered and conflicted," unable to situate him- or herself in a stable site (6).

Multiple Interpretations of Author:
The Author/Narrator/Protagonist Triad

The hybridity of Lispector's movements into and out of the text as an exploration of the reconstruction of identity is first revealed on a metatextual level. This analysis is begun in the "Dedicatória" with the subtitle "(na verdade Clarice Lispector)." As Gotlib observes:

> [And the very Clarice doubles herself. She is the author, with her name on the cover and signature on the cover page, among the thirteen novel titles, and also in "The Author's Dedication (alias Clarice Lispector)."]

> E a própria Clarice desdobra-se. Ela é a autora, com nome na capa e assinatura na folha de rosto, entre os treze títulos do romance, e também na "Dedicatória do autor (na verdade Clarice Lispector)" (Gotlib, 467).

Lispector's declaration in the "Author's Dedication" that she, not her constructed narrator Rodrigo, is the real author, emphasizes her simultaneous positioning both outside of and within the text. Her study of the act of writing as a means of telling another's story and as a forum where the personal can be explored is ultimately a means of exploring the idea (and construction) of identity—both of the self and the Other, particularly given the limitations of language itself. This process of self-realization is not new to Lispector's works. Her work in the 1970s is especially characterized by what Anna Klobucka describes as "the autobiographic project—the writing of the self" (30). Later works also reveal similar examinations of the self:

> These patterns of solipsistic allusion may be traced in all of Lispector's later works, coalescing into a slippery dialectic of disguise and disclosure that is probably nowhere as prominently on display as in the notorious opening passages of . . . *A hora da estrela*. . . . *A hora da estrela*'s prefatory manoeuvres establish thus a pendular vacillation of the writing subject between the affirmation of self-sameness and the overt practice of narrative *fingimento,* accentuated by the emphasis on the distribution of discursive agency across the dividing line of sexual difference. (29)

This interchange of disclosure and *fingimento* is found in the author's dedication, amid the enumeration of important influences in the text, through a declaration to the reader of the overall themes of multiplicity of identity and collective that will be found. This includes references to the plurality of her own (the true author's) identity: "I dedicate it to the deep crimson of my blood as someone in his prime . . . to all those prophets of our age who have revealed me to myself and made me explode into: me. This me that is you, for I cannot bear to be simply me, I need others in order to stand up" (*The Hour of the Star* 7, 8). Though Clarice presents herself as a refracted entity that is the result of the "explosion" of influences, she nonetheless emphasizes that she is the product of a collective. All the "prophets of our age" and the text's reader, whether real or virtual, are what support her and make up her identity. For Lispector, the collective connections with the reader, and the other influences she mentions, are a necessity to maintain her creative capacity. As a result of these unions Lispector begins the movement in and out of the text that is a preliminary indication of its hybrid nature.

The first example is the establishment of an interior/exterior movement between the author and reader. Lispector's "This me that is you" serves as an open invitation to the reader to be an active participant in the text and dialogue by stating that the two are in fact one. Lispector breaks down the boundary between the author or creator as sender of the message and the reader as solely the recipient of the text or message. The reader is instead one of the "others" that the author needs in order to creatively progress and consequently, shares responsibility for the development of the text. Therefore one can say that both author and reader, who begin outside the text, are mutually dependent for each other's entrance into the text.

The second link she creates in order to reflect on her voice is between herself and Rodrigo S. M. (whose initials are never defined in the text). Lispector's declaration uncovers the claims of complete (although problematic) authority that Rodrigo makes throughout, revealing his dependence on her. He has authority only insofar as she allows him to have it, and even then has it problematized by her commentary. This results in the reader questioning throughout the text the veracity of Rodrigo's assertions.

The relationship between author, narrator, and protagonist along with the multiple reader interpretations of their voices in particular serves as an important indication of their interconnectedness. Their varied positionings are especially affected by social, economic, and psychological factors that create another level of movement between centralized and marginalized spaces internally and externally.

An analysis of Lispector's oeuvre shows the common theme of the boundaries of language as a manifestation of reality—whether it be impersonal, individual or collective. In "The Making of a Novel," in *Discovering the World* Lispector expresses her frustration with the constraints of words:

> What I write does not refer to past thought, but to thought in the present: whatever comes to the surface is already expressed in the only possible words, or simply does not exist. As I write them down, I am convinced once more that, however paradoxical it may sound, the greatest drawback about writing is that one has to use words. It is a problem. . . . I would do what so many people do who are not writers . . . I would live and no longer use words. And this might be the solution. (371–372.)[2]

Once a given thought is converted into a written discourse it loses its original form. The paradox that Lispector expresses is the inability to represent a thought, or reality, in its true form without the distortion that words bring.

Such a dependence on words to express reality despite their simultaneous destabilization of meaning is an example of Lispector's poststructuralist, particularly Derridean, influence:

[T]his constantly self-destabilizing semantic tension is the basic
building block of Lispector's narratives and it explains why,
in her themes, structures and characterizations, her work para-
doxically exudes both a sense of "unity" and "control". . . .
Lispector's fiction shows us how language . . . structures our
awareness of our existence at the same instant or moment . . .
that it "deconstructs" it. (Fitz, *Sexuality and Being* 13)

Her subversion does not however stop at the smallest common denomi-
nator of writing but aims itself at the next level—a type of communication beyond words. Just as marginality and centrality are represented on
a socioeconomic level in the author and her protagonist, so too are they
used as discursive dividers of identity that Lispector seeks to break down.
The first step for her, therefore, would be the deconstruction of one of the
elements used to mark alterity and reinforce dominance—language.

In the case of *A hora da estrela* the discourses of self-representation
and representation of the Other occur through the presentation of a triad:
the author, Clarice Lispector, and the narrator Rodrigo S. M. The narrator's
interaction with the protagonist Macabéa serves as a rhetorical device
used by the author to subvert the domination of centralized discourses
here represented as a masculine one—of being and writing—over the
marginalized, here feminized one. The central metaphysical discourse,
which Lispector undermines, is achieved in part through an attack on the
phallocentric discourse that Rodrigo in particular represents.

Lispector's insertion in her text further blurs the boundaries of this
dichotomy of marginality and centrality through subtle manipulations of
the text, its tone, and its characters. She rejects the restriction of the
author to one space and instead erases the boundaries of fiction and
nonfiction by adopting the dual role of author and character. As Fitz
observes, "It is as if Clarice slips, very unobtrusively, into Rodrigo's
character and, with only a faintly discernible shift in tone to mark it, then
proceeds to make her final accounting to us, as a writer, and as a human
being" ("Point of View" 204).

By focusing on the idea of gender, one can begin to understand the
discursive play that is at work:

[Parallel to that history of social violence and virtual love,
another occurs: it is the story of two novels, by two protagonists: Rodrigo, narrator created by the author, and thus implicit, in order to tell Macabea's story; Clarice, author and
narrator . . . in order to tell that story fairly. . . . In the doubled
structure-Clarice/Rodrigo/Macabéa—the three mirror each
other like "interchangeable identities."]

> Paralelamente a essa história de violência social e de amor virtual, uma outra acontece: é a história de dois romances, por dois protagonistas: Rodrigo, narrador criado pela autora, aí implícita, para contar a história de Macabéa; Clarice, autora e narradora . . . para justamente contar essa história. . . . Na estrutura desdobrável—Clarice/Rodrigo/Macabéa—os três espelham-se entre si, como "identidades intercambiáveis." (Gotlib 467–468)

The interplay between a "feminine sentimentalism" and "masculine rationalism" is another way of framing the question of the representation of identities, especially given the oppressive presence of the phallocentric discourse:

> [And there is a dialectic of genders. The "feminine" of Clarice has the "masculine" of Rodrigo as a counterpoint that empties into the "neutral" of Macabéa. Thus, the "sentimentalism" of the first is contrasted with a "rationalism" of the second, and both, to an extent, mutually unmask themselves: the first is not so feminine, nor the second so masculine, since such stereotypes are demystified.]

> E há uma dialética de gêneros. O "feminino" de Clarice tem por contraponto o "masculino" de Rodrigo, que deságua num "neutro" de Macabéa. Assim, o "sentimentalismo" da primeira contrapõe-se a um "racionalismo" do segundo, e ambos, de certa forma, desmascaram-se mutuamente: nem a primeira é tão feminina, nem o segundo é tão masculino, já que tais esteriótipos são desmistificados. (Gotlib 467–468)

As Gotlib's model attests, the result in this text is a mirror that refracts identities and manipulates the relationship between the stereotypically central rationalism and the stereotypically marginalized sentimentalism.

A horas Titles: Multiple Perspectives of the Other

An important structural representation of Clarice Lispector's influence on and presence in the text is the list of alternate titles that immediately follows the dedication. Again, the most salient feature is the varied possibilities of interpretation that each title represents as a statement of the multiple narrative voices. Upon reading the list, the first aspect that calls our attention is the variation of subject. Two titles are written in the first person: "The Blame Is Mine" and "I Can do Nothing," while two others are written in the third person with a specific reference to Macabéa: "Let Her Fend for Herself," and "She Doesn't Know How to Protest."

As in the Dedicatória's declaration of multiple narrators, Lispector presents us with information whose meaning changes the narrative perspective that the reader assigns to it. Maria Cristina Vianna Figueiredo, in her discussion of the various titles, points out that there are two interconnected approaches the reader may take to their interpretation. As a preface to the fictional story of Macabéa and Rodrigo S. M., the reader uses these titles to formulate ideas about possible meanings of the text with no influence by prior knowledge of actual details. The direction of interpretation is thus from external knowledge to an interpretation of the dedication that influences an analysis of the titles. This in turn influences the reader's understanding of the text.

A second reading of the titles in the context of the complete work therefore reveals the mixing (and therefore hybridity) of voices that was present in the dedication and permeates the text. During this process the reader uses information gathered from the complete text to reevaluate the meanings of the titles as indicators of the emotional and textual development of the characters. As a result, in this second level of analysis, previous opinions and the text interact to inform the interpretations of both. It is on this second level that Figueiredo reads the thirteen titles presented before the text. In particular there are six titles that are especially indicative of the interplay of authorial, narrative, and protagonical voices.

For the first title, "The Blame Is Mine," Figueiredo associates this declaration of guilt with a narrator who "assume toda a responsabilidade de construção da personagem principal. Ele se identifica com ela e sofre com a narrativa a ponto de precisar de uma trégua" (2). [assumes all the responsibility for the construction of the main character. He identifies with her and suffers with the narrative to the point of needing a rest.] The second, "The Right to Protest," represents a moment of intersection of the author's, narrator's, and protagonist's voices. On one level it represents Macabéa's future and the right to self expression while on the other hand it could be a reference to northeasterners (Nordestinos) in general and their condition of still being "ainda teimosa por lutar o que insistem em resistir apanhando" (Figueiredo 2). [still fearful of fighting what they insist on resisting catching.] This second seemingly objective assessment could therefore correspond to Lispector's perspective on the group out of which her protagonist originates. Such an observation is an interesting, subtle, preliminary reference to Macabéa's marginalization in Brazilian society and the resultant sense of impotence it causes. This aspect of her protagonist's identity and its impact on both the narrator's and reader's interpretation of her is a subtle thread that runs throughout and links Lispector's representation of marginalization with the racialized and gendered dislocation in Jesus's diary.

There is a third crucial meaning that in part begins to address the racial, ethnic, and class alienation of Macabéa and its effect on outside definitions of her identity. What this title may allude to when taken in this context is Rodrigo S. M.'s feelings of entitlement to Macabéa's story: "[I]t is my duty to relate everything about this girl among thousands of others like her. It is my duty, however unrewarding, to confront her with her own existence" (*Hour of the Star* 13). Here the narrator expresses his perceived power over Macabéa's story as his social right to present the injustices of her life. It is important to look at the reasoning Rodrigo uses specifically at the end of this passage. He ends by saying that there exists a general entitlement to exercising one's voice (specifically about the miseries of life) but follows this declaration not with an affirmation or hope of Macabéa one day finding her voice but rather of his decision to speak for her. The underlying supposition is that she is silenced in society and as such is invisible, even to herself. This criticism is reminiscent of the observations made about favelados in Jesus's *Quarto de despejo*. In this short statement, the silencing of Macabéa is an act that will continue throughout the text.

"As For the Future" is not only another of Lispector's alternate titles for the novel but also a phrase mentioned twice in the text as commentary and as a declaration posed by Macabéa. One of these references is by the narrator when trying to explain to the reader the structure and character of the story he will be telling: "A story that is patently open and explicit yet holds certain secrets—starting with one of the book's titles 'As For the Future,' preceded and followed by a full stop. . . . If, instead of a full stop, the title were followed by dotted lines, it would remain open to every kind of speculation on your part" (Lispector, *Hour of the Star* 13). This is a reference to not only the title but also to Macabéa's last words before she dies. As Figueiredo stresses, at the moment of her death Macabéa "encontra um ponto final logo adiante quando é atropelada. Os dois pontos finais . . . delimitam o futuro a um presente vigente. O futuro é inatingível para o ser humano, reduz-se a um simples pensamento totalmente falível." (3) [[F]inds a final point as soon as she is run over. The two final points . . . delimit the future to a valid present. The future is unobtainable for the human being, it reduces itself to a simple totally fallible thought.][3]

The following title, "Singing the Blues," is a significant reminder to the reader of the multivocality of the text and the structural ties that link the three main voices outside of and within the text. The title represents, for Figueiredo, the structuring of Lispector's text as a rhapsody. When we examine the origins of this musical category we see this reference as a metaphor for the text's multiplicity.[4] Rhapsody was synonymous with polyphony and was represented in poetry and prose as a method of forming a collage of discourse. In musical terms a suite that is surrounded by its variations characterizes the rhapsody. In relation to Lispector's work, the most relevant characteristic is polyphony, through the interweaving of Lispector's, Rodrigo S. M.'s, and Macabéa's voices. It is this simultaneity of voices (that is ironically achieved by layers of communication with silence) that creates the blurring of the boundaries between author, narrator, and character, and thus, the polyvalent rhapsody of the text.

The next title, "A Sense of Loss," is an apparently objective description of Macabéa that on closer look has a double reference. It can refer to her daily struggle for survival or the progression of Rodrigo S. M.'s engagement with his subject. The first reference is to Macabéa's continuous losses each day as she attempts to survive in metropolitan Rio. This title reveals the constant tension between Macabéa's perceptions of herself, the narrator's perceptions of her and the story told by her actions as opposed to her words. These points of tension or friction, according to Peixoto, are examples of the violence so often found in Lispector's narratives.[5]

It is the second reference to Rodrigo S. M. that extends the insider/outsider–exterior/margin–interior/center paradigm. As the narrator/author of the protagonist's story, Rodrigo progresses from a self-imposed indifference to a deep involvement with his creation. One consequence of this involvement when combined with Macabéa's assertion (in her own subtle way) of her constructed identity is his sense of a loss of control over her.

The sense of loss he feels is progressive as Macabéa gradually becomes the subject and Rodrigo the object. The result is a sense of powerlessness, feeling that Macabéa "slips through my fingers" (Lispector *Hour of the Star* 29). This helplessness reaches a climax at the end of the novel when Macabéa dies, for Rodrigo is confronted with his lack of authority—not just over his text, but also over "his" protagonist and over death itself: "Macabéa has murdered me. She is finally free of herself and of me. . . . I have just died with the girl. Forgive my dying. It was unavoidable" (Lispector, *Hour of the Star* 85). An act that on first glance leaves the protagonist helpless in fact becomes a tool for her power over and freedom from the narrator. Nonetheless, as Rodrigo observes, this freedom is also from the protagonist herself, releasing her from the societal conditions that from the beginning condemned her to a life of marginalization.

Because of its multiple points of articulation one can place the declaration in the first person: "I Can Do Nothing" alongside "A Sense of Loss." Lispector clearly describes a feeling of helplessness that was evident in the earlier "A Sense of Loss." This title can also be seen as a declaration made by both the narrator Rodrigo and the protagonist

Macabéa about the individual transition from object to subject. If we refer back to Rodrigo's deliberations over whether to save his creation or not, and the conclusion he reaches about his impotence against the combined powers of Death and Macabéa, we can easily attribute this statement to Rodrigo—in a final surrender to forces that in the beginning he felt able to control.

By contrast, in the mouth of the protagonist these words represent her own depersonalization combined with the narrator's continuous objectification of her by divesting her of any agency. The characterization is thus of a woman who feels unable to act and control her life but finds herself instead led by situations around her: "More and more, she was finding it difficult to explain. She had transformed herself into organic simplicity. . . . For other people, she didn't exist" (Lispector, *Hour of the Star* 62).

As the narrator's and Lispector's observations on Macabéa's upbringing suggest, this feeling of loss is one that we can trace back to birth. For the narrator Rodrigo S. M. in particular, she is aware of her inability to completely belong with or to be on equal footing with those around her—whether it be linguistically, socially, economically, or even, to a certain degree, racially.

As a migrant identified as originating in the northeastern state of Alagoas, Lispector presents the reader and narrator with an identity for her protagonist that is charged with historical, economic, racial, and social connotations of alterity and oppression. In the context of national representation de Madeiros notes that Macabéa is "a misplaced 'nordestina,' orphaned so long ago that she no longer remembers ever having parents, and of whom it is known that her roots were bad" (155).

The last title, "A Discreet Exit by the Back Door," attributed to the narrator Rodrigo, occurs during one of his reflections on writing as his salvation: "I can no longer bear the routine of my existence and, were it not for the constant novelty of writing, I should die symbolically each day. Yet I am prepared to leave quietly by the back door" (Lispector, *Hour of the Star* 21). In this confession the reader is given a glance at a narrator who is not as invincible as he initially leads us to believe. The truth revealed here is that he is in fact quite vulnerable. Writing is the only activity that gives Rodrigo S. M. a reason to live, because it provides him with the possibility of change and is the only thing that keeps him from death. Nonetheless, he still expresses a resignation to be able to confront death at any time, and leave writing behind.

This quote also opens up questions about the intersection between Lispector, Rodrigo, and Macabéa. Is it just Rodrigo speaking here, or is this an example of Lispector's insertion in the text? A possible alternative analysis of this statement is that it is Lispector's acknowledgement of the significance of writing in her life as well, anchoring her despite her daily routines. This last title is one example where Lispector and Rodrigo S. M. as writers in search of the self through an engagement with the other reveal the willingness to renounce it all if writing fails to bring salvation. For both, life is a constant search, a process whose usefulness lies in the possibility of revelation.[6]

Salvation of the Authorial Voice: Understanding the Other

The varying points of view of the novel's multiple titles highlight the fluidity of the voices and Lispector's challenge to the human tendency to try to establish and maintain an objective evaluation of the Other. The effect of this interweaving of voices is twofold. The first result is to deconstruct and ultimately dispel the idea of objectivity and reveal it as an always flawed endeavor. Consequently, any attempt to dispassionately portray the Other is in itself false and wrought with subjective judgements. The second consequence of this criticism is to therefore establish a more level field of observation, where the undermined authorial voice is removed from its privileged place, leaving a space where the Other can speak, or attempt to speak.

The deconstruction of a centralized narrative voice ultimately becomes a recognition of the position from which one may speak the Other, and of the impact of that position. By blurring the lines of author and narrator, Lispector questions not only the shortcomings inherent in not only Rodrigo's narrative project but also in her own. The ramifications for her project of understanding the Other are consequently negative. Such an endeavor would be an unbridgeable gap by definition. In the end Lispector's narrator's salvation—and her own—is the creative act. It is not just telling Macabéa's story or writing in itself, but a combination of the two. Rodrigo's constant references to his identification with his creation is a representation of Lispector's awareness of this familiarity. As Olga de Sa notes: "Clarice sabe que todo narrador inventa o mundo à sua imagem e semelhança e o 'ele' ou 'ela' das fábulas é sempre um disfarce do 'eu' do escritor" (273). [Clarice knows that every narrator invents the world in his image and resemblance and the 'him' or 'her' of the fables is always a disguise of the 'I' of the writer."] As a result, there is never a clear line between the I and the Other: one is always blurred into the other.

As Archer indicates, this subversive tension, which she defines as ambivalence, is indicative of the text's feminization: "It is my contention that this ambivalence indicates Lispector's feminine mode of expression; her hesitancy and indecision reflect her overriding concern with receiving and speaking for the "other," while establishing the proper distance between herself and her protagonist... without appropriating her" (253). According to Archer, the use of simple language is an example of not only subversion and tension, but more specifically, of the feminine text based in part on the theories of Cixous and Irigaray of a "libidinal economy": the "desire-that-gives" instead of appropriates:

> It makes no sense to Lispector to write a richly-worded sophisticated tale of a poverty-stricken illiterate; that would be appropriation, a vulgarization and a colonization of the other. "I will give you a voice and you will speak my language"— the bourgeois mentality, the masculine "gift-that-takes."... This is how Lispector makes the text more than a text; she relinquishes her privileged position to language so that she may accommodate Macabéa's tiny voice. (Archer 257)

What is important about the symbiotic relationship Archer describes is that it is constantly changing in order to resist concretization. "The effect is a symbiotic relationship between the novel's form and content, as well as a correspondence between author, narrator and protagonist.... Lispector, Rodrigo, Macabéa are at some moments blurred, at others distinct; the right closeness, the right distance" (Archer 257). The relinquishing of a position of privilege allows hybrid moments of approximation and of difference while emphasizing the tactics of using space (as in the use of Macabéa's silence) in the text to reveal the elements of individual identity that dominant discourse hides. Lispector contemplates the possibility of discovering the self through an interaction with the Other in her essay "In Search of the Other": "When I can fully sense another's presence I will be safe and think to myself: here is my port of call." (Discovering the World 158)

Deconstructing the Authorial Voice and Its Implications for Feminine Writing

Throughout the text, Macabéa's struggles to find her own voice are a constant subversion of the imposition of an authorial voice over the Other. However, by having the protagonist find her true importance in a tragic death, Lispector is presenting us not with a clear-cut answer to the authoritarian discourse but a problematic one that rejects a strictly methodical application of theories of feminine writing. For Gotlib, this death is both a symbol and culmination of the at times conflicting relationship between author, narrator, and protagonist:

[The quality of that novel is . . . in the system of dialectic tension created by the conflict between the various constructions, each one bringing a history of love and death in relation to the other: to create is to kill oneself as subject, or rather, it is to give voice to the other, which is done with autonomy, already as a subject of her own history, a creature disconnected from the creating subject. . . . He kills Macabéa just at the moment when she inserts herself as a subject that desires the other, taking the risk of constructing or inventing her own story, impossible in a system rooted in the horrors of discrimination.]

A qualidade desse romance está . . . no sistema de tensão dialética criada pelo conflito entre as várias construções, cada uma trazendo história de amor e morte em relação à outra: criar é matar-se como sujeito, ou seja, é dar voz ao outro, que se faz com autonomia, já como sujeito da sua própria história, criatura desvinculada do sujeito criador. . . . Mata Macabéa justamente no momento em que esta se insurge como sujeito que deseja o outro, arriscandò-se a construir ou inventar uma história sua, impossível num sistema fundado nos horrores da discriminação. (470)

In order for any being to realize its subjectivity it must have the space to develop its own autonomy. For the individual wishing to generate life, the "I" must decenter itself. On a textual level this means that in order for Macabéa to have any possibility of achieving individuality and power, she has to take it from her creator, Lispector, via Rodrigo S. M. Although this appropriation of autonomy is achieved through a symbolic death, Lispector chooses to represent Macabéa's emergence as a subject, from margin to center, literally through her death.[7]

This erasure of Macabéa's past and present can also be seen as a deconstruction of her personal histories that have held her in specific marginalized identities. Although recognizing a dangerous ahistoricity in deconstructive practices, Mary Poovey's proposal of this strategy in analyzing women's identity provides a useful approach. As she states:

The second contribution deconstruction can make is to challenge hierarchical and oppositional logic. Because the practice of deconstruction transforms binary oppositions into an economy in which terms circulate rather than remain fixed, it could . . . mobilize another ordering system in which the construction of false unities intrinsic to binary oppositions would not prevail. . . . Even as an ad hoc strategy the "in-between"

constitutes one tool for dismantling binary thinking. . . . [I]t
would enable us to rethink "power" (along with identity) so
as to perceive its fragmentary quality. (263–264)

In the realm of linguistic constructions the masculine syntax never disappears, and the feminine never completely escapes from it. Nonetheless, Macabéa's death is not an end, as I have pointed out, but a transferal, therefore allowing the feminine and the masculine to coexist in a discourse that is neither one nor the other. This coexistence is not a sudden one, but rather represented throughout the text by the multiplicity of voices that Lispector establishes. As Galvez-Breton notes, "Lispector, it must be stressed, chooses to superimpose narrative voices that speak of with voices that speak as. This is the post-feminist choice: the choice of masculine and feminine: multiplicity (71). This multiplicity is emphasized ultimately by Rodrigo S. M. Relato Antigo's final reflections, when he declares his death with Macabéa and his realization of the inevitability of death for all human beings: "Dear God, only now am I remembering that people die. . . . Don't forget in the meantime, that this is the season for strawberries" (Lispector, *Hour of the Star* 86). Although the feminine dies, with it and through its death is the opportunity for affirmation. The masculine, however, cannot escape from this fate: it too must die. Yet here Lispector presents the reader with two possible sources of comfort: the belief that death is less menacing because of its transitoriness, and the revelation of the meaning to be found in Macabéa's death.

Even within the masculine discourse the feminine is able to find a space of empowerment and strength. If we look once more at the principles Lispector expresses in "In Search of the Other" we can understand more clearly the final lesson that Macabéa's passing represents. When Lispector states that feeling the Other brings safety she uses Rodrigo, Macabéa, and herself to teach a lesson on both a social and metatextual level. Through their voices she informs the reader that this recognition of herself through an awareness of the Other is not impossible. In the spaces left by silence, Lispector is able to represent through Macabéa the possibility of asserting a definition of the self through a process that incorporates both the marginal and the dominant discourse.

A hora da estrela's exploration of the independent subject, as we shall see, continues on an even more defined textual level. Through the complex relationships of the narrator, protagonist, and other significant characters Lispector is able to subvert and deconstruct gender in order to create hybrid conceptualizations of self and Other. Symbolically these manipulations answer the question of the possibility of establishing agency, subjectivity, and, ultimately, individual autonomy that Lispector poses to herself and her readers.

Chapter Four

Textual Cross-Gendering of the Self and the Other in Lispector's *A hora da estrela*

Hybrid Structures: Author-Narrator-Protagonist Interactions

My study of Carolina Maria de Jesus's use of writing as reconstructive tool explored her personal project as an example of hybridity in a strictly autobiographical text. By contrast, Clarice Lispector's story of a young northeastern woman struggling to find her place and voice in Rio de Janeiro exemplifies a metafictional text that crosses the lines of author-narrator and protagonist on a metatextual and intratextual level and in so doing creates a hybrid dialogue of voices fighting for subjectivity.

As a result of Lispector's multifaceted identity there is a continuous search to restore a personal balance. Yet there is also a counteracting representation of these internal dualities as hybrid structures. She creates a text that is conscious of yet questions definitions of the self and of historical positioning as constructive factors in the representation of the individual and the Other. The hybrid discourses of identity are presented on a textual level through the analysis of three factors: (1) the specific dynamics of the narrator-protagonist interaction; (2) the gendered sub-versions of this relationship, and (3) the protagonist's establishment of an autonomous yet hybrid voice that counteracts racial, economic and linguistic restrictions. From the "Author's Dedication (alias Clarice Lispector)" Lispector presents the inter- and extratextual complexity that will be one of the chief elements of the novel, along with a nontraditional dynamic between the author-narrator. The first indication of this complex relationship can be seen in the blurring of lines of authorship and consequently, a decentralization of power within the text. As Galvez-Breton notes, the interplay among characters and ever-changing distance

85

between them is one of the ways in which Lispector undercuts "the power of the singular, the One, ... of authorship per se (69)," thus refusing to recreate a masculine order, or center.

Galvez-Breton describes the relationship between the authorial voice and the other characters in the text with a variation of the insider/outsider framework. According to her center-edge model, in the moments when the authorial voice—specifically Lispector—wants to speak through a character we can see a movement from center to edge to center. In contrast, when the narrator, Rodrigo, stresses his voice, to the exclusion of other viewpoints by enforcing their silence, one can see a distancing from the character, ". . . a reaffirmation of subject-object, . . . a recentering reterritorialization of the narrator as the One" (69). Such an alienation and reinstatement of narrative hierarchy is an important factor in explaining Lispector's conception of feminine writing as by necessity rejecting any unilateral structure of domination.

Lispector uses the shifting interactions between her characters to subvert the phallocentric hierarchy and the traditional order of gendered definitions in general on both an intertextual and metaphysical level. This is achieved by the connection of a social critique, esthetic questions and commentary on the strategies of representation, and a metaphysical study of reality (the role of language in influencing these representations). As Fitz points out:

> But operating in close consort with the two more obvious themes in this novel, the ruinous and as yet unresolved human tragedy of Brazil's northeastern region, and the attempt of an essentially philosophical and lyrical writer to show a barren, blighted personality struggling, blindly and futilely, to develop into something more satisfying, there exists a subtle yet powerful third theme. This tertiary though no less vital impulse of A hora da estrela comes to grips with the implications inherent in being an artist, the ethical, humanistic and philosophic meaning of creativity, what it really means to connect words with reality and then to give them form, to turn them into art, into literature. ("Point of View" 201, 203)

Fitz's observation emphasizes that instead of two separate focuses there is instead a complementary relationship that exists between the social and the esthetic, especially when the two are used to represent a reality foreign to the writer: the reality of the Other. The narrator's (author's) dilemma is how to make language represent reality and more particularly, how to make the text's language represent the reality of Macabéa ("Point of view" 201, 203).

The first part of this process is the narrator's representation of the object/subject Macabéa and its illustration of the intersection of esthetics, language, and social reality. When Rodrigo S. M. explores which is the best technique to represent Macabéa his decision on the narrative style of her story is based on an evaluation of her life that takes into consideration that her future capabilities will be affected by his belief that "her existence is sparse." (Lispector 23) Because her life has always been uncontrolled and lacking in brilliancy and distinction, the narrator concludes that the techniques used to represent it must display the same characteristics: "But that is the problem: this story has no technique, not even in matters of style. It has been written at random. Nothing would persuade me to contaminate with brilliant, mendacious words, a life as frugal as that of my typist" (Lispector *Hour of the Star* 35–36).

While in the "Dedication" (Dedicatória) the simplified linguistic approach is put aside in favor of "a story in technicolour to add a touch of luxury" (Lispector, *Hour of the Star* 8), later complications in the representation of Macabéa occur when the narrator includes references to "explosions" at important moments in her life accompanied by references to the music of the piano and of the violin that accompany her death. These cinematographic inclusions highlight another way in which Lispector subverts the text: through the variety of voices and strategies that continually undermine one absolute, authoritarian approach.

Nonetheless, returning to Fitz's commentary we find a reference to "representation" as the exploration of the self as well as the Other. This issue is dealt with by Macabéa, "struggling, blindly and futilely to develop into something more satisfying," the "artist"/narrator Rodrigo who seeks to understand "what it really means to connect words with reality and then to give them form, " and the "artist author Clarice Lispector who by being the original creator of the above mentioned is tackling the very same issue of turning art into literature" ("Point of view" 198). Part of the answer to these questions lies in the discourses used to bring the subject to life: an approach in part influenced by gendered considerations of hierarchy, voice, and subjectivity.

The Self and the Other: Rodrigo S. M. and Macabéa

Lispector interweaves and problematizes these multiple identities through the creation of a narrator whose representation of and relationship with the other, Macabéa, exemplifies the interaction of centralized and marginal voices. An understanding of the problematic relationship of Rodrigo S. M. with writing the Other, Macabéa, and consequently with Lispector must take into consideration five important points: (1) Rodrigo S. M.'s unease with his powerlessness in representing both himself and the other; (2) the implications of his historic, social, and racial representation of Macabéa as Other; (3) his attempts to establish centrality in the text; (4) the beginning of his hybrid discourse with Macabéa through cracks within his hegemony; and (5) the attempt to reestablish agency over his subject. As Peixoto observes:

> Instead of using a narrator who could in some way merge with the author, or an impersonal narrator who would dilute a personal vision in anonymity, Lispector chooses to empha-size the dilemma of the approach to the other as she inter-poses a mediator between writer and character, the narrator Rodrigo S. M., who dramatizes the difficulties that confront him as he attempts to write Macabéa. (59)

The progression of the narrator's voice reveals that his dilemma is pre-cisely the inability to merge with the author or remain anonymous. Part of the process of discovering the complications in such an undertaking is by attempting—unsuccessfully—to merge with the Other or at other times to cloak himself in anonymity. Our first introduction to the narra-tor and his participation in this process is on the second page of the text. From his opening statements the reader is made aware of the narrator's attitude toward the act of writing, part of his motives for engaging in this act, and his ability or inability to record his own personal experiences. Although at the outset we are given no official name of the story's nar-rator he does give the reader a partial explanation of his reasons for writing: "I only achieve simplicity with enormous effort. So long as I have questions to which there are no answers, I shall go on writing. . . . The more genuine part of my life is unrecognizable, extremely intimate and impossible to define" (11–12). One interesting duality in this confession that runs through the rest of the text is the combination of the social commentary of the text and its metalinguistic function. It is, as the nar-rator reveals at this point, not exclusively due to a desire to explore this activity as an esthetic tool, but due to his own personal motivation: writing as part of his own ontological exploration.

This multiplicity of purpose complicates the phallocentric discourse upon which the narrator will base his self-characterization by inserting the personal into the act of writing. As Sandra Gilbert notes in "Literary Paternity," drawing on the previous works of Said and Hopkins, embed-ded in "Author" is an identification with father and paternity—one that initiates, founds, continues, and controls his product. Part of the source of this power, and simultaneously a manifestation of it, is an unques-tioned belief in the word as an accurate tool to represent any reality.

Consequently, he who has access to and control over the word is afforded the same control over reality and experience (Gilbert 487). In these opening pages however, instead of presenting a man who is omniscient and objective, detached from writing and therefore from his text, we are presented with one who is instead struggling between a command of his text and recurring uncertainty, while hopeful that writing will serve as a tool to resolve those questions.

The inability to understand his own life, and bring that understanding out into the open, an act which would make the experience a shared one, is compounded by and a result of an inability to accurately represent experience (a personal reality) with words. Here, nonetheless, Lispector uses Rodrigo S. M. to present some important ontological ramifications of the narrator's self-examination. If he is uncertain, on a metalinguistic level, of his ability to find a word to represent his life, there is consequently an uncertainty about his capacity to represent Macabéa's life through words.

In order to counteract this unease Rodrigo S. M. establishes early on his centrality in the text and therefore in Macabéa's life by approaching her story with a cold, distant eye which he also describes as [without pity.] "The story—I have decided with an illusion of free will—should have some seven characters, and obviously I am one of the more important. . . . I want my story to be cold and impartial. Unlike the reader, I reserve the right to be devastatingly cold" (13). He emphasizes this supposed objective centrality by beginning the story with a self-presentation, rather than with a presentation of the protagonist. Despite a momentary vacillation Rodrigo establishes his primacy in the text not only by choosing the time, the number of characters, and the text's development (beginning, middle and end), but also by stressing his positioning as one of the key characters. Yet again he emphasizes his ability to control the reader's perception and reception of the text. What seems to be free choice and randomness ("an illusion of free will") governing the narrator's organization of the story is actually false, structured instead by carefully constructed passages yet continuously questioned and subverted from the start by the author Clarice Lispector and by Rodrigo's own momentary admissions of weakness.[1]

Once Rodrigo S. M. has sufficiently introduced himself to the reader he relates the encounter with an unknown northeastern girl that compelled him to write her story. It is important to note, as I stated in the introduction, that this encounter is based on Lispector's own encounter with a young girl from the northeast: "How do I know all that is about to follow if it is unfamiliar and something I have never experienced? In a street in Rio de Janeiro I caught a glimpse of perdition on the face of a girl from the Northeast" (12). The narrator begins relating the encounter with

what at first is another reminder of his authorial/narrative power yet ends
with an admission of a certain ignorance of his subject's personal experience because it is not his own. One means of reestablishing himself over
the text is by appropriating Macabéa's struggles as his own. In doing so,
Rodrigo S. M. draws on historical and social presuppositions about the
northeast to inform his judgments and consequently, influence ours: "What
I am writing is something more than mere invention; it is my duty to relate
everything about this girl among thousands of others like her. . . . So, I am
shouting. . . . But the person who I am about to describe scarcely has a
body to sell; nobody desires her, she is a harmless virgin whom nobody
needs" (13–14). The image conveyed here is that of an unknown—representative of a group of women without meaning in their lives and without
any space in society from which they can speak or shout. The young
protagonist, and these women as well, are not, in the narrator's opinion,
valorized persons in society. Therefore, the social obligation toward her
story that Rodrigo S. M. expresses in this declaration is to be the voice of
this young girl and shout for her because of the silence imposed upon her.
As in other reactions to his subject's plight, Rodrigo's decision here straddles
the boundary between subjectivity and objectivity, between what Peixoto
has described as the narrator merged with his creation and the dispassion-
ate observer.

Nonetheless, Rodrigo S. M.'s attempted dominance over his subject
is equally informed by a racial and economic classification of her based
on origin—an interesting parallel with the displaced author, Lispector.
As Earl Fitz observes, this young northeastern girl's significance as a
symbol of the effects of one region's poverty on its inhabitants' physical,
intellectual, and emotional growth represents one of the principal social
themes around which this text is centered:

> Macabéa . . . is an individualized character. . . . But at the same
> time Macabéa is portrayed as a distinct social type, as a sym-
> bol of sorts, a painful reminder of how the poverty of life in
> the Northeast stunts one's physical and intellectual develop-
> ment and how it effectively blunts a person, rendering him
> useless as a contributing member of society and hollow as an
> individual. ("Point of view" 201)

As a representative of a region characterized by extreme poverty, unemployment, and malnutrition, the representations of northeasterners by
larger Brazilian society also acquired a racialized tone because of the
ethnic difference from the more industrialized southeast (Burns 419).
Because of its size, each region's ethnic makeup could differ vastly, yet
in comparison to the more indigenous influences in the north, the more

African-influenced coastline from Pernambuco to São Paulo, and the predominantly White south, "the Northeast revealed an even wider variation caused by the amalgamation of Indian, black and white" (Burns 318). In his answer to the question, "O que é Nordeste Brasileiro" [What is the Brazilian Northeast?] Carlos Garcia states that:

> [The society that was formed in the region is, more than in any other part of Brazil, a mestizo society. . . . The stratification of the social levels, defined in the colonial period and consolidated during the Empire and Old Republic, although weakened, predominates even today in the sugar plantation zone.]

> A sociedade que se formou na região é, mais do que em qualquer outra parte do Brasil, uma sociedade mestiça. . . . A estratificação das camadas sociais, definidas no período colonial e consolidada no Império e República Velha, embora atenuada, predomina ainda hoje na zona canavieira. (46)

Given this combination of racial mixing and economic underdevelopment, the general perception of the northeasterner was that of a racial, intellectual, and economic inferior. These stereotypes can be considered, because of their predominance in history and the literary history in Brazilian society, as perceptions that influenced Rodrigo S. M.'s sense of power and superiority over his subject. To this end, when placed in this historical context, his reference to her origin serves as an introduction and added explanation of his at times overt objectification and appropriation of Macabéa. Macabéa's racial and social displacement by the narrator, as well as its effect on the reader's interpretation of her character, parallels the racial and economic marginalization of Jesus in *Quarto de despejo*. Consequently, the protagonist's oppression by and resistance to such norms exemplify another facet of the insider/outsider dynamic I have established in the other subjects.

The injustice that denies Macabéa the right to self-expression also serves as an example of the social violence that Peixoto speaks of, and more specifically, the replication of that social violation on a narrative level. In Rodrigo's descriptions of Macabéa's social victimization what especially stands out is the way in which his language reinforces her marginalization by emphasizing her anonymity and silence.

The narrator's declarations therefore are a means of inspiring confidence, albeit false, in the reader that this is Macabéa's story (both her life and her emotions) without intervention. By emphasizing their shared condition and the ease with which their lives could have been even more closely linked, he is attempting to erase issues of class, race, and gender that would lead us to question the objectivity of his descriptions of her.

Once Rodrigo S. M. has related the facts surrounding his first encounter with the Nordestina that would inspire him to write this story, and developed an initial sketch of her personality for the readers, he feels a certain level of freedom to include more of his personal observations as well as the significance of his involvement in the writing of her story.

In spite of attempts to remain objective Rodrigo becomes emotionally involved with his subject, experiencing emotions ranging from love and passion to what one could possibly call obsession. Although the social commitment toward the protagonist is in part because of a need to be the voice of those he sees as voiceless and powerless, it is not completely under his control: "I must write about this girl from the Northeast otherwise I shall choke. She points an accusing finger and I can only defend myself by writing about her" (17). As Damasceno points out, the growing emotional attachment in actuality undermines this authority over her representation:

> As her portraiture increasingly escapes him, she acts as the mark of both his impotence and growth, and as reference to Lispector's power. In fact, as Rodrigo's narrative progresses a kind of cross-identification occurs: Macabéa's sensitivities show through despite Rodrigo's authorial and existential desperation, and he gradually falls in love with her. (5)

Although Rodrigo never completely becomes his protagonist, in the sense of leaving behind the influences of his dominant class origins, he does "fall under her spell," changing him temporarily from the subject to the decentralized object of his discourse. As he himself observes, "The action of this story will result in my transfiguration into someone else and in my ultimate materialization into an object" (20).

According to Rodrigo S. M. the process of writing Macabéa's reality slowly becomes one that is carried out with his whole body. "I write with my body. . . . I can scarcely invoke the words to describe this pattern, vibrant and rich, morbid and obscure, its counterpoint the deep bass of sorrow. . . . I shall attempt to extract gold from charcoal" (Lispector *Hour of the Star* 16). Peixoto's study of the textual violence of *A hora da estrela* provides a clearer understanding of the narrator's role as a device used to question writing, in particular when dealing with issues such as the aggressor/victim, male/female discourse as represented socially, textually (between the narrator and his creation), and metatextually (between the author and the narrator):

But how, from what perspective, and with what investments does one write the victim's experience? . . . [H]ere, the strategy for writing the victim no longer entails a containment within ideological and narrative structures that minimize the violence, but involves, on the contrary, an unleashing of aggressive forces. . . . *The Hour of the Star* foregrounds and calls into question the perverse components of the pleasures of writing and reading and the suspect alliances of narrative with forces of mastery and domination. (83)

In this context the adjectives used previously by the narrator to express Macabéa's existence demonstrate the uneasy partnering of a reality rich yet sorrowful with words that uncomfortably and antagonistically represent it. Despite this friction the narrator's last words repeat his insistence on his ability to create from Macabéa's reality a cohesive narrative by changing charcoal into gold. As Barbosa remarks, S.M. believes that he can ". . . leash the process of writing through his many roles in this narrative", allowing him to "transcend mere pity for Macabéa's social condition as he tells her story. In his furor poeticus, he thinks that he will be able to grasp the fleeting moments of revelation, have the ultimate glimpse into the essence of things, and create a coherent unity" (*Parodies of Narrative Power*, 117). As someone accustomed to exercising complete control over the text, Rodrigo S. M. frequently has difficulty recognizing and coming to terms with the limitations placed on his authority by the independent aspects of the text and the realities of the marginalized life being portrayed. In moments of weakness when he is overcome by life's complexities—by the contrasts for example of pain and vibrancy expressed in the earlier quote—his reaction is to attempt to regain a position of superiority and centrality.

A second strategy that his introductory comments have shown is an equal desire to displace himself along with his subject. However, as Galvez-Breton observes, while the authorial voice wants to speak through his character and in fact is able to recreate a sense of marginalization alongside her, on many levels it is not lasting. Despite Rodrigo's narrative power and belief in the absence of class distinctions, the reality of his privilege can never be erased, making the otherwise difficult task of knowing the Other further complicated by the social and economic bridge between them. Rodrigo S. M.'s attempts to control Macabéa's voice are the result of a sense of communal responsibility, and to a greater degree of his belief in a shared marginality with his protagonist, yet ironically an underlying sense of privilege in being able to portray her. However, his most compelling motivation for writing her story is a need for redemption: "Why should I write about a young girl whose poverty is so evident?

Perhaps because within her there is seclusion. Also because in her poverty of body and soul one touches sanctity and I long to feel the breath of life hereafter. In order to become greater than I am, for I am so little" (20–21). Through Macabéa, Rodrigo S. M. can analyze the existential problems he continually grapples with and personally redeem himself from an anonymity that to him is an indicator of the inconsequentialness of his being. Therefore, because of his constant need to define himself through the Other, tempered by the difficulty of such a task, the relationship of narrator-protagonist vacillates between center to edge to center, marked by a distancing and a reterritorialization of power.

The Gaze, the Face, and the Racialization of the Other

The "poverty of body" that Rodrigo S. M. uses to describe this redemptive project does still open up a space for the social appropriation of Macabéa's identity that cannot be disregarded as influential in his strategies of representation. Through *A hora da estrela*, Rodrigo's representations of Macabéa's physical being, particularly her face, reveal the stereotypes of northeastern inferiority, European superiority, and their effect on the narrator's and reader's reading of her. A particularly charged adjective used to describe Macabéa is the word "sallow." This "grayish greenish yellow color" is not only a possible indicator of a circumstancial physical deficiency but is also significant in the context of northeastern ethnicity because it is not White, and therefore not privileged:

> She reckoned that it might not be such a bad thing being a vampire; for the blood would add a touch of pink to her sallow complexion. For she gave the impression of having no blood unless a day might come when she would have to spill it. (25)

Later, the narrator observes Macabéa's desire to physically fit in:

> She collected newspaper advertisements, and pasted them into an album. The advertisement she treasured most of all was in colour; it advertised a face cream for women with complexions so very different from her own sallow skin. (When I consider that I might have been born her—and why not?—I shudder.) (38)

Macabéa's sallow, nonwhite skin, in the narrator's view, is representative of her condition as an outsider—someone who is seemingly dead (bloodless) and not a "real," "beautiful" woman.

Her Otherness is further expressed by Rodrigo's at times detailed descriptions of her overall facial features:

> She examined herself mechanically in the mirror above the filthy hand basin. . . . [T]he dark, tarnished mirror scarcely reflected any image. Perhaps her physical existence had vanished? . . . She studied herself and mused: so young and yet so tarnished. (24–25)

> Her eyes were enormous, round, bulging and inquisitive. . . . Lost in thought, she examined the blotches on her face in the mirror. In Alagoas they had a special name for this condition—it was commonly believed to be caused by the liver. The girl concealed her blotches with a thick layer of white powder which gave the impression that she had been whitewashed but it was preferable to looking sallow. (26)

> There was nothing iridescent about her, although the parts of her skin unaffected by the blotches had the subtle glow of opals. (26–27)

In the second reference Rodrigo S. M. links Macabéa's physical defects to a physical deficiency. Not only is her face tainted, but so is her body. The connection with the common belief that it was a liver disease also subtly ties the body to place. Not only is she the embodiment of an inferior Other, but possesses a body influenced by her origin in a marginalized place. As Rodrigo notes through his narration, although Macabéa uses the face cream to erase or at least conceal her otherness with a literal and figurative "whiteness," her sallow complexion—and consequently her racialized identity—can never be erased.

The fact that this revelation occurs in front of a mirror is significant. The reader is not only dependent on Rodrigo S. M.'s gaze, but is for a brief time, given the opportunity to witness a rare moment of self-analysis by Macabéa. However, as de Medeiros points out, the result of this moment of subjective analysis is not empowerment but further alienation:

> This moment of the confrontation before the mirror is crucial in several senses: one might be tempted to recall Lacan's mirror stage, the moment at which a child for the first time upon seeing its own reflection on a mirror recognizes it as belonging to him—or herself and thus assumes consciousness of the Self. But Macabéa is often described as not having any such conception of herself. (152)

Unlike a later moment where Macabéa does seem to achieve a temporary moment of subjectivity and power, the two mirror references here
only emphasize her impotence. This revelation is reminiscent of and
holds certain similarities with Jesus's gaze into the mirror. What she
sees is a face like her mother's—an identity and future locked in the
poverty, deprivation, and powerlessness of her Black Brazilian mother's
life in poverty. Similarly Macabéa does not see a future when she looks
in the mirror—only an identity already determined by lack. As readers
seeking connection with the protagonist, we are also disempowered by
these moments—to the point that Rodrigo guides our perceptions of
Macabéa. Consequently, his equation of racial, social, and physical identity with victimization threatens to become ours, unless Macabéa's voice
is heard.

Marginality as Subjectivity: Macabéa's Voice

The question then becomes, what space is available for the object to speak
as subject? Where is the voice of this northeastern girl? These questions
can be answered by examining the principal tool used by Lispector to
demonstrate difficulties and possibilities for the marginalized Other to
assert her voice: Macabéa. In *Jewish Voices in Brazilian Literature* Vieira notes
that on one hand, " In true Talmudic fashion, . . . the process of writing
becomes the process of questioning, a way of evoking insights into self-
awareness, subjectivity, and the possibilities of the other " (140–141).

Through the presentation of a protagonist who seems on one level
powerless to establish a place in Brazilian society, an act that includes
developing and cultivating a sense of self (whether this be as an active
or reactive response to the pressures of surviving in a metropolitan setting), Lispector uncovers the deeper, more subtle ways in which Macabéa
actively constructs a hybrid identity that allows her to survive by uniting
her marginalized position with the discourses and consciousness of her
narrator, subverting them and thus establishing an ever increasing sense
of agency. Like Jesus, who uses her diary to bring together at times
opposing discourses to reflect and rise above the limitations of her marginality, Lispector presents a tale of a marginalized woman seeking agency
socially, racially, and through gender. However, whereas Jesus as a writer
used this medium as her principal tool and focused on asserting a historically positioned identity through race, class, and gender as well as
exploring metafictive questions of writing as self-portraiture, Macabéa
has no such recourse. While her path to subjectivity also deals with issues of racial, class-based, and ethnic marginalizations, as a symbolic
representation of Lispector's examination of the challenges in the por-

trayal of the self and Other there is also an ontological aspect of her investigation that is replicated on the level of narrator and protagonist that is less a part of Jesus's process.

Macabéa's acquisition of a voice is part of a process that can be defined by five important factors: (1) the legacy of survival in her name; (2) the masculine attempts to appropriate her voice; (3) her use of mirroring, marginal, and central discourses to reformulate her identity; (4) her subversion of silence and the masculine perspective to establish a personal voice; and (5) her death as a final assertion of subjectivity.

The protagonist's movement from marginality is already alluded to by the first outstanding fact that the reader notices about her: her name. According to Macabéa, this name was given to her by her mother as a result of a promise made to one of the apparitions of Mary. Many critics believe that one of the origins of this name has to do with the biblical brothers—the Maccabees. They were the sons of the priest Matathias Maccabaeus who took turns as commander of the Jews against the king of Syria, who wanted to import the Hellenic culture in order to destroy Judaism (N. Vieira, *Jewish Voices* 136). Vieira adds that Lispector's use of the history of the Maccabees allows her to comment on her protagonist's resistance and heroism, deconstruct concepts of faith, justice, and representation, and serve as a useful approach to the possibilities of movement from a marginalized position of power: "By reappropriating the myth of the Maccabees, the novella allows us to perceive the human spirit in unexpected places and unheroic-looking beings" (*Jewish Voices* 140–141). By analyzing these concepts in the context of Jewish resistance, Lispector uses her female protagonist as a double for her racial displacement and exploration of marginalization, inclusion, and power.

Vieira distinguishes between a social definition of an "unheroic figure" and the heroism Macabéa displays. Similarly Gotlib believes that the characterization of the protagonist as antiheroic masks the connection with Lispector and her background that in truth highlights the protagonist's ability to survive.

Under the form of the shout of rebellion, denouncing hunger, and the impotence of the character, Macabéa is also a prisoner, like the Maccabees. However, like them, she resists, a northeastern girl in the big city, massacred by an inhuman social system. Her shout of rebellion is the contemporary equivalent of their stand against the efforts by King Antiochus of Syria to divest them of their essential identity through forced assimilation. Their rebellion was on behalf of their religious beliefs while Macabéa's is on behalf of her instincts to survive despite forces that together consort to keep her on the periphery.

Olga de Sá , like Vieira and Gotlib, sees Macabéa as a heroic descendant of the Maccabees. She connects the protagonist with temptation and the forbidden by tracing the origin of her name to an apple [maça]. Sinilarly, a related work by Lispector is entitled *A maçã no escuro*, chronicling the protagonist Martim's search for his own language, means of exploring the world, and sense of self. Macabéa's constant engagement with issues of culture, class, and language could be said to be like Martim's in that she is reaching out for what society has forbidden her to have, trying to find her own language and way of navigating through reality.

Other critics, like Cristina Figueiredo, however, disagree, and observe that although the seven Maccabean brothers are killed in a heroic gesture, Macabéa's death converts her into an antihero, being reborn for another life (2).

Othering and Alienation: Macabéa and Olímpico

One area in which Lispector establishes Macabéa's alienation and victimization and her attempts to counteract it is through her relationship with her boyfriend Olímpico, or as he calls himself, Olímpico de Jesus Moreira Chaves. This character is another northeasterner trying to find some type of success in the city. He grew up without a father but tried to reinvent himself socially into someone with a good family background. His goals are to be a man of class, become wealthy, be a bullfighter, and show his bravery by killing. His last and possibly most ambitious goal is become a deputy from Rio de Janeiro. Although he does not understand social norms and language, he uses his aspirations to cover up his ignorance and continually show his superiority over Macabéa. However, beneath the false charm lies a darker side: "He enjoyed taking his revenge. Revenge gave him an enormous satisfaction and the strength to go on living" (47).

The narrator reveals that Olímpico's flaws are also his strength, however. He belongs to this masculine world and is therefore strong and capable of redemption, albeit through violence as empowerment. Unlike Macabéa he was not an outsider, "a crossbreed between one 'quiddity' and another" (57). Like the narrator, Olímpico can find salvation. While the narrator's is through writing (and specifically, writing Macabéa's story), Olímpico's is through "masculine" behavior that gives him "class" and through activities that will give him a sense of privilege. Like Rodrigo S. M., Olímpico exhibits a continual desire to define and change Macabéa. Although he too is culturally ignorant and uneducated, he constantly corrects her and points out her supposedly inappropriate behavior while highlighting his own supposed superiority.

As a fellow northeasterner from Paraíba, Olímpico is also racially and economically inferior. However, the narrator's earlier distinction that Macabéa, not Olímpico, is the "crossbreed" again shows the importance race plays in their respective isolation from and incorporation into dominant culture. For Olímpico, like the narrator, Macabéa will always be the racialized outsider, never accepted into mainstream, White Brazilian society:

> [Macabéa] . . . Did you know that Marilyn Monroe was the color of peaches? And you're the colour of mud. What makes you think that you've got the face or the body to become a film star? (53).

Olímpico's description of her complexion as the "colour of mud" subtly alludes to her racial impurity while concluding that, along with other physical defects, she will never succeed socially or economically. The reference to Marilyn Monroe internationalizes the desire for this symbol of success: it is not purely a White, Brazilian ideal but also the American ideal: White, blond, and beautiful, which is a model to emulate.

Such an ideal is in fact what Olímpico also aspires to, through his relationship with Glória, Macabéa's coworker. She represents the racial ideal that Macabéa is not, a key to unlock society's doors to power:

> When [Olímpico] set eyes on Glória . . . he felt at once that here was a girl with real class. Glória had rich Portuguese wine in her blood and a provocative way of swinging her hips as she walked, no doubt due to some remote strain of African blood. Although she was white, Glória displayed that vitality one associates with a mulata. . . . [E]ven without the peroxide she was fair, and that made her superior as far as Olímpico was concerned. . . . To be *carioca* identified Glória with the privileged class who inhabited Southern Brazil. (58–59).

The irony of Glória's identity and privilege was her proximity to a privileged race and place: from Rio and white enough to have access to the image of social capital, despite the reality of her struggling class position and employment, her manipulation of an imagined "mulatta esthetic," and, according to Olímpico, her lack of any real physical beauty. Despite these weaknesses his valorization of her symbolic identity demonstrates the symbolic power that race and class position can have.

Olímpico's overall indictment of Macabéa is reminiscent of Jesus's many detractors who did not believe a Black woman could be literate or ambitious. Although she was not judged by the same physical standards as Macabéa, both women of color had to navigate racial prejudices in order to find their own voice. Olímpico, by comparison, sees himself in many ways as powerful, ambitious, and educated, the arbiter of knowledge for both himself and Macabéa. As Barbosa points out, "By portraying them parodically, Lispector shows that their behavior is socially acquired and, at the same time, she subverts and calls into question the 'sexual textual' politics in *A hora*" (Barbosa, "Parodies of Narrative Power" 118).

The behavior that both have socially acquired is reinforced and perpetuated by the rewarding of stereotypical masculine behavior (Olímpico's aggressive and domineering actions) and the subsequent punishment of any feminine behavior perceived as atypical (Macabéa's attempts at acquiring "culture"). In her work Lispector brings to light the "sexual textual" politics of male-female relationships and the obstacles to hybridity of the subject voice by exposing the hypocrisy and double standard of the rewards of Olímpico's behavior contrasted with the punishments of Macabéa's attempts at bridging the gap between her identity as a marginalized person and the dominant discourses of culture only accessible to her in part. However, the scope of Lispector's critique goes beyond the binary male-female interrelation in *A hora da estrela* and beyond just highlighting the feminine subversion of these dualities. Barbosa elaborates on this theme when she emphasizes that on one level Rodrigo, Olímpico, and the Author are examples of the phallocentric discourse seeking to exert itself on a literary level: "She does not treat their discourses simply as a system of polarities, but rather exposes and parodies the ideologies present in this system of hierarchized oppositions" ("Parodies of Narrative Power" 120).

The chief difference however, is that while textual and social discourse of dominance represented by the narrator and Olímpico seem in the end still able to manipulate language and identity to their advantage, Macabéa must learn to use other textually or socially marginalized methods available to her, like her own self-definition and the subversion of the silence to which she is often relegated.

Macabéa's Voice: Textual Interruption as Self-Affirmation

Macabéa's reformulation of the self occurs on one level through the moments of self-definition that are not controlled by the narrator. They create a second level of hybridity characterized by a reformulation of the marginalized-dominant interaction between narrator and protagonist. This occurs when the narrator's commentary is interspersed with spaces of dialogue and thoughts by the protagonist that escape manipulation and allow the reader increasingly greater insight into Macabéa's opinions of herself. One revelation in particular that demonstrates her ability for self-affirmation is the following:

> So she had recourse to a lie that sounded much more convinc-
> ing than the truth: she informed her boss that she would be
> unable to turn up for work the following day because she had
> to have a tooth extracted that might be troublesome.... The
> following day, therefore,... she could enjoy at long last the
> greatest privilege of all: solitude. She had the room all to
> herself.... She danced and waltzed round the room for soli-
> tude made her: f-r-e-e! (Lispector, *Hour of the Star* 41)

Macabéa allows herself to participate in the previously unknown activity of celebration and then uses the mirror to reinforce her framing as subject and reformulate a more positive sense of self: "As she drank, licking her lips between each sip, she studied her own enjoyment in the mirror. To confront herself was a pleasure that she had never before experienced. I have never been so happy in my whole life, she thought. She owed nothing to anyone, and no one owed her anything" (41). By creating a solitary time (even at the cost of deceiving someone in authority over her), Macabéa is able to enjoy a freedom (dancing in front of a mirror while drinking tea) and a chance to dream heretofore inexperienced. Leslie Damasceno highlights the importance of this mirror image to both the narrator's and the protagonist's power in the text:

> [T]he most prominent of these interrupting images—that of
> the mirror—clearly fragments identification at the same time
> that it indicates a mirroring process. Macabéa enters, physi-
> cally, into the book via a mirror image. But the image reflected
> is of the narrator, not of his creation.... This initial mirroring
> sets the tone for identification and confusion. Hereafter, the
> mirror is given over to Macabéa, a narrative gesture of non-
> verbal self-scrutiny that allows the narrator distance from her,
> at the same time that Macabéa's gaze becomes progressively
> a self-framing device. (7)

These moments of self-affirmation are not perfect, given the emotional, cultural, and economic deficit that Macabéa has inherited. The overrid-ing importance however of this positive moment of self-definition is to present the reader with a contrast to the frequently flawed moments when Rodrigo S. M. interprets Macabea for us. Through a self-framing act, she is able to step ever so briefly out of the constant victimization by others (narrator, boss, coworker, or society in general) and be a central figure in her universe.[2]

In these references one sees the relevance of the mirror as a tool of self-affirmation.[3] As Leslie Damasceno notes, "*The Hour of the Star* has what might be called a frantically verbal narrator and an almost preverbal protagonist. In Lacanian terms Macabéa remains until the end of the book essentially in the preverbal mirror stage where outside world and inside reality are contiguous and non-differentiated" (7–8). By placing Macabéa in this framework we can begin to understand the obstacles to her self-representation and consequently, the extent of the changes she experiences throughout the text.

Silence as Subjective Subversion

A second strategy of resistance that Lispector utilizes to demonstrate Macabéa's attempts to free herself of Rodrigo S. M.'s marginalizing objectification and phallocentric discourse is the use of silence. The subjectivity that Macabéa achieves is another example of hooks's theory of a site of contestation of which one chooses to take advantage. As hooks states, "We are transformed, individually, collectively, as we make radical creative space which affirms and sustains our subjectivity, which gives us a new location from which to articulate our sense of the world" (hooks, *Yearning* 153).

In this quote hooks is stressing the subversion of a peripheral positioning into a central one in terms of individual agency. While neither hooks's reference nor Macabéa's reality reflects an initial choice of marginalization, the radical change occurs with the recognition of the power available. For Macabéa this recognition is intimately tied to instincts of survival.[4] It is important to consider when applying hooks's modern assessment of feminine power to Macabéa's condition that it is not a completely matched prescription. As a poor young girl from the Northeast living as almost an invisible entity in Rio, Macabéa's access to power and her ability to wield it are extremely limited. Although she is racially marginalized like the contemporary African American women to which hooks originally directs her strategic advice, the added historical cycle of poverty in which northeasterners lived also limits her in additional ways. Nonetheless, hooks's belief that marginality can in a sense be subverted can in a general sense be applied to certain behaviors in which Macabéa engages.

The silence represented in *A hora da estrela* has either negative or positive connotations depending on the position from which it is viewed. Rodrigo S. M.'s view explains Macabéa's silence as the result of an inability to express herself in a language that dominant discourse would define as constructive: "I now want to speak of the girl from the Northeast. . . . For she had reduced herself to herself. . . . .The girl worries me so much that I feel drained. And the less she demands, the more she worries me. . . . Why does she not fight back? Has she no pluck?" (18, 25–26) In this passage, Rodrigo S. M. criticizes Macabéa for her inability to react verbally or emotionally in a way that he deems appropriate to the given situation. Her lack of what he would interpret as an assertion of her rights and of her oppression (by affirming for example her loneliness and distrust of others) is seen here as the equivalent of silence:

> How I should like to see her open her mouth and say:—I am alone in the world. I don't believe in anyone for they always tell lies, sometimes even when they're making love . . . . The truth comes to me only when I'm alone. . . . Maca, however never expressed herself in sentences first of all, because she was a person of few words. She wasn't conscious of herself and made no demands on anyone. (42, 68)

However, Lispector is able to invert Rodrigo's criticisms to point out the difficulty that nevertheless exists in approaching and appropriating the Other. He is unable to see the value of her silence because his imposition of his circumstances and reactions on the protagonist blinds him to her worth. As he confesses, "I can see that I've tried to impose my own situation on Maca" (68–69).

Barbosa notes that this negative silencing of the subject converts *A hora da estrela* into a testament to "how the female voice faces the implications of male norms and is penalized for the complex web of her own discourse in the narrative tradition" ("Parodies" 120). In this light it becomes in one sense another textual forum in which Lispector represents the negative side of silence: as an indication of the inability to appropriate a personal voice, stressing what critics identify as the postmodern elements of her writing. As Elizabeth Lowe observes:

> Pervaded by a sense of blockage, of isolation and frustration, however, Lispector's fiction can be revealingly read as a discourse of silence, a lyrically rendered yet ironically self-conscious commentary on the evanescent relationships among language, human cognition and reality. In focusing on these metafictional issues, the novels and stories of Clarice Lispector exemplify the kind of writing described as "post modernist," writing that takes as a primary subject the nature of fiction itself, the processes through which it makes its statements. (qtd. in Fitz, "Discourse of Silence" 420)[5]

Nonetheless, *A hora da estrela* is in fact more than a testament to the impermeability of male norms as Barbosa suggests. What Lispector does to counteract this vision is to present the development of Macabéa's character through the empowering significance of silence.

When we look again at the periods where the protagonist does reveal herself through moments of introspection, we are looking at moments of silence that are productive and not negative. These positive redemptive aspects of silence that Lispector illuminates in the text begin with references to the fascination that the protagonist's silence evokes in Rodrigo: "The facts are sonorous but among the facts there is a murmuring. It is the murmuring that frightens me" (24). Even this quote alludes to what in the end will be the importance of silence: its ability to carry meaning that is lost in facts. According to Fitz the greatest meaning of silence for Lispector's characters is its function as a path to self-knowledge, going beyond "the silence that lies forever beyond the speech act" ("Point of View" 421).

This level of autonomy that they can achieve creates a fear in the narrator of the reversal of hierarchy that is seen to a certain extent here and occurs as the text progresses, represented by his transferal from subject to object. Although Rodrigo again tries to maintain a distance from Macabéa, the potential that her silence has to convey meaning draws him to "write himself through her," thus giving her a certain control over his self-expression:

> [[W]hat one sees is an ever greater closeness between these elements: subject (narrator) and object (character), because he, upon writing, surprises himself, just like Macabéa, who doesn't know herself by living aimlessly. . . . [H]e will write himself through her.]

> [O] que se percebe é uma aproximação cada vez maior entre esses elementos: sujeito (narrador) e objeto (personagem), porque ele, ao escrever, se surpreende, assim como Macabéa, que não se conhece através de ir vivendo à toa. . . . Ele vai se escrever através dela. (Xavier 141).

This approximation of subject and object opens our discussion up more to the role of silence in the author's subversive tactics. While doubt is created in the narrator's interpretations (as we have seen) the silence serves as a quiet reflection of a more accurate verbalization of Macabéa's life (because of its increased subjectivity) and proof of the distance that exists from the narrative viewpoint. Damasceno again relates this to the reversals of power in the text:

> First of all, construction of identity by way of silences and negation is one of the most radical procedures of the novel. . . . Feminist theorists have often pointed out that

women, even as heroines, are bearers of meaning, but not makers of meaning in the narrative. The ironized reversals of narrative power in *The Hour of the Star* are explained in part by Macabéa's magnetic and absorptive passivity. But they are also given force by inverting symbols of subjectivity and objectification that rupture the narrative flow. (7)

Macabéa's seeming passivity and silence is not condemned to be nothing more than an indication of a lack of agency and control in her self-definition. Ironically it becomes a powerful tool of self-awareness through reversed roles of subject and object. These inversions of perspective and self-framing not only manifest themselves through structural breaches but on a deeper level show the ways in which Macabéa becomes more of a maker of meaning as it relates to her life.

The question Lispector poses in *A hora da estrela* is in a sense the same one Jesus posed twenty years earlier in *Quarto de despejo*: how do the powerless acquire the power to construct their identities on their terms, and more specifically, how can a woman construct her identity when society has placed barriers in her way that seem insurmountable? Once again, like Jesus, Lispector examines this dilemma on two levels: on a social level, exploring how her female protagonist can actively affirm a sense of self, and on a metatextual level, analyzing how she as a writer can break through this discourse. However, the answer she proposes is the reading and careful use of silence—by paying attention to the narrative and social spaces present in the text:

> Literary postmodernism aspires to silence, to the kind of nonexpression and noncommunication that occurs when, living in a Babel of verbal noise, words come to lose the meanings we expect them to have. Turning against itself, the literature of post modernism shows us that the more we talk,the less we communicate, that silence, because it leads to a pure, undetermined preverbal state, ironically begins to do what we want language to do. (Fitz, "Discourse of Silence" 435)

Through silence Macabéa found a voice and opportunity to leave a legacy that the lack of complete access to language and the logocentric masculine domination had always denied her.

Macabéa's Death: The Hybrid Voice

The final example of Lispector's subversion and empowerment of her protagonist's search to reformulate her self-definition is ironically found in a death that is linked with the theme of silence previously discussed. Because of the hit-and-run accident by a Mercedes Benz after her visit to the fortuneteller, Macabéa experiences her "hour of the star" as Rodrigo had predicted: "For at the hour of death you become a celebrated film star, it is a moment of glory for everyone when the choral music scales the top notes" (28). In death the protagonist finally receives the identity that she never had in life and the importance that always evaded her. In the end, at the moment of her death, when the narrator finally recognizes Macabéa's significance as representative of an illumination that each human being desires to experience, it is in part in silence that this new consciousness is found: "She is finally free of herself and of me. . . . I now understand this story. She is the imminence in those bells, pealing so softly" (85). Figueiredo concurs, stressing that in the end this silence is more important than facts: "Por este motivo o 'gran finale' denunciador de sua história se faz ao mesmo tempo de palavras (a narrativa em si) e silêncio (a morte)" (3). [For this reason the accusatory 'grand finale' of her story is made of both words (the narrative in itself) and silence (death).] She adds that this end can be seen as Macabéa's epiphany, her moment of enlightenment and transport to another level of being, ripping apart the shell of the everyday (which is routine), through the mechanism of the vacuum, and what is silent and internal. This epiphany is achieved in various stages: contemplation, sacred silence, an explosion of profane joy, the revelation of life, the appearance of the angel and of glory, and nausea—vomit:

> [The grandiloquent final that she (Lispector) plans for history is connected to a type of interior and voiceless genesis. It is made in one single phrase, "As for the future," which is con-nected much more to interior radars than to reason and intelligence. . . . The epiphany, in Macabéa, is unleashed in the moment when she dares to dream about happiness, break with a status quo, transgress an already crystallized structure, within a dominating and rotular regime.]

> O final grandiloqüente que ela (Lispector) planeja para a história se conecta a uma espécie de gênese interior e surda. Se faz em uma só frase "Quanto ao futuro" que se liga muito mais a radares interiores do que à razão e à inteligência. . . . A epifania, em Macabéa, se desencadeia no momento em que ela ousa sonhar com a felicidade, romper com um "status quo," transgredir com uma estrutura ja cristalizada, dentro de um regime dominador. . . . (Figueiredo 3)

It is through Macabéa's death that Lispector affirms, as Damasceno notes, the reversal that has taken place throughout the text. In this moment Lispector brings together once again the narrator and protagonist in one final hybridized destiny: "In effect, the narrator is absorbed back into the initial mirror image, and loses the certainty of language as his protagonist ironically gains independence and control of the symbolic realm of language by implicit affirmation of the power of silence" (Damasceno 8). Through the parallel existence of the two characters, the narrator "interweaves Macabéa's story with his philosophical questionings in a desperate attempt to read himself at the same time that he writes Macabéa's story. Throughout the narrative they proceed side by side until the end where Macabéa's death is Rodrigo's end" (Barbosa, "Reinforced Affirmative" 235). As Xavier summarizes:

> [The narrator starts from a masculine position but proceeds, slowly to discover himself and surprise himself in a process in which writing corresponds to submitting oneself to a rite of passage: that of a situation connected to the environment, . . . [the narraror] lives the moment of the dream . . . the moment of cleansing . . . until the mystic instant in which destiny/ liberty/death are integrated.]

> O narrador parte de uma postura masculina mas vai, paulatinamente, se descobrindo e se surpreendendo num processo em que escrever corresponde a submeter-se a um rito de passagem: de uma situação ligada ao ambiente, . . . vive o momento do sonho . . . o momento da purgação . . . até o instante místico em que destino/liberdade/morte se integram. (145)

The indication of this reversal and Rodrigo's end is his inability to control his characters and his text just when his protagonist's very life is at stake:

> I could turn the clock back and happily start again at the point when Macabéa was standing on the pavement—but it isn't for me to say whether the fair-haired foreigner looked at her. The fact is that I've already gone too far and there is no turning back. . . . I could resolve this story by taking the easy way out and murdering the infant child, but what I want is something more: I want life. (79, 82)

As Sá observes:

> [The truth that the narrator invents, he does not know com-
> pletely... he still does not know the end of the story.... The
> narrator dies with Macabéa. And he advises the reader that to
> die is an instant and belongs to the human condition.....
> Macabéa died; the narrator died with her.]

> A verdade que o narrador inventa, ele não o conhece inteira....
> Não conhece ainda o final da história.... O narrador morre
> com Macabéa. E avisa o leitor que morrer é um instante e
> pertence à condição humana.... Morreu Macabéa, morreu com
> ela o narrador. (274)

What is subverted here at the end is the reader's belief in and even
reliance on the narrator's invincibility, thus creating a doubt and uneasiness about a narrator who throughout has attempted to portray himself
as omniscient and omnipotent.

While we can see the capacity of silence to be used as an instrument
of subversion on a structural level, it is its metaphysical function that
Lispector recommends as a possibly effective tool for combating the
prohibition of the Other from self-realization and from the strictures of
phallocentric discourse.

Lispector's work in *A hora da estrela* has raised important questions
about the possibility of constructing a fictional space in which to explore
the redefinition of the self. How is this impacted by changes in the dislocation of the subject? Can conditions like silence that are socially defined
as positions of weakness be turned into actions and viable methods of
empowerment? In the examples of writers like Julieta Campos we see a
process of reformulation of identity that shares common ground with the
authors I have studied. Campos shares with both Lispector and Jesus a
representation of the movement incorporating marginal and central discourses in order to redefine the self and a common element of dislocation
from which they begin this process. By contrast, she especially explores
these issues on a structural level while grappling with similar problems
of the limits of the word in representing reality and the efforts of the
individual to mold both language and time in ways that show the complexity of identity.

Chapter Five

Campos's *Tiene los cabellos rojizos y se llama Sabina*: The Multivocality of Identity

Hybridity and Multivocality in Campos's Text

While Jesus's diary of her life in the favela presented a seemingly direct representation of one woman's struggle that revealed the complexities of her redefinition of the self against society's strictures, Lispector's *A hora da estrela* used the story of a young northeastern woman's survival in metropolitan Rio as a basis for the author's exploration of the process of understanding and redefining the self. This awareness was achieved in part through a greater comprehension of interactions with an Other and through the exploration of issues of geographic and social dislocation in the construction of identity. As part of this ontological exploration Lispector also incorporated an analysis of the dynamics of female identity as a counterpoint to phallocentric discourse. Through her deconstruction of traditional gender roles and expectations she was able to expose the problems in both and demonstrate how an individual could use hybrid forms of discourse to rewrite herself.

While both Jesus's and Lispector's texts presented protagonists who represented marginalized individuals at a given moment in history, Campos's text presents both its characters and its author in a space whose historical positioning cannot be easily identified. While there is no one specific historical base, there are historical references, both past and present, in a nonlinear style, which the text's principal voices navigate. In addition, the author's own geographic instability serves as a nonfictional referent that possibly informs the characters' and novel's overall sense of displacement. The foundation from which Campos analyzes the reformulation of identity can be understood through an analysis of the positioning first of the authorial voice and second of the multiple voices—both authorial and fictive—present in the text with regards to time, space, and the socioeconomic factors that I have defined as historical positioning.

These varied subject positions demonstrate how Campos, in her text *Tiene los cabellos rojizos y se llama Sabina* [*She Has Reddish Hair and Her Name Is Sabina*], uses a multiplicity of voices that are not historically stable in order to represent her theory of the interaction and responsibilities of the artist and his or her work as defined in her critical texts *La imagen en el espejo* and *Función de la novela* while also examining to an extent the ramifications of a gendered and geographic marginalization. As she states, "Y en el espejo, desvanecida la imagen, queda la imagen definitiva, su creación, . . . ese objeto donde todo se aclara" (*Imagen* 98–99). [And in the mirror, the effaced image, remains the definitive image, his creation.]

Campos therefore uses the text as a forum for reflection on the creation of an individual voice. Her novel originates from the principle that art allows her to contemplate the world around her as well as examine the different aspects of personal identity. As with Jesus's *Quarto de despejo* and Lispector's *A hora da estrela*, included in this contemplation is a process of self-representation both influencing and in turn influenced by the structure of this text. The result of this dual influence is the revelation of the text's presentation of the possibility of time, language, and text without limits. Consequently, the text reflects a hybridity on two levels: first, structurally, through the interweaving of fictive voices with an authorial and narrative voice, and second, chronologically, through the erasure of boundaries between past, present, and future. The text becomes a reformulation of the self that exhibits characteristics of feminine writing yet also explores issues of the parameters of such a categorization.

Outside the "Boom": Theoretical Influences in Campos's Writings

Born in Cuba in 1932, Campos received her education in France and at the age of twenty-three moved to Mexico, where she became a citizen and continued to write novels, short stories, and literary criticism. For this reason, one interesting aspect of Campos's work is seeing the similarity or distance from her other Cuban contemporaries, as well as the presence or absence of Cuban influences in her work. Campos's emigration to México in 1955 raises questions about the existence of any impact of definitive historic moments like the Cuban Revolution four years later on her writing. In biographies and interviews, however, this topic is not usually discussed, thus leaving spaces for a questioning of the references to Cuba in her texts, including *Sabina*. One wonders if they are references to a pre- or postrevolutionary Cuba, or to a possibly nostalgic image of Cuba that corresponds to neither.

Despite the absence of a marked historic *cubanidad* in her works, Campos's migration from Cuba does in fact tie her to other citizens and artists of the Cuban diaspora who in part are defined by a sense of exile. Women writers in particular, like the poet Gertrudis Gomez de Avellaneda, and more contemporary novelists like Zoé Valdés and Cristina García have incorporated questions of displacement and identity in their works, at times engaging in the creation of what Anderson calls "imagined communities." In the foreword to her anthology of contemporary fiction by Cuban women writers Ruth Behar comments on this act: "The question of homeland is so vexed for Cubana writers, and women writers very much need homelands to write, no matter what Virginia Woolf says. For us, truly, the island is an absence of water surrounded by water. Ours is an embattled homeland, divided by revolution and exile; the ocean is our border and bond, the mark of our loneliness and longing" (xv). Behar sets up the themes of water and fluidity, longing, and absence from the beginning with her quote from the poem "Geography" by Cuban writer Dulce María Loynaz:

> question: Define: island
> answer: An island is
>   an absence of water surrounded
>   By water; An absence of
>   Love surrounded by love (vii)

Both quotes set up interesting themes that are connected to Campos's text, and specifically *Sabina*. The tropes of water as both a defining factor of Caribbeanness and a symbol of fluidity and instability, exile and longing as consequences of geographic but not necessarily emotional distance, and the idea of longing and absence are all, I contend, elements of the thoughts and emotions of the protagonist Sabina. Similarly, Campos's physical displacement from her homeland is an experience that links her to Jesus and Lispector. For all women, their lives and identities are marked (whether to a small or large degree) by a sense of dislocation and the readjustment it provokes. Their experiences (whether long lasting or short lived) of not belonging, and being the Other in a new social or national context, as we have seen, are reflected to differing degrees in their works. A careful look at these themes in *Sabina* demonstrates that this can also be considered the case with Campos, although the degree to which it informs her character representations may differ from the two Brazilian writers.

Campos's work, because of its time of publication, can also be considered in the context of the Latin American "Boom" of the 1960s. One
notes that despite certain thematic and stylistic characteristics—particularly of narrative experimentation—in common with the writers of this
literary current, her works also exhibit significant differences that place
her more in the company of writers like Beckett, Robbe-Grillet, Simon,
and Mauriac, especially in terms of the problematization of language and
the increased degree of experimentation with structure and time. In a
comparison with works by Cortázar, Cabrera Infante, and Elizondo,
Evelyn Picon Garfield concludes:

> Novelistic structures which create an atmosphere of simulta-
> neity abound in contemporary Spanish American fiction. . . . In
> them logical transitions between episodes disappear or are
> hidden, voids are created, and information is deferred in or-
> der to goad the reader into participating in the reconstruction
> of a fragmented plot. . . . Nevertheless, in the aforementioned
> novels, text and texture do not usually form a unified focus
> since the disjointed framework of those novels generally serves
> only as a scaffolding for their various themes, not as the theme
> itself. . . . None of these novels achieves success as an "open
> work," replete with ambiguities and contradictions, to the
> extent that Sabina does in its constant metamorphosis. (78)

In *Sabina* Campos comments briefly on the relation of novelists to the
boom of Latin American literature. She uses a conversation between two
of the narrative voices—"El Laberinto" and the voice that incorporates
aspects of Campos's theories—to question the future of the Latin American novel.

The first narrative voice points out the qualities of Latin American
reality that, once explored, could lead to distinctive, successful literature.
For him the boom's success, particularly in Europe, is due to the Western
world's desire for nonmimetic literature. In order to stress the need for
a distancing from mimetic writing, this narrative voice refers subtly to
Campos's text *La imagen en el espejo*, in which she defines the current
literature as creating an image in the mirror that does not correspond to
reality but rather distorts it. By advocating the investigation of characters
and myths found in the region, this narrative voice is stating his approval of the direction in which the authors of the boom have taken their
writing. The second narrative voice, corresponding to Campos, stresses
that her literature will also not be mimetic but will be different by not
recurring to myths in order to explain the world. The result in *Sabina*

therefore is a battle between the two approaches to literature and the myths used to define a society at any given point in time.[1]

In 1965 Campos published her first novel, *Muerte por agua* (Death by Water), and her first book of literary criticism, *La imagen en el espejo*. This was followed by two more texts of literary criticism: *Oficio de leer* (1971) and *Función de la novela* (1973). In 1974 she published her second novel, entitled *Tiene los cabellos rojizos y se llama Sabina*, for which she received the Xavier Villaurrutia Prize. 1979 was the year of her third novel, *El miedo de perder a Euridice (The Fear of Losing Eurydice/a novel)*, followed by the critical essay *La herencia* (The Inheritance 1982), analyzing a collection of Nahuatl folk tales based on the theoretical principles of Claude Lévi-Strauss, Vladimir Propp, and Sigmund Freud. Along with her literary activity as a writer and critic Campos has served as the president of the P.E.N. club of Mexico and has written for the literary magazines *Plural* and *Vuelta*. She was also involved as editor with the journal *Revista de la Universidad de México* and has translated books on the social sciences, history, and psychoanalysis from French and English (Campos, *Sabina* xiii–xix).

One of the reasons why Campos' literary style is not wholly representative of the Latin American boom of the 1960s is her theoretical and literary influences. Two important influences that can be recognized are Proust and Umberto Eco. Eco's theory of the "open work" structure in a literary text, for example, is perfectly exemplified in *Sabina* (Martin 77).[2] In *La imagen en el espejo* Campos discusses the theoretical approaches of writers like Simone de Beauvoir, Nathalie Sarraute, and Virginia Woolf— whose influence on the development of her literary strategies is seen by the incorporation of their theories into *Sabina*. From Beauvoir, Campos has been influenced by the author's questioning of the concept of freedom, its definition, and how we as humans live with it, as well as seeking an understanding of the role of the past in deciding the present and future: "La causa de todo hombre es la causa de la libertad de la humanidad entera: sólo puede proyectarse válidamente si lo hace en relación con un futuro" (Campos, *Imagen*, 121). [Every man's cause is the cause of the freedom of all humanity: it can only be validly projected if it is done in relation to a future."] Two points that are especially important to Campos's structuration of *Sabina* are the subjective approach to reality and the elusiveness of language: "[C]on la idea todavía fresca en la mente hay que buscar la palabra y meter al pájaro en la jaula antes de que vuele y se le caigan las alas. . . . Y las palabras se buscan entre si y se ajustan a una forma que tiene sus propias reglas: la frase" (Campos *Imagen* 121). [With the idea still fresh in the mind one must seek the word and put the bird in the cage before it flies away and its wings fall off. . . . And the words seek each other and adjust to a form with its own rules: the phrase."]

From Sarraute, Campos has found a model from the nouveau roman to help guide her attempts to develop a nonmimetic novel, especially with relation to the narrator. For this reason Campos stresses that the use of the personal pronoun "tu" is so meaningful:

> [[I]t is like a mirror in front of which life marches by. . . . If the narrator is the mediation between the narrated world and the world where one narrates, his intervention represents as much the author as the reader. . . . The second person is the very reader, with whom communication is established, unknown in the traditional novel.]

> [Es] como un espejo frente al cual desfila la vida. . . . Si el narrador es la mediación entre el mundo narrado y el mundo donde se narra, su intervención representa tanto al autor como al lector. . . . La segunda persona es el lector mismo, con quien se establece una comunicación desconocida en la novela tradicional. (*Imagen* 123)

Virginia Woolf's impact on Campos's work is equally strong, serving as the inspiration for the opening chapter of *La imagen en el espejo*. In Woolf's arguments Campos sees an appreciation of an individual's inner life, which is in turn reflected in an artist's character depiction, the importance of not presenting an objective representation of reality but rather a subjective one that serves as a commentary on the concept of reality, and the difficulty every writer (and possibly every individual as well) faces in capturing language in any meaningful, permanent way (Campos, *Imagen* 52).

Together, these influences have allowed Campos to develop her own theories on the subject's interaction and interpretation of reality that serves as a subtle foundation to her fiction. Such an approach is representative of the analysis of literature adopted by various feminist critics. Spivak notes, "A deconstructive critical approach would loosen the binding of the book, undo the opposition between verbal text and the biography of the named subject . . . and see the two as each other's 'scene of writing.' In such a reading, the life that writes itself as 'my life' is as much a production in psychosocial space as the book that is written by the holder of that named life" (149). Campos's theory of the relationship between fiction and critical discourse in her work operates along similar lines as she states in her interview with Evelyn Picon Garfield:

Now my reflexive and critical discourse and my fiction slide so imperceptibly by each other that it is difficult to separate or distinguish them. Don't you think it seems so in *Tiene los cabellos rojizos y se llama Sabina*? The writing and its criticism comprise a single text: a weaving in which strange voices and other works converge, incorporated within me so that I felt them to be my own. Each time, my criticism is less isolated from narrative forms in a kind of symbiosis between criticism and fiction. (82)

On the more specific level of the author as subject of her writing, the presence of the novelist or author in the text is a theme that runs through many of Campos's critical texts. Years later, in *Función de la novela*, she expands on the interiorization of the writer in her work that she had addressed years earlier in *La imagen en el espejo*:

[The author who changes into his own character gives himself a role within a story more extensive than his own novel, a story that includes him as a character, at the same time it covers the characters invented by him. . . . The author dares to expose himself to the gaze of the reader, who he also includes at times as a character.]

El autor que se convierte en su propio personaje se atribuye a sí mismo un papel dentro de un relato más amplio que su propia novela, un relato que lo comprende a él como personaje, a la vez que abarca a los personajes inventados por él. . . . El autor se atreve a exponerse a la mirada del lector, a quien incluye también a veces como personaje. (62)

Anäis Nin and Campos: Tessera as Structural Hybridity

When we look at the literary influences in Campos's latest novel, *Sabina*, the writer whose work serves as a direct inspiration and an initial blueprint for understanding the structual hybridity of the text is Anaïs Nin. As Juan Bruce-Novoa points out, the protagonist from Campos's work is a reference to Sabina, the protagonist in Nin's prose poem "House of Incest," one of three in her prose pentology. Nin's Sabina represents unfettered freedom. She does daily what the other characters only dream of at night. Sabina's talent is creative talking, expressing phrases the narrator describes as "Talk—half-talk, phrases that had no need to be finished, abstractions. . . . The muffled, close, half-talk of soft-fleshed women" (Nin 181). However, behind the incessant talk is what her lover describes as lies: "arrows flung out of your orbit by the strength of your fantasy" (185). While other characters, like Lillian, accept logocentric male, readings of herself, Nin's Sabina challenges male figures. Her desire for freedom encompasses all areas of male-female relationships—a rejection of any domination by man and a desire for sexual freedom: "Sabina was no longer embracing men and women. Within the fever of her restlessness the world was losing its human shape. . . . She was spreading herself like the night over the universe and found no god to lie with" (183). For Nin's Sabina, people fall into two categories: the slave or the enslaver. As a woman espousing the principles of what Bruce-Novoa has characterized as "militant" feminism, she chooses the latter. It is important to problematize however the use of the term militant to define the attitudes reflected in Nin. Unlike a militant feminism defined by a total rejection of the masculine, Nin's Sabina moves between a distancing of men and women to a oneness with her lover that instead reflects the union of masculine and feminine. This coalescing of voices is an important preamble to the multiplicity of voices exhibited in Campos's *Sabina*. The connection the male character feels with Sabina is an important contrast with the ties between the fictive voice in "The Labyrinth" and the fictive voice Sabina in Campos's text. However, the imprint he is able to make through the attempted appropriation of her presence brings to mind the female voice in "El Mirador" and her desire to incorporate Sabina into a novel she would like to write.[3]

Bruce Novoa, however, indicates that Campos's representation of Sabina in her text is not an exact copy of Nin's protagonist but rather a combination of types, employing a technique that Harold Bloom has defined as *tessera*: "completion and antithesis." One example of tessera is the physical appearance of Sabina. Campos fuses three female types in one slightly revised character. While Sabina had black hair, Lillian's was red. From Campos's title *Tiene los cabellos rojizos y se llama Sabina* we are immediately made aware of this tessera: Campos's Sabina has Lillian's hair color. Another example of tessera that Bruce-Novoa emphasizes is Sabina's rhetorical style—continually shifting, ambiguous, unreliable, and allusive with often borrowed text (59–60).

Bruce-Novoa compares not only the protagonist Sabina as she is represented in Nin's and Campos's text but also the two authors themselves, in order to emphasize that their literary techniques have important similarities as well as points of divergence. While Nin utilizes extraliterary references in her text, Campos's references, especially in *Sabina*, remain purely literary. Another important contrast highlighted is the nature of the images used in their texts. As Bruce-Novoa points out, while Nin believes that somewhere is an original image, a unique source, Campos's assertion is that "every image is an intertextual reference to yet another image" (61).

Structural Hybridity as Ontological Study

It is in part this intertextuality and the resulting belief that no original image exists—whether it is literary or simply of an individual—that makes *Sabina* an interesting text to study in terms of reformulating identity through interwoven textual and structural devices. Campos's "open structure," temporal manipulations, and references to both masculine and feminine texts provide an important contrast with Jesus and Lispector. On one hand all demonstrate strategies of hybridization. As three authors crossing fictional and nonfictional boundaries as part of this hybridity, what also unites them is a personal displacement played out in their textual strategies of identification. At the same time what distinguishes Campos's process of identity reformulation is the use of unstable temporal and textual conditions where the subject is not tied to one specific historically positioned context. The subject's identity in terms of race and class can only be vaguely inferred by certain subtle textual indicators, but never as explicitly as with Jesus as favelada or Macabéa as the poor young woman from the Northeast.

Consequently, instead of a plot with suspense, climax, and anticlimax, Campos produces a site that strongly fosters ontological reflection. The reader immediately becomes aware that the text is an interaction of voices in various historical and temporal sites, creating a work that has aspects of an antinovel, reminiscent of Cortázar's *Rayuela*, but which can best be described as an example of the *nouveau roman* (Bruce-Novoa 45).

Nonetheless, Bruce-Novoa defines Campos's literary style as one that, while returning to earlier traits found in the nouveau roman, also incorporates other important influences:

> In short, in her early prose Campos tended towards the *nouveau roman*, with its de-emphasis of traditional mimetic devices, plot, and character. Within that orientation, there was an apparent evolution from a resemblance to Sarraute and towards a descriptive emphasis closer to Robbe-Grillet. Yet, as she says above, the figure of the character does not completely disappear, and that character is a woman. . . . The obsession with the descriptions of fields of vision, spatial relationships, and the narrative act itself again place it in the camp of the *nouveau roman*. (44–45)

Campos's relationship with the nouveau roman and its historical origins is a noteworthy connection of form, voice, power, and politics. In more specific terms, the nouveau roman was a revolt against the literary representations of a coherent universe, completely decipherable by the reader.

"It was a reversal of the formal stereotypes which we accept because we suppose them wrongly to be absolute or essential in the philosophical sense. . . . The responsibility of the novelist is now to show what a fiction consists in, and by extension, what the role of the imagination is in our daily lives" (Sturrock 10). In this sense, Campos's use of nontraditional chronology and character development to make the reader work to understand Sabina's universe owes a strong debt to the nouveau roman.

In part Robbe-Grillet's development of this aesthetic was a reaction to Sartre's and Camus' more ordered, unified literary world and Sartre's belief in political engagement and commitment as an integral part of literary production. In his impersonal descriptions Robbe-Grillet attempted to demonstrate that "the tragedy and alienation that haunt human beings stem from a falsified sense of a relationship between people and things. There is no such relationship, just a gulf "(137). This alienation and questioning of the relationship of people and objects is in a sense part of what the protagonist Sabina undergoes as she questions the nature of language, its connection with reality, and her own identity. The alienation she feels now can be seen as multiple in nature: First, in one sense it is a textual mirror that represents the feelings of dislocation that are a part of the author's experience. Second, it is a representation of the crisis of the gulf of reality and their signifiers. For proponents of the nouveau roman like Robbe-Grillet and Natalie Sarraute, their lack of cohesive structure and progression is a subversion of the structural hierarchies of the text and exploration of the adventure of writing. Similarly, as further analysis of *Sabina* will reveal, the aesthetic philosophy of Campos and the author is to similarly undermine definitive narrative strategies and canonical guidelines. Laura Beard emphasizes this act of contestation, particularly for the female narrators who "do not find it easy to narrate their visions, visions that are 'other' than those of the male narrator. They must struggle not to drown in the sea of male-authored images of women. . . . [T]he female narrators . . . must work to clear the water of such debris so that female names and works may surface" ("Navigating the Metafictional Text" 53). Such a subversion is therefore a battle for power of expression and identification.

The historical context within which the nouveau roman develops is also a commentary on power in a postcolonial context. French colonial identity, particularly in the Caribbean and sub-Saharan Africa, was projected onto these lands as an imaginary reality through an imposed structured discourse and linguistic uniformity. The fictional production of the time demonstrated just such uniformity and hegemony. However, in the late 1950s these power structures began to unravel. Between 1954–1962 many African countries fought to gain their autonomy. While Algeria received its independence in 1960 after a prolonged war, other countries peacefully became independent nations throughout the decade. Just as the political strongholds were being torn down, so too were literary discourses of authority. Precisely in 1957 Robbe-Grillet published his first new novel called *La jalousie* when Natalie Sarraute had already published her first novel *Martereau* in 1953. In both cases the espousal of the tenets of the nouveau roman was a way of taking politics (and commitment) out of literature and, while not supporting explicitly the wars and movements of independence, in Africa and the Caribbean, supporting the ideologies of destabilization. It is this principle of displacement that both Campos and Sabina grapple with throughout the text. Together with this instability is a tendency, consequently, not toward structural homogeneity but rather toward hybridity.

Another historical curiosity, possibly irony, is that this form developed not only during a time of political upheaval but particularly at a time when former Francophone colonies were grappling with and trying to resolve their own insider/outsider relationships and identities with dominant French linguistic and political discourses and their own marginalized histories and structures.

Intersecting Voices: Authorial Interruptions and Gendered Voices

Of the characters and voices in *Sabina* who interact most, the primary is a young woman on a balcony in Acapulco. It is the end of her vacation, and her decision to stay or leave is dependent on her ability to recapture a moment of truth that she has experienced about herself and her life. However, competing for the right to interpret her reality are a masculine voice alone in a room called "The Labyrinth," and another female voice that is writing the protagonist into a novel. The struggle between these three voices is revealed through dialogue and the interpretations of a fourth narrative voice. As the reader slowly learns from the references that this narrative voice alludes to, it is a vehicle the author Campos uses to insert herself in the text.

The text as a result serves as a fascinating, complex study of the endeavor to define and extend the limits of the work itself as well as those of the self. It is this multiplicity, and specifically the interaction of constantly changing narrative points of view with constantly changing novelistic possibilities (rather than conventional plots), that serves as an example of what Bruce-Novoa terms "metaobservation":

> But it is always clear that the points of view, and what lies in the field of vision or imagination, are not settings for a narrative, but rather perspectives or possibilities to be discussed as

just that, potential perspectives or potential texts. Instead of describing or narrating from a particular perspective, the perspective is discussed by a narrator, and often not the same narrator who inhabits the vantage point in question, but by another who imagines the other. . . . The result is that metaliterature—metaobservation—replaces narrative. (47).

The metaobservation described above has two important elements in the text. First is the exploration and commentary on the act of writing (and specifically, writing this text) and the conflicting discourses that shape it—be it a dominant male discourse or a female-centered discourse. This analysis of language leads to an analysis of how the self is represented and represents itself in this medium. What we find in carefully studying the relationship between the female narrative voices and the male narrative voice is an attempt to use language for self-definition in a way that promotes empowerment. As Bruce-Novoa states in describing the principal narrative voice's project, "In the end, her search is the text, and the text is her self-image, the only one available to the reader" (56).

What is particularly interesting about this text is that the author is also present—converting herself into one of the many narrative voices that the readers encounter. Her presence in the text thus becomes more than just a literary exercise or experiment but rather a means to exploring her own identity as writer, individual, and gendered subject, particularly as it is articulated through words. For Campos her incorporation into the text is more than just an interesting textual strategy. It is a metafictive commentary on the difficulty and possibly inability of writing to reproduce reality by purely distanced spectators. One such obstacle and at the same time tool for shaping reality is language, and particularly the written word. For Campos, these words have the power to create reality more so than reality itself (including representations of class, race, and gender that are the principal components of historical positioning). As Campos states:

> [The function of the artist is to reveal in such a way that, once the work is carried out, it seems as necessary as reality itself and detaches from its roundness, from its totality, a reality even more real. For the writer, the universe becomes a succession of words and nothing was clear for him before the utterance of those words.]

> Poner en evidencia es la función del artista de tal manera que, una vez realizada la obra, parece tan necesaria como la realidad misma y desprende de su redondez, de su totalidad, una realidad

todavía más real. A el escritor, el universo se vuelve una sucesión de palabras y nada había sido claro para él antes del proferimiento de esas palabras. (*Función de la novela* 14–15)

Campos's presence in the text also serves as a model for her readers to follow, inciting them to actively enter the text in order to interpret the signs at their disposal and make their own reality.

Authorial Restructuring of the New Novel

Part of the reconceptualization of reality that occurs in *Sabina* takes place through a transformation of the narrative structure that encompasses this reality. As Rivero-Potter notes, the text, once written, becomes an independent entity that takes away the power and predominance of reality as the determining interpretation of itself. The author, for Campos, can have special insight into fiction and reality, but once the text is written ceases to be privileged. Then the text, its suggestions to the reader, and the reader's interpretations become important. One can see in *Sabina* how this textual autonomy is used by Campos to break with the traditional unifying function of the novel and instead create a personalized, multifaceted universe ("The Role of the Reader" 637). In this sense we can see how Campos also uses this text as a means of breaking the once traditional structure and purpose of the novel.

These textual and temporal manipulations are therefore an important part of the dual searches for the text and self-image that Bruce-Novoa referred to previously. To illustrate this dual exploration I will begin by establishing Campos's presence within *Sabina* and then examine the key aspects that, as I have pointed out, serve as an important part of her reshaping of the text and the textual self through her protagonist. As in Jesus's and Lispector's works there is a dynamic at work of movement between inclusion/exclusion and insider/outsider positions. On the level of structural patterns it is represented in the interweaving of several narrative voices that move between positions of marginality and centrality.

In *La imagen en el espejo* Campos shows how art, in this case, the text, serves to clarify the artist's image by giving her a privileged position in which to view herself:

[The painter, the writer, is not at the edge of the world, contemplating it only as a spectator and with a singular authority for creating other universes within that world. He is one more object within this world and can be contemplated from outside, by a spectator capable of contemplating his work, of

contemplating him creating his work, of contemplating the
world that he has created within this world.]

El pintor, el escritor, no está al margen del mundo, contem-
plándolo únicamente como espectador y con una facultad singular para constituir otros universos dentro de ese mundo. Es
un objeto más dentro del mundo y puede ser contemplado
desde afuera, por un espectador capaz de contemplar su obra,
de contemplarlo a él creando su obra, de contemplar el mundo
que él ha creado dentro del mundo. (90)

As a result of this self-contemplation, the artist or, in this case, Campos,
is able to keep herself alive and thus cheat death: "I peel off a skin every
time I write and give it to my characters, who live a borrowed life. So as
not to die altogether, I give pieces of my being to my literary progeny;
they keep me alive with every reading" (qtd. in Garfield 91).

Campos weaves her voice into the text in three important ways: (1)
through personal references based loosely on her own life—mainly geographical, (2) through references to her other texts, and (3) through her
own at times subtle, at times direct admission of her presence in the text.
The first method is the subtlest of the three. By references to her biographical information Campos begins to apply this information to her
characters, in order to incorporate herself into the text on a similar level
as the other narrative voices and provide a subtle commentary on her
own geographical displacement. In a discussion of the protagonist's
manipulations of time and death, and the role of writing in representing
this, one of the narrative voices addresses the unavoidable importance of
symbols in any novel, giving as an example the symbol of the sea: "It
will be necessary to describe the sea. . . . I am thinking of the Caribbean,
of the ocean surrounding Capri, of the ocean on the northern coast of
Cuba. There are two cities. . . . The other city, the longed-for, the one that
is dreamed, because, although it too shelters death in its most secret
nature, it negates death with its obstinate survival" (*Sabina* 41–42). This
is followed by a supposedly fictitious announcement for a steamline that
travels from New York to Havana and various Mexican ports, the latter
two being two important sites in Campos's life. A few pages later Campos provides another extensive reference to her native island: "Havana,
this year which commemorates the fifth centenary of the discovery of
America, recalls the exploits of the immortal Latin race. . . . Tourists who
wish to escape from the rigors of a winter in the north, seekers after fun-
time experiences eager to enjoy a gentle, delightful climate, will fulfill all
their desires on the Island of Cuba. Key to the Gulf. Queen of the Antilles"
(44). This quote also reveals the manipulation of time that occurs through-

out the text. While this is a reference to actual places, Campos moves ahead eighteen years from the time that *Sabina* was written to comment on the social climate in the country at that point in the future.

As Martha Martinez points out, these references are part of Campos's interiorization of not the memory of just a physical place but more importantly, of a personalized sense of Cubanness in her works:

> [And it is that lyrical side of Julieta Campos that makes her recreate the Cuban, to try to translate the ungraspable climate of the Cuban, the longing for the familiar yesterday, the customs. . . . Julieta sees Cuba with the love of the far away.]

> Y es ese lado lírico de Julieta Campos el que le hace recrear lo cubano, tratar de traducir el clima inasible de lo cubano, la añoranza del ayer familiar, las costumbres. . . . Julieta ve a Cuba con el amor de lo lejano. (794)

Martinez, like Behar, describes the alienation and longing as part of any Cuban identity in exile. By recalling qualities of a culture she left behind, Campos is incorporating into this discourse a physically distanced part of herself. This can be seen when we look at several other references to Mexico, Cuba, or at times to the Caribbean in general that are interspersed throughout the text: "I scarcely am familiar with Havana, with its freezing winds that blow from the north" (65). "They only happen in the Caribbean after a fleeting storm such as this one" (66). One result of the multiple references to her homeland at different points in the personal and national history is to use writing, like Jesus and Lispector, as a site where the tension of displacement can be worked on, in an attempt at some resolution. These references, particularly those made about the sea, also symbolically point to the text as a fluid entity that merges different temporal moments to help reveal personal development.

Accompanying Campos's incorporation of personal biographical information into *Sabina* are references to her other texts. The first is in the same passage where the narrative voice refers to Cuba and Mexico, as part of a conversation with one of the female voices, a conversation which in itself is a metafictive analysis of writing. Her reference here is to Campos's first novel *Celina o los gatos*, using it as yet another possible identity that the narrative voice can adopt (*Sabina* 43). The use of this fictitious identity is just one of the options Campos's works provide. On another level, it is proposed as a possible scenario for the novel being written (by several of the narrative voices): "You will write a book in the form of a travel diary. . . . And one day you will disembark in Vancouver, British Columbia, the very place a character I have invented (a character

who is also writing a kind of diary, although not exactly a travel diary—
or perhaps it is really a memoir—about a woman who liked to surround
herself with cats and mirrors)" (73–74). Campos's other text, *Muerte por
agua*, is also mentioned by the female writer as a possible novel to be
written by the woman watching the sea: "She might be able to write a
novel in which the rain would dissolve beings and things until it resulted
in annihilation. That novel would be called *Death by Water*, alluding to
Heraclitus and T. S. Eliot at once 127)."[4] Both quotations also illustrate
the discursive options that Campos's narrative voice presents for writing
the self: the nonfiction diary (as Jesus chose) or the novel (as Lispector
chose). Therefore, the individual is able to choose her mode of interpreting reality where the subject aspires to a close or more distanced representation of her world. As we see in the instances where Campos herself
is part of the textual dialogue, *Sabina* employs a hybrid strategy to redefine
her identity that is between the two interpretations.

Lastly, Campos references herself both in conversations with the
other narrative voices, and conversations with *Sabina*'s readers. An example of the first category is a subtle description of Campos's self representation through the multiple voices she has created: "A writer is
nothing at all—or, if you will, a writer is an empty sounding board
where the echoes of other voices make themselves heard, magnified, all
out of proportion" (67). Again, Campos emphasizes that the whole is the
sum of its parts: the writer's selfhood is intimately linked to the voices
that constitute her. This fact is repeated in other instances when Campos
subtly refers to herself as the other presence in the text that in fact is the
creator of all the other voices: "Nevertheless, for both of them (and for
myself, who have invented them), the woman on the terrace is imposed
as an indisputable presence: as mirror and as enigma" (79). Campos's
references share certain key similarities in language with Lispector's
Dedication, her admission of the creation of Rodrigo S. M., and consequently, of Macabéa. In both cases, the authors navigate the fine line
between individual control and collective dependence. Like Lispector,
this collectivity is a testament to the intimate link between the creative
act and the text's structure. In describing the protagonist's dual purpose
as mirror and enigma, Campos presents the reader with another example
of multiplicity, a possible paradox of the text. While Campos is the creator of the narrative voices, and thus in a position of privilege and power,
they are at the same time a part of and reflection of her that place them
all on the same level in terms of interdependency.

It is this simultaneous privilege and interdependency that Campos
emphasizes in the latter stages of the novel when her references become
more direct: "Julieta Campos, the one who I am and am not, has written
an essay on a novel titled *The Secret Vault* and another on a novel called

The Amplification. In both cases she deals with the same theme, which is an obsession with her: the motif of the image in the mirror, or in other words, the representation of the world within that representation in the very act of representing it" (107). Through the intertextual references to Elizondo's work, *La amplificación*, and her own critical text, *La imagen en el espejo*, Campos confirms the thesis presented in the latter: of the text as, in one sense, a reflection of its author, while maintaining the delicate balance of presence and distance from the text and the other narrative voices in it.

Temporal Manipulations and Intersecting Voices

The author's direct references to herself within the context of her protagonist's struggles for autonomy are just one strategy employed to explore her own complex identity. In keeping with the multiplicity of voices interacting in the protagonist's journey, Campos weaves together multiple techniques to redefine herself. One such strategy is the manipulation of the narrative voices' temporal positioning, in part to reveal the instability and flexibility of identity. Campos illustrates the reformative qualities of time when she explains, in a conversation with one of the other narrative voices, the text's temporal multiplicities:

> For now I want it said that this character belongs both to me and to two other narrators who are my characters as well. I would say, then, that there are several time frames within the novel: the time during which I am writing this novel: the time when the character gazing at the promontory plans a novel . . . and above all, the time during which she attempts to discover that image of hers, that is, when she tries to be her own person. (100)

In this statement Campos clearly defines the correlation between the textual and structural hybridity in her work through the description of the temporal possibilities of *Sabina*. She sees the three possible times as significant, equating the active time that created the novel with the projected time in which the protagonist hopes to create her own story and finally a future time where this process leads to the reformulation of an independent identity. For Campos all three are part of memory, and form a discursive, revelatory unit only when they coincide: "The dimensions of time which her memory brings up are incommensurable, and the miracle of the discourse is to make coincide, at four o'clock on the afternoon of the eighth of May 1971, the time of a female character . . . the

time of those who are the others; the time frame that could be *my* time"
(101). Just as the connections between the narrative voices leave the reader
unable to distinguish between them with complete certitude, so too does
time become communal. Therefore, Campos's aim is not only to translate
the protagonist's life-changing moment of revelation watching the sea
(an understanding of reality that defies chronology), through her discourse,
but also to create a link that makes the moment equally revelatory for
another narrative, or even authorial voice.

In this statement Campos points out three diferent referents each of
whom seeks to distort time: "my"—referring to Campos, "a female character"—referring to Sabina, and "the discourse"—the text. While Sabina's
motives are clearly stated here, Campos's and the text's can also be understood in the context of the revelatory moment the protagonist experiences and in light of additional statements made in the text: "I, for
example, I am writing a novel about the longest minute ever recorded in
literary history. . . . That was just a game, and what I propose is a serious,
categorical measurement of the meaning of reality for each one of you"
(92). In Campos's *Función de la novela* she describes the division that the
novelist asks the readers to undergo in the text:

> [Author and reader of novels like you, probable reader, imag-
> ined and imaginary, also perhaps author and without doubt the
> reader of one or an infinite number of novels, we are all con-
> demned to assume an identical rupture. . . . A rupture that we
> experience upon letting ourselves be swallowed by his invented
> world, upon letting it devour us as well and convert us into
> another of his many characters. [That rupture] obligate[s] the
> reader to take a step and situate himself within and convert
> himself, at the same time, into the subject of fiction.]

> Autora y lectora de novelas como tú, lector probable, imaginado
> e imaginario, también quizás autor y sin duda lector de una o
> de infinitas novelas, todos estamos condenados a asumir un
> idéntico desgarramiento. . . . Un desgarramiento que experi-
> mentamos al dejarnos tragar por su mundo inventado, al
> permitir que nos devore también a nosotros y nos convierta en
> otros tantos de sus personajes. . . . [Ese desgarramiento] obliga[r]
> al lector a dar el paso y situarse adentro y convertirse, a su vez,
> en sujeto de ficción. (156–157)

Campos asks her readers to cross the same narrative boundaries that she
has transgressed and to a certain extent erase the boundaries between
fact and fiction. Just as the text is able to witness its own genesis and
development, and the author is able to insert her voice into the text, so

too is the reader asked to become an author and take part in the moments of self-exploration and revelation.

The Author's Creation and the Possibilities of Feminine Writing

Campos's request to have the readers join her as coauthors has at its foundation an understanding of the subjectivity of each individual's representation of reality and fiction. This difference can be affected by a range of factors, including the class-based and gendered ones I have examined throughout this chapter. The identity Campos reformulates through her protagonist is one of a woman in search of her voice, but not necessarily looking for the answers in historically positioned structures. Her voice can be found in the manipulation and molding of structures—of writing, time, and memory that transcend history. However, the text and the author's role in it can still aid in our understanding of its applicability (or not) as feminine writing. When speaking of the representativeness of such a category one can point to the protagonist and author's search for their own empowering means of expression, rather than depending solely on an expression of qualities that would define them as feminine.

Campos's conceptualization of a feminine text in particular cannot however be classified primarily based on thematics. For example, if we look at the author's theories on the novel as elaborated in *Función de la novela*, we see that she believes that the feminine text is distinguishable from a male text:

> [If the novel helps the novelist to fill the vacuums of the world, when the novelist is a woman the dispersion of the person is emphasized; the fragmentation of the person, that is distributed even more among numerous demands, demands that the world gives you as a gift, in surrender.]

> Si la novela sirve al novelista para colmar los vacíos del mundo, cuando el novelista es mujer se acentúa la dispersión del ser, la fragmentación de la persona, que se comparte más entre numerosas exigencias, demandas que el mundo le hace de donación, de entrega. (141)

Campos explains that this fragmentation is more common for several reasons:

> [A woman tends to sustain a more immediate relation with reality than a man. . . . [H]er contact with objects . . . that obligatory closeness with the everyday erosion of the real, sharpens

her uneasy perception of the separation to which she is sub-
jected and the strength that she must gather in order to integrate so much dispersion and find her room in the work that
will be for her, much more than for the reader, that "room of
one's own" that Virgina Woolf speaks of, with a much more
concrete connotation.]

La mujer suele sostener con la realidad una relación más
inmediata que la del hombre. . . . Su contacto con las cosas . . .
esa obligada vecindad con el desgaste cotidiano de lo real le
agudiza la inquietante percepción del desgarramiento al que
está sujeta y del acopio de fuerzas que debe hacer para integrar
tanta dispersión y encontrar su aposento en la obra que viene
a ser para ella, mucho más que para el escritor, ese "cuarto
propio" del que hablara Virgina Woolf, con una connotación
mucho más concreta. (*Función de la novela* 141)

According to Campos a woman has an especially immediate relationship
with reality because she is able to perceive the split between her individual identity and the reality that constitutes it. However, Campos's
declaration does not end with the woman—herself—as a helpless witness to this rupture. Through the text, and specifically hers, the female
author is able to use it as a site of contestation and resistance on the level
of the text. Within the literary work the narrative voices, of which the
author is one, are able to interact in multiple ways to demonstrate how
the female narrative voice in particular can create her own subjectivity.

Chapter Six

Telling My Story: Campos's Rewriting of the Feminine Voice in *Sabina*

Introduction

By recreating herself within a fictive world Campos is able to use the literary space to represent her theories of the creative act, specifically as it relates to a subject's interpretation and narration of the world around her. Her insertion into the open work of her novel *Tiene los cabellos rojizos y se llama Sabina* is characterized by an instability and fluidity of representation because of the fleeting nature not only of reality, but also of language as a signifier. As in Lispector's novel the multiplicity of identity is also textually represented through the interaction of fictive characters whose struggles with gender and subjectivity serve as a mirror and at other times a counterpoint to the author's self-exploration. Her reconstruction of identity not only exhibits and influences the fluidity present in her text, by taking place on the nonfictional and fictional plane, but is marked by a sense of dislocation that informs the reformulative act, both personal and aesthetic.

Intersecting Voices: Tensions of Gendered Voices

The text's opening thoughts are from a protagonist who, alone in her room called "El Mirador," [Widow's Walk] is looking out to sea at four o'clock in the afternoon on the last day of her week-long vacation ending Sunday, May 8, 1971, trying to decide if she will leave or stay. The reason for her indecision is her desire to photograph the sea in an attempt to capture a moment of "revelation" that she experienced. While this scenario is revealed only later in the text, the opening image is that of this same woman transporting herself mentally to another beach twenty-two years ago, facing the same dilemma and the same search for knowledge and self-definition. This voice, however, is only one of several that Campos weaves throughout the text. Three voices in particular interact with "the woman on the balcony" to represent the constant struggle between masculine patriarchal language (and texts) and feminine language (and texts). An anonymous man, also in Acapulco, in a hotel room called "The Labyrinth," personifies the masculine voice. As a male writer, he hopes to make the woman looking out to sea a protagonist in his novel.

However, his desire is to use her as a marginal character in a novel very much like Truman Capote's *In Cold Blood*, incorporating elements of sex and violence. On the other hand, a woman seated at her maple desk, observing the protagonist looking out to sea, trying to write a novel where the protagonist is the central figure, personifies the female voice. Unlike the novel attempted by the man in "The Labyrinth," the woman at the desk hopes to empower the woman looking out to sea through the story and not relegate her to passivity. Campos makes the reader aware that these are voices that give us access as readers to their thoughts and motivations but exhibit limited patterns of psychological progression or of physical action in the text that would advance a plot. Together with these two outstanding narrative voices is a third voice that weaves in and out of the text, interacting primarily with the woman on the balcony. As I have examined in the previous chapter, this voice is not represented by any character within the text. This voice represents another level in the fictitious world created that bridges the extratextual and the textual as the author's forum for self-examination.

The presence of these narrative voices is entwined with other "false" voices that appear throughout but actually have very little impact on the development of Campos's text. These "false" voices include a woman taking notes in a notebook, a photographer, Celina, and a journalist. The reader must become lost within these voices, which are the "masks, faces and voices in order to find evidence of their own images" (Campos, *Sabina* 90). Therefore, when the woman looking out to sea states that she is the character Celina, she is using her as an intertextual reference and not referring to a narrative voice that will incorporate her perspective into the text on a significant basis (*Función de la novela* 61). The narrative masks are later revealed to in part be some of the possible memories the protagonist could have in order to construct an alternate narrative. Included in the possible memories of the protagonist are "the memory of someone who has already written fictional texts and whose settings and characters do not cease to haunt her; the memories of those waiting in the air-conditioned room; the nearly blank memory of a photographer on the hunt for snapshots; . . . the memory of a woman who as a little girl lived through the war in Spain" (Campos, *Sabina* 119). Just as Campos's characters display a different development, so also does she establish a nontraditional plot in terms of introduction, development, climax, and denouement. The protagonist's desire to recapture on film, and through words, a moment of enlightenment serves as a springboard for many "possible plots" that are never fully realized. In terms of the actual inspiration for the text, Campos notes in an interview that she was inspired by a newspaper article she read while in Acapulco about an unsolved murder, which she refers to at the end of the text: "The report says: 'A woman of uncertain age died yesterday when she fell fifty feet into a ravine from her room in an Acapulco hotel. The fall was due to the fact that the woman was completely intoxicated' " (*Sabina* 132).[1]

This suicide then becomes one of the many possible stories of the text, and specifically, one of the possible endings to the story of the protagonist watching the sea. She either commits suicide in an attempt to free herself from the control of the two writers, in "The Labyrinth" and "El Mirador," [Widow's Walk] who attempt to define her, goes crazy as another way of seeking refuge from the voices that try to appropriate her, or finally takes the photograph she originally intended to take (Bilbija 144–145). The multiplicity of possible outcomes is paralleled within the text by Sabina's uncertainty about her identity, an incertitude that is part of the text's foundation. Because of the intervention of the various voices, Sabina's struggle for control of her voice leads her again to attempt to choose between five options that range from writing her own novel to becoming one of the characters that others see in her (that is, the man in "The Labyrinth," or the woman watching her and writing), from changing herself into one of the characters she imagines surrounds her, to becoming one of the characters she dreams she could be, or finally, incorporating her childhood and her lifetime personae.

Presence and Absence: Temporal Flexibility and Narrative Development

All of the choices the protagonist has at her disposal, in particular the last one, indicate the importance of time to the representation of the narrative voices. In her study of *Sabina* Francescato analyzes the idea of absence in the context of Barthes's conceptualization of linguistic Utopia in his text *Writing Degree Zero*:

[Together with the narrator we drown in that sea of words that, at heart, do nothing but manifest the absence and artifice.

This is, therefore, the ground zero of writing, the absence, the project in which "literature is converted into the Utopia of language." . . . Everything returns and is reduced to the word. To exist and not to exist: to be and not to be: the novel affirms and denies at the same time.]

Junto con la narradora nos ahogamos en ese mar de palabras que, en el fondo, no hacen sino materializar la ausencia y el artificio. Este es, entonces, el grado cero de la escritura, la ausencia, el proyecto en el que "la literatura se convierte en la Utopía del lenguaje." . . . Todo vuelve y se reduce a la palabra. Ser y no ser: estar y no estar: la novela afirma y niega al mismo tiempo (122).

From early on the text defines itself as a revelation of the mutual existence of presence and absence, possibility and impossibility: of the word, the text, and the individual. This is evident from the beginning of the novel with a declaration of location: "I am not here; I am on another shore" (*Sabina* 3). While the use of the first person sets the tone of the writing as subjective, the use of the negative establishes the uncertainty of this narrative voice. The first sentence is a negation of location, of an assumption made prior to the text's beginning. The protagonist states that she is not here, but rather on another beach.

This quote is important because it sets the tone of uncertainty and displacement in regards to physical and temporal position. This uncertainty and negation is accentuated a few lines down when the narrator reveals the artifice of the opening statement: "If this were the beginning of a novel it should have begun this way . . . but I do not know how it would have ended because the narrator would have been someone else and it would not have had water lilies . . . or, above all, that inconceivable confidence in the power of the word" (*Sabina* 3). It is the beginning of this text and at the same time only a possible beginning for a novel not yet written, not yet realized because had it been, the narrator would be different. As Beard observes, this declaration is a rejection of more than a possible reality by the narrator: "Campos signals Proust's narrative as the definition of what a novel should be. . . . [T]he sentence can be read not only as a tribute to Proust but also as an ironic acknowledgment of the oppressive weight of the literary canon. Real novels, as established by canonical criteria, follow certain rules. If one does not write in accordance with such criteria, one is not writing a novel, at least not a novel that will be admitted to the canon" (47).

Campos is not only aware of this canonical model but challenges it by destabilizing words and the reality they construct. Although everything can seemingly be reduced to the word, including time, one additional result of the instability of Campos' narrative is a crisis of historical positioning.

While in Jesus's *Quarto de despejo* and Lispector's *A hora da estrela* the protagonists that existed at the same time as either the author, as is the case in the former text, or part of the author's representation within the text, as in the latter, possessed identities that had been formulated and reformulated according to social and economic criterion, *Sabina* presents a different case. Just as the text begins with a negation of fixed time, so the many memories that Campos, Sabina, and the other narrative voices refer to serve to constantly keep the reader decentered, unable to fix on one voice, nor on its historical positioning because in the end, the words used to represent these memories only serve to stress the distance from the actual place or reality they attempt to represent and recall.

In this precarious, fictive world, time becomes another narrative device, objectified and molded according to the purposes and desires of the multiple voices. As the feminine narrative voice in El Mirador [Widow's Walk] states: "My novel would not attempt to reproduce life but rather describe a moment when a character would try to deny that the cycle is never interrupted; she would attempt to deny, with her imaginary presence on a balcony facing a spectacular promontory, that the sequence of time is inalterable" (*Sabina* 60). By attempting to go against the limitations one is subject to in reality, the character, and the author who is expressing her desire through this character, is attempting to create her own interpretation of time and of memory (through the character's recollections of varying episodes in her life) and her own position in time. Consequently, if one can alter one's position in time, then it is very likely that one's historical positioning is also unstable and subjective.[2]

These objectives are achieved by distorting time and the protagonist's position in it in three variations (which are not mutually exclusive, but rather, intertwined): (1) traveling through time, (2) changing her physical orientation, and (3) the distortion of memory. The first we have already seen in the protagonist's reference to a fictitious beach twenty-two years ago. The second variation on Sabina's physical orientation is seen in her many imagined travels (or reference to travels) to other lands, like Cuba, and to other seas. This particular reference bears repeating because of its significance: "It will be necessary to describe the sea. The sea of Ulysses? Ahab's sea? Maybe it is the Saragosa Sea? I am thinking of the Caribbean, of the ocean surrounding Capri, of the ocean on the northern coast of Cuba" (41–42). The reference to these voyages is important for two reasons: (1) as a reference to the sea which serves as mirror—as reflection, and (2) the struggle to counteract the dominance of male referents with a female-based model for her self-articulation. As Bruce-Novoa states, what is being reflected is the constant referentiality and intertextuality of language and particularly the dominance of male referents:

> Every text, an effort to structure experience, must contend with the presence of the previous efforts that are contained in language itself. Those previous texts, accumulated over centuries, have determined the rhetorical possibilities of the language Campos' narrators have available to them. And the vast majority of those persistent texts came from men. The mirror's surface, encrusted by years of male dominance, reflects a distorted, false image. The world and literature are a multilayered palimpsest. (50)

These referents to male-authored texts by writers like Proust, Tennessee Williams, Balzac, and Mallarmé are attempts to problematize the hold they have on the discourses of Campos, Sabina, and the woman in "El Mirador" [Widow's Walk]. These literary and theoretical authorities are contrasted with the female narrator who is being advised as to how to structure her novel. Their opposition reveals another aspect of the interaction of the marginalized feminine and centralized masculine discourses. The intense questioning of the female protagonist is an attempt to find a path to her identity that is trapped within the strictures of the male discourse.

Memory, therefore, serves as a tool to reconcile multiple conceptions of time and the memories that accompany them in order to create a new conceptualization of the self not tied to old patterns:

> The options in the tale attempting to impose itself upon my character on the balcony are many, with its tone, nuances, and implications, but it wavers principally between the recurrence of sea images, some of them splendid and others fateful; a literary memory which gradually is less and less distinguishable from that other one, the memory of a reality... the memory of someone who has already written fictional texts... and—of course!—*my* memory. (*Sabina* 119)

Sabina cannot achieve her independence without passing through the sea of memory. Male and Female alike—all are memories, texts and spaces she must navigate: memories that are individual and collective, male and female, hers and belonging to Campos. These memories consist of not just intangible ideas and images, but also of more concrete matter: words.

It is on this battlefield that Campos/Sabina continues her struggle for self-definition. The author's/protagonist's attempts to manipulate time are attempts to manipulate memory and consequently how it is represented textually—through words. However, it is not just a reformulation of memory and temporality that is achieved through such an act, but also a relocation of the subject. As a dislocated voice whose identity is as tied to place as any other element, the questioning of the necessary descriptions of the sea (including the Caribbean) to reorient oneself is in a sense the question, Who am I ? For Jesus and Lispector such an act involved a reimagining of their relationship to Brazil. Interestingly, the narrative voice here incorporates some of Campos's biographical background by reimagining a relationship with the Caribbean, and particularly Cuba, as a way of redefining her identity.

Separate Yet Connected:
Individual Perspectives and Multiple Narrative Voices

Such freedom of representation and temporal manipulations only serve to further destabilize the narrator's perceptions and belief systems. As a result, another accompanying cause and simultaneous consequence of the narrator's uncertainty is the plurality of voices used to express her identity. Three voices in particular interact with each other yet can also be seen as important separate entities: the narrator, the man in The Labyrinth, and woman in "El Mirador" [Widow's Walk]. The first of the nonauthorial voices, corresponding to the narrative voice that could be called the novel's protagonist, is present from the very beginning: "I am a figure who is gazing at the ocean at four o'clock in the afternoon. But I am also the one who imagines this character that I am. And I am the words that I imagine and that, once imagined, compel me to be watching the sea from a balcony in Acapulco" (*Sabina* 3–4). Beginning the text in the first person leads to certain conclusions about the scope of the characters' narrative view. The reader immediately expects that this voice will not be aware of everything that is going on within the text because of the naturally limited view of any individual. This is combined with the creation of an intimacy with the reader that is absent when the narrative voice is third person and omniscient. These, however, are the expectations that a specific narrative point of view once carried. In Campos's novel, as the previous quote suggests, the situation is considerably different. While each voice indeed possesses a limited awareness of its surroundings, this consciousness of the other is increased because of the interconnectedness of the voices: the "I" is at the same time another "I," which it will refer to as "you," and yet a third voice referred to as "he." Bruce-Novoa sums up the role and dual search of the female narrator:

The female narrator is lodged in the Mirador ["widow's walk"], a word meaning both a lookout point and a looking glass mirror. The first corresponds to the hotel, the balcony, and the woman's contemplation of the seascape. The second relates to Campos' idea of the artist finding self-images in art and the world. The woman's orientation, thus, is dual, both outward and inward simultaneously. As a synthesis of meanings, the Mirador is a vantage point from which the woman explores her own image in the world, while seeing herself viewing herself in nature as a reflection of herself—and we find ourselves very close to Elizondo's concept of writing. (54)[3]

Thus, the female narrator's continuous movement from marginalized to more central positions in the text is accompanied by a process of reflection that is both inward and outward toward her surroundings. One important manifestation of the female narrator's inward orientation is her desire for the power of expression. After imagining a possible beginning to her story she confesses a doubt that has constantly plagued her: "The truth is I have never known where to start. There are so many words and so little to say. And if one tries to tell about something, it is because one assumes that things happen which are not self-explanatory, things which seek after words to stay afloat just as someone on the point of drowning looks for a piece of wood to hold onto for support" (*Sabina* 3). Although by her own admission the female narrator has never had a considerable story to tell, whenever there has been the desire to communicate an important occurrence in her life, she has never had confidence in her ability to sufficiently express the experience with words. This problem resurfaces again during her vacation when she finds herself trying to relive a special moment of revelation through the lens of a camera and not through words, which she has never been able to use effectively. The female narrator's desire to capture photographically this significant moment is revealed in the text through various voices, at times conversing with each other. One such conversation begins with the woman's reflections on the events leading to her moment of insight and ends with the man in "The Labyrinth," who engages in a conversation with her, questioning her attempts to distort time in order to gain wisdom and insight.

This moment is especially important to the protagonist watching the sea because her life in general seems to be so insignificant: "I too am playing a role but a much more modest one, almost minimal, I would say virtually nonexistent; I am playing a role that no one would care to steal from me . . . I would have had to write a novel but novels, it is said, are written from things that happen, and nothing has ever happened to me"

(*Sabina* 4). The inability to write a novel because she has no story to tell leaves the female voice on the balcony with no written means of self-expression. Although she speaks here, her words and actions are indecisive, in part because the part of her life that she claims as solely her own is in her opinion relatively unimportant. "Unimportant" however is a subjective term, as evidenced by the male narrator's declaration later on in the text that female characters in his novel could be relegated to minor roles because of their unimportance. Its subjectivity can also be understood in light of Bernd's (and Didier's) explanation of the beginning factors that lead to *écriture feminine:* namely "successive losses and displacements created by the insertion of the woman into a universe which has not invited her to participate in its organization" (26).

One way in which society denies a woman's participation is by convincing her that she has nothing of value to contribute. In this light, the narrator's search for words to "keep afloat," to give her story importance is another facet of her writing that can be classified as a means of empowering the feminine.

An important point illustrated by the reflections of the woman in "El Mirador" [Widow's Walk] in the two previous quotes is her awareness that her present identity is a construct. Whereas these quotes reveal her knowledge of her status as a character who is playing a part, the woman recognizes from early on in the text that she is not the only fictionalized being:

> I realize that we are here for an experiment, as if the arrival of each one of us has been planned in order to give testimony about something or in order to participate in something or to avoid something . . . only when I have some ominous inkling for the motives for his stay in "The Labyrinth" can I be clear to myself. . . . [H]e is moving us about to suit his whims and that the danger lying in wait for us is that of acting like marionettes managed by a will belonging to someone who lacks all scruple. (*Sabina* 12)

The other narrative voices have also had their power controlled by a force not their own. All share a common origin: that of a construct created for a specific purpose. Although the woman remains vague about what end she believes they will serve, she clearly realizes that their common fate, at this point in time, can and will be decided by the man in "The Labyrinth." One important effect of this realization is to emphasize the weakness the woman feels. She slowly becomes aware that her greatest danger is to give in to the feeling of helplessness and let herself be a puppet, manipulated by the man in "The Labyrinth." This decision is one facet of the outward process Bruce-Novoa alluded to earlier. By assessing her external situation, as well as that of those around her, the female protagonist is able to better recognize the dangers that threaten her and from there, attempt a strategy of attack. As Bilbija states, the woman, despite the lack of control she feels, seeks ways to reverse these emotions and create her own space:

> [The fear that she expresses is the fear of any human being of being captured in the reflection of his existence, it is the anguish, terror, and above all, the humiliation comparable to what the wizard feels in "The Circular Ruins" upon realizing his own illusory existence. How, then, to hide oneself from the gaze of the writer of The Labyrinth, how to appropriate one's own destiny, how to prove that the silence between words means as much as the words themselves, how in the end, to obtain "a room of one's own" without words. A private entrance, but, at any rate, a personal space from which dialogue would arise?]

> El miedo que ella expresa es el miedo de cualquier ser humano de ser captado en el reflejo de su existencia, es la angustia, terror y más que todo, la humillación comparable a lo que siente el mago de "Las ruinas circulares" al darse cuenta de su propia existencia ilusoria. ¿Cómo, entonces, esconderse de la mirada del escritor de El laberinto, cómo apropiarse de su propio destino, cómo probar que el silencio entre las palabras significa tanto como las palabras mismas, cómo en fin, conseguir un "cuarto propio" sin las palabras. Privado en la entrada, pero, de todos modos, un espacio personal desde el que surgiría el diálogo? (139)

The observation of this narrative voice is yet another example of the intertextuality prevalent throughout the text by referring to Cortázar's "Las ruinas circulares" and in the author's exhortation at the end of Woolf's *A Room of One's Own*, "So that when I ask you to earn money and have a room of your own, I am asking you to live in the presence of reality, an invigorating life, it would appear, whether one can impart it or not" (114).

Explorations of the Self: Inward and Outward Dialogues

Now aware that she must fight for control of her self-definition, the principal female narrator attempts to find her own space in which to dialogue, through reflection: a reflection that manifests itself in two ways: by looking outward at the sea, and by searching within to question her understanding of herself and reality.

The first method, as I previously mentioned, is through a contemplation of the sea, hoping to capture in a photograph the revelation that she found in one fleeting instant. The importance of water, in fact, is evident in a quote from Chateaubriand that Campos places at the beginning of the text before chapter 1: "Je reposerai donc au bord de la mer que j'ai tant aimée" (*Sabina* ix). [I will rest now on the shores of the sea I have loved so much.] From the beginning Campos establishes the possibility of a connection with the sea as well as emphasizes its role as a resting place where one can stop and gather oneself.

For Francescato, the sea is just one of the "traditional oppositions" Campos uses in her text. Throughout *Sabina* Campos juxtaposes images of death, the sea, and water in general with life, the land and the promontory, as in her reference to Ingmar Bergman's film *The Seventh Seal*. However, as a nonfictional text written by a displaced Caribbean author, the sea, as I have shown, takes on a more significant role as a possible reference of a once stable site of identification.

Part of Campos's overall textual approach is to combine and contort new structures with traditional ones in order to create something completely different. Francescato stresses that these "traditional oppositions" do not mean that what is being represented in every textual reference to a journey is the archetypical hero and his search, because this text is not a traditional text. One can look to the characters' state of self-awareness for further evidence that the text does not fit traditional standards:

> [In *She Has Reddish Hair and Her Name is Sabina* there are no traditional characters because all the characters that appear are 'conscious' of their imaginary existence, since all are products of the mind of the narrative voice.]

> En *Tiene los cabellos rojizos y se llama Sabina* no hay personajes tradicionales porque todos los personajes que aparecen están 'conscientes' de su existencia imaginaria, ya que todos son productos de la mente de la voz narradora. (Bilbija 137)

As constructs of a narrative voice seeking a sense of individuality, the novel's characters use reflection and other strategies to convert an objectified, imaginary existence into a subjective one.

The protagonist's development of an individual, empowered identity as subject can be understood, in part, in accordance with Lacan's theories of the development of the subject. In such a model the protagonist watching the sea—or the subconscious—is engaging in the first stage of the three-fold process, the imaginary:

> [The imaginary takes places in the phase of the mirror, where fantasy and imagination play an essential role, since through these the subject attempts to integrate his alienated image. One seeks an identification or dual relation with objects, with other bodies and principally, with the mother.]

> Lo imaginario tiene lugar en el estadio del espejo, donde la fantasía y la imaginación desempeñan un papel esencial, ya que mediante éstas el sujeto intenta integrar su imagen alienada. Se busca una identificación o relación dual con objetos, con otros cuerpos y principalmente, con la madre. (532)

I would like to stress Agüera's reminder that Lacan's theories do not discuss the subject's role in identity per se: "sino en términos de su función o lugar que ocupa dentro del sistema simbólico-lingüístico" (536) [but in terms of its function or the place it occupies within the symbolic-linguistic system.] This is important to my thesis about the reformulation of identity because it addresses a determining element of identity that we have seen to a certain degree in Jesus and Lispector: namely, the link between self-definition and the symbolic linguistic register used to represent it. When the symbolic linguistic register is questioned, as it has been in Lispector's text and here, the speaker is also questioning the stability of the self-definition that results from this framework.

In *Sabina*, the access to the subconscious and the verification of the protagonist's existence in the imaginary state is exemplified in the beginning by the image of the sea as something that can return the protagonist's gaze, as her mirror: "I have only said that she is gazing at the sea and that as she gazes at it she is gazing at herself. The ocean is her mirror" (*Sabina* 95).

One reference in particular is significant because it highlights four important functions that the sea fulfills in the text. This reference states, "The sea is the dream of the unknown, the fantasy of the voyage, the hope of other destinies, as well as the fear of pirates and storms" (110). In this quote there are four applications that stand out: (1) "the dream of the unknown" on one hand referring to the sea as a means of personal exploration, (2) "the hope of other destinies," (3) "other destinies" as a reference to cultural transport, and (4) "the fear of pirates and storms" referring to the fear of anything that would take away control. Of these four I will focus on the first function.

First, the sea as the dream of the unknown is on one level a reference to the hidden parts of the protagonist's subconscious to which, until now, she has had limited access. The sea symbolizes the promise that Bilbija spoke of: to delve into the subconscious, not with words, but in silent contemplation and uncover hidden truths that in the end are what make up a person's identity. Nonetheless, this promise is not easily achieved. Several times the narrator expresses her fear of the water and of the process of self-realization that its contemplation signifies: "This thing that is happening to me is something I have dreamed before but the dream is always interrupted and I have never known the ending. In that dream I was gazing at myself in the mirror but the mirror was not looking at me. . . . I am afraid that the ocean is not the ocean" (*Sabina* 122).

The narrator's fear expressed here stems from an uncertainty of her future because of an inability to find answers where they were promised her: in the mirror/sea. When she states that she fears the sea is not as it appears there is a questioning of whether it can deliver the insight into her inner self as she believed or leave her uncertain about her future.

On yet another occasion this fear of the sea is expressed in a conversation between the narrative voice representing Campos and the woman in "El Mirador" [Widow's Walk]: "Come with me. Come closer. Don't be afraid. It's not dangerous. . . . Just let yourself float, pretend you're a little corpse, relax, rest, don't be afraid of the ocean. Remember that it's a stage-set sea, an ocean invented by someone on a lined notebook. . . . You will not really drown, except in a sea of words" (119–120). This identity crisis represented through the interaction of the subject with the gaze can be contrasted with the use of the mirror to comment on identity in both Jesus and Lispector. Despite moments of self-affirmation in Lispector, all three feminine subjects have more often than not faced nonaffirming moments in front of the mirror that have forced them to recognize the different factors influencing their identities.

There are two points expressed here that can be specifically contrasted with the dynamics of identity reformulation in Lispector's *A hora da estrela* and Jesus's *Quarto de despejo*. The first is the mirror as an object that reveals doubt. In Lispector's text this is represented at the moment when Macabéa, after being informed by her boss that she is being fired, looks at herself in the mirror but only sees a tarnished, distorted gaze looking back. In *A hora da estrela* the narrator's conclusion is that Macabéa is lacking in what she needed to be a whole person. Only at the time of her death, after she expresses her hope for the future, is she able to find meaning in the silence that accompanies her. In *Quarto de despejo* Jesus is faced with the question of to what extent her life has been strongly determined by the cycle of poverty and oppression that the gaze in the mirror provides. In *Sabina* the narrator reassures the protagonist that the life she perceives is a construct. Therefore, her search for answers by immersing herself in the sea of words can and must continue.

In both Lispector's and Campos's texts the word in its simplest form is problematized as an adequate conveyor of meaning. For Rodrigo the struggle is to find the right words to represent the reality of an Other than he can never truly know. For Sabina and the other narrative voices there are also doubts as to the ability of words to represent a reality when their limitations make them unable to represent the present in its complexity (for example, the movement of time): "To write that novel . . . there would have to come many words capable of being precisely the opposite of that ambiguity and capable of taking its place" (*Sabina* 30).

Both narrators doubt the ability to express the moments of self-revelation through words but acknowledge the possibility of expressing this moment of awareness through death. While in *Sabina* the revelation through death is one of several suggestions, in *A hora da estrela* it is a reality—and not a construct. Despite the narrator's efforts to prove his control over the text, his protagonist, and death, both he and Macabéa do fall victim to it. However, unlike the promise never completely fulfilled in *Sabina*, in the end Macabéa is able to experience a brief moment of self-revelation through death and for one instant to affirm her existence.

In *Sabina* however, the protagonist's second fear is of drowning, of losing control. The external narrator reassures her that this sea is not real, but only fiction. Like everything else in *Sabina*, there is just an illusion of reality, but reality itself is never achieved—not for the protagonist, the other voices, or up to this point, for their respective projects.

The reality the protagonist wants to represent is one where, as the earlier quotes attest, she is in control. She realizes the difficulty of doing so when her identity is so intimately tied to the other voices around her—so much so that they too form mirrors into which she can see an image of herself: "Some time ago, in a dream, I am motionless on a balcony as now on this terrace. . . . A woman is looking at me, and I at her. For both of us it is as though we were looking into a mirror" (*Sabina* 95). Just as Lacan's model of the imaginary states, the protagonist uses fantasy and imagination—her dreams—to analyze and attempt to reformulate her own identity. However, unlike the dreams of the sea I have spoken of, the protagonist's image is not reflected in the water but rather in the gaze of another, the woman at an American maple desk who is attempting to write the protagonist's story. In this dream that mirrors reality the protagonist and the writer seem to be copies or mirror images of one another. This serves as an example of what Lacan was describing when he spoke of the protagonist's search for any dual relationship with an Other in order to discover herself.

In the case of the female protagonist in "El Mirador" [Widow's Walk] the subject development leads not to an acceptance of the primacy of the Law of the Father (as Lacan's theory of subject formation posits) but rather to a self-awareness achieved by action and contemplation:

> If anything distinguishes this story from others like it, it is merely that she, the woman, is imagining the possibility of writing a story about a woman who is gazing at the ocean without making the decision to leave it. She has a wild notion of being able to be her own person and in that way fulfilling a destiny which, she perceives darkly, has something to do with the sea. At the same time, two narrators, a woman and a man, persist in making her their own character, in one case a figure of central importance and in the other only a marginal one. . . . Let us say, metaphorically, that both are attempting to get control over her mind. (96–97)

The narrative voice here, that of the woman at her desk, wants to write a novel where the woman on the balcony is the protagonist—as she is in the text in the reader's hands. She does note, however, that she is not the only one who has these intentions. The protagonist herself, although fictional, also wants to write her own novel and in so doing, extricate herself from the web the other two narrators, the one speaking at this moment and the man in "The Labyrinth," have created for her. The protagonist attempts to follow the strategy feminist critics like Cixous have proposed: to write "from and toward women" in order to free themselves from the silence that the symbolic relegates them to (312).

The female protagonist of "El Mirador" [Widow's Walk] finds herself not only caught between the intentions of the two narrators but also unsure of how to best redefine herself. She ultimately becomes aware of a certain interdependency with the other narrative voices that further complicates the process:

> I, the one who is/am seated on the pier—I have never wanted to write books. She has been the one who has forced me into it. She, the one who speaks in second person, though sometimes I myself am the one who assumes the second person singular, that ambiguity of my character without which the novel that I might be able to write, that perhaps I am writing, could never have been, would not have had to be, nor would it ever have been necessary to have been written. (Sabina 32)

It is the female narrator's desire for independence that causes her to question the advantages of authorship of a formalized text of the self. As Bilbija states:

[The body of *She Has Reddish Hair and Her Name is Sabina* consists of an oceanic paragraph in which the subject radically changes her position, thus reflecting the complexity of the feminine identity that wishes to escape the position of the Other, the mythification, that wants to take control of her destiny.]

El cuerpo de *Tiene los cabellos rojizos y se llama Sabina* consta de un oceánico párrafo en el que el sujeto cambia su posición radicalmente, reflejando así la complejidad de la identidad femenina que quiere escapar la posición del Otro, la mitificación, que quiere apoderarse de su destino. (143)

However, it is important to note that while the female narrative voice's quote points to her recognition of the struggle between her independence and a submission to the control of the other narrative voices, there is also an implied acknowledgement of the significance of the interaction of the voices to the articulation of her selfhood. In this sense the protagonist subtly acknowledges the narrative hybridity as ironically part of the development of the individual.[4]

The Transition from Subject to Object: The Use of the Gaze

One way of taking hold of one's destiny is through the development not only of an autonomous voice, but also of an informed subjective positioning as opposed to the object of another's gaze. Such is the case with the protagonist. While the woman watching the sea is aware that she is being watched by others attempting to manipulate her, she also is watching them—making them the object of her gaze:

[Sabina's gaze sees "him," the promontory and the analyst-reader. One can see that in Julieta Campos's hands Lacan's framework is inverted. He who has always appeared as the Other, the symbolic, he who always invents and writes plots of Oedipal, thematic, or testimonial novels, is left displaced to a position and vision of realistic imbecility.]

La mirada de Sabina ve a <él>, el promontorio y al analista-lector. Se puede ver que en manos de Julieta Campos queda invertido el esquema de Lacan. El que siempre ha aparecido como el Otro, lo simbólico, el que siempre inventa y escribe tramas de novelas edípicas, temáticas o testimoniales, queda desplazado a una posición y visión de imbecilidad realista. (Agüera 536)

The expectations of subjectivity and vulnerability that the first person narration implied is subverted. She who has been fighting the other two narrative voices for greater control of her identity is revealed to be the one with the objectivity, and therefore, with greater power:

> Sabina, attached to the imaginary and who, supposedly, suffers the dissolution of the subjectivism of a private and phantasmal knowledge, is placed in a privileged position: not only does she see the promontory-significant, but she also sees "him" and the reader-analyst . . . . Sabina makes the reader the Other.

> Sabina, apegada a lo imaginario y que, supuestamente, sufre la disolución del subjetivismo de un conocimiento privado y fantasmal, se coloca en una posición privilegiada: no sólo ve el promontorio-significante, sino que también ve a <él> y al lector-analista. . . . Sabina hace del lector el Otro. (Agüera 536)

The protagonist on the balcony confirms this fact when she explains the limited vision of the writer in The Labyrinth:

> From up there he does not see the promontory. Of course his angle of vision does take me in, but I think it only reaches this far and that he cannot see what is happening further down. . . . The view from the balcony where I am is something else. Things tend to assume their proper place on the stage, to grow calmer, to lose their lack of proportion. (*Sabina* 23)

The last line establishes the primacy and privilege of the woman's gaze: it is her gaze, and not that of the man in "The Labyrinth" that organizes things, puts them in their rightful place and causes them to lose their sense of excess. Her gaze allows her to move from a position of marginality to one of dominance. The writer in "The Labyrinth," on the other hand, clings to his reality—insisting that his vantage point is privileged.

Naming as Self-Representation

Another significant step in the protagonist's acquisition of greater agency in determining her identity deals with an area of representation that at times is overlooked: a name. Up until this point I have referred to the protagonist as the woman watching the sea: using a description of her actions as my primary point of reference, as is the case with the narrators who do not have a formal point of reference other than their positions.

This is because of the inability to separate the multiple voices from each other: "The character has no name because she has no identity or, if you wish, because many latent or possible identities converge or are exchanged in it, in her" (*Sabina* 57).

This anonymity as a result of the objectification and marginalization of the Other is similar to the process in *A hora da estrela* and *Quarto de despejo*. Just as in *Sabina*, the narrator refers to Macabéa with third person singular pronouns like "ela," "a nordestina," or "moça" for approximately one-fifth of the text. While Sabina does not exist as a unified entity, Macabéa is, for the narrator, nonexistent because she is a marginalized one. In the opinion of Rodrigo she is barely alive: "But the person whom I am about to describe scarcely has a body to sell; . . . nobody needs her" (Lispector, *A hora da estrela* 14). Similarly, Jesus comments on various occasions that as a favelada she has no name and no recognizable place of power in Brazilian society.

Whereas Sabina's anonymity is due to the multiple voices within her identity, the narrator chooses to keep Macabéa anonymous because of her embodiment of the multiple voices of poor northeastern girls who disapper once they migrate to the South. Jesus on the other hand combats her anonymity through her authorship of the diary and the affirmation of her vocation as a poetess. This does not mean however that one can easily classify Sabina's anonymity as an ontological statement while Macabéa's and Jesus's are purely social. For Macabéa in particular, the narrator's decision to keep her marginalized for so long is also part of Lispector's study of individual representation.

The acquisition of a name therefore is the acquisition of power by establishing an identity separate from the other voices. This confirms Agüera's point that the protagonist's privilege is in making the man in the room called "The Labyrinth" the Other. Similarly, Macabéa's naming becomes part of the reversal of subject-object relation that she has with Rodrigo, resulting in his "transfiguration into someone else and in my ultimate materialization into an object" (Lispector, *Hour of the Star* 20), while Jesus's calling as a poet inscribes her within Brazilian society as an object with greater agency.

In *Sabina* the first time the protagonist's name is given is in the midst of a reexamination by the other narrators of her possibilities of telling her own story through literary texts or film. In the midst of these inquiries one of the narrators reveals the name as a French translation of the title, "Elle a les cheveux roux et s'appelle Sabine" (*Sabina* 82). In the spirit of the self-reflexivity of the text this quote is referred to twice at the end. In this, the first of the two last references, the narrative voice addresses the reader to assure him or her of the only certainty in the novel: the aspect of the protagonist's identity that refers to her proper name, position, and physical description. As I stated earlier, the choice of this name is important because of its reference to one of Campos's influences, Anaïs Nin:

> Nonetheless, I, who know this character better than anyone because I invented her, independently of the facts and even of her will, I suggest that the only piece of information the reader can rely on . . . appears on page 82, where the reader must have discovered it already if he or she is provided with a certain perspicacity. . . . [S]he has reddish hair and her name is Sabina. That is absolutely the only certainty, it must be; and all the rest is a mirage or a dream. (*Sabina* 133)

While Sabina's name is an intertextual reference to Anaïs Nin's protagonist, so too is Macabéa a reference to the Maccabees who fought to keep their religion in the face of persecution. However, of even greater importance is the relationship of both narrators, Campos and Rodrigo, to their protagonists. On one hand, both feel they know their creations better than anyone. While Rodrigo admits that Macabéa has become so much a part of him that "I seem to know the most intimate details about this girl from the Northeast. . . . [S]he has clung to my skin" (*The Hour of the Star* 21), the narrative voice above also refers to a confluence of identity: between the "yo" that invented Sabina—referring to Campos—and Sabina herself, identifiable only by her name and physical feature. One important difference however is that while both narrators see themselves as the creators of their protagonists in *A hora da estrela* Lispector emphasizes the difficulty of knowing the self and the other by contrasting a confident narrator, who initially feels that every detail he determines about his creation is a certainty, with a protagonist who is subtly able to subvert this confidence. By doing so she forces him to realize the limitations and illegitimacy of his power and knowledge. On the other hand Campos is constantly aware of the artifice of language and reality, and therefore the uncertainty of establishing or understanding identity. The only certainty she admits to is Sabina's name. The uncertaintly about the other facts surrounding her becomes an obstacle of sorts to be navigated as she recreates herself, but also serves as a benefit by providing her with a possible neutral space where her agency is as valued as the other narrative voices attempting to control her.

The Navigation of Discursive Space: Silence as Voice

Despite the promise of the principal narrative voice's strategies of empowerment, there is still a recognition that the literary and linguistic baggage that words and memories carry make it difficult to establish any autonomy from previously established realities. For this reason the nar-rator/writer is cautioned to try to avoid that trap, and is advised that the one possible solution, the one answer that could lead to words capable of portraying her reality, is silence:

> The material of this book cannot be composed out of memo-ries. Build it up literally from nothing. Embody that definitive absence in words. . . . Avoid the snare of memory. Let yourself be devoured by silence. . . . [Y]ou are forgetfulness, you are the promise of a mystery that will culminate in an image, a word-only if you allow yourself to work tenaciously through silence. (*Sabina* 30)

As with the contrast of presence and absence, the plays on silence is another theme prevalent throughout Campos's text. Through the si-lences—or, in other words, spaces between the conflicting memories, words, and discourses—there is the possibility of writing the novel that Campos/Sabina/the female narrator wants to write, to represent the revelation and reality they have been seeking to explain.

Silence as a means of empowerment is another theme shared with the vision expressed in *A hora da estrela*. Macabéa on the other hand is from the beginning a silenced individual (by the society and the narra-tor) and is given very limited opportunities to speak. Her goal therefore is to use any tool to empower herself. What Lispector succeeds in doing is to show how silence can be one of these effective tools, a realization that Sabina experiences later in the text. Just as Macabéa is accompanied by silence at the moment when she achieves the freedom and peace she longed for, Campos's greatest hope is to let the imprecision of reality (of time and of memory) that words cannot capture be reflected through silence. In both texts the embracing of silence is a movement below the word to a site where what is present is reality and insight to the self that words and dominant discourses distort.

Contesting Dominant Discourse:
The Challenge of the Masculine Discourse

Nonetheless, despite the awareness of the limitations of the word, the importance of using writing in any form to record one's personal reality is emphasized as a necessary step in the reconstruction of identity. Throughout *Sabina* we have seen how Campos explores this process through textual experimentation consisting of the manipulation of voice, space, and time. This is achieved first through the development of multiple narrative voices (including the principal female narrative voice) that continually intersect with one another on a psychological level and second, through the contrast in particular of the male and female narrative voices found in the text.

The narrative voice that represents the challenge of a dominant discourse to Sabina's autonomy is the male narrator situated in "The Labyrinth." His symbolic position in the exchange of discourses is represented physically by his position in the hotel: this male narrative voice is a writer locked in a private room with limited access, only reached after passing through a labyrinthine hallway. Just as we established that Sabina represented the existence of the imaginary in Lacanian terms, so Bilbija concludes that The Labyrinth represents the symbolic:

> En el espacio del hotel, igual que en el espacio del consciente, es posible distinguir dos modos expresivos—correspondientes a dos hemisferios cerebrales, o dos terrazas: [el primero es] el modo verbal, racional, lógico, activo, claro, analítico que se identifica con lo masculino y funciona linealmente, elaborando cualquier información en secuencias ordenadas, generalmente cronológicas. (140)

> In the hotel space, just as in the space of the conscious, it is possible to distinguish between two expressive modes—corresponding to two cerebral hemispheres, or two terraces: [the first is] the verbal, rational, logical, active, clear, analytic mode that identifies with the masculine and functions lineally, elaborating on any information in ordered sequences, generally chronological.

This is an accurate description of the man in "The Labyrinth's" role in the text: he is the one who attempts to maintain order, and more importantly, maintain control over the other narrative voices. This is exemplified in the novel that he would like to write using Sabina as a protagonist: "Anything else that might be said concerning, relative to, or about that woman depends only on the will of a narrator situated on another terrace, that of the room called "The Labyrinth," who may or may not turn her into a marginal character of a story on the model of *In Cold Blood*" (63). His desire is to write a novel that exploits the protagonist not as a central figure, but as just another character in a novel whose focus would be the elements of sex and violence that constitute any bestseller. Later in the text the writer himself defines his literary purpose: "In my novel, which I've been writing for two months now in this room called "The Labyrinth," and in which I try to be an objective narrator without concessions, I need a fragile femenine character who might be the victim of a sordid plot and who at worst might opt for suicide" (36). In his text the writer in "The Labyrinth" intends to recreate the position of marginality of the female narrative voice in order to create a work wherein his position and power are not jeopardized. Ironically, although he wants to incorporate a weak woman into his text to serve as the object of his structural and linguistic manipulations, the woman in "El Mirador" in fact occupies a position of power of sorts as the subject whose existence is necessary for him to tell the story he wants to: "That woman, I can't make out her age, who arrived a week ago and who at this moment is staring toward the promontory . . . from the terrace of a room whose name I don't know but which might well be called "The Balcony" because of its privileged location, would serve me as a point of reference" (*Sabina* 36).

The challenges of the narrative voice in "The Labyrinth" to the feminine discourse as agent can be contrasted with the narrator Rodrigo S. M. In *A hora da estrela* he engages in a discourse that specifically underscores the difficulties in the comprehension of the other as part of a metaphysical exploration of being, while on another level exposing the interaction between masculine and feminine discourses in their struggle for power.

The Challenge of Multivocality: Contestations of the Feminine Voices

In the continuing representations of multivocality, Campos employs a collaboration and navigation of masculine voices and feminine ones that together oppose to varying degrees the masculine voice's attempts to appropriate Sabina's story and are incorporated into the principal narrative voice's process of autonomy. Their challenges are not only a response to the threats to the protagonists' autonomy but also an effort to articulate through words a sense of reality where the female narrative voice is the subject and not object. While neither voice is excluded, the feminine voices are able to move into a more central position in Campos's text and leave the marginal sites that they were relegated to in masculine discourses. One such feminine voice is that of the woman at the maple American desk. While Bilbija described "The Labyrinth" as linear and rational, the female narrator at the maple American desk represents the opposite: another representation of the imaginary. As she observes:

> [On the other hand, the intuitive, passive, dark, mysterious, artistic mode that identifies with the feminine and that is marked by the instability of the discourse, rejecting the stability of the word and its symbolic capacity.]

> Por otro lado, el modo intuitivo, pasivo, oscuro, misterioso,
> artístico, que se identifica con lo femenino y que está marcado
> por la inestabilidad del discurso, rechazando la firmeza de la
> palabra y su capacidad simbólica. (Bilbija 140)

In the search for a sense of time that fits the demands that this reality imposes, a second female narrator is described as the one who may have the answers. As opposed to "The Labyrinth's" novel, hers would highlight Sabina, presenting her as a protagonist who would be able to exercise her own agency.

Assessments of Feminine Writing: Destabilization as Empowerment

By understanding the ways in which Sabina and the other feminine voices exert their agency one can also gain insight into the text as a commentary on the concept of feminine writing. One important theory that aids in our evaluation of such a process is Minh-ha's recognition of the significant uses of plurality. As she states:

> The to-and-fro movement between the written woman and
> the writing woman is an endless one. . . . She is "woman
> enough" to slip out of herself and go, then to return almost
> without self and without denying the going. For writing, like
> a game that defies its own rules, is an ongoing practice that
> may be said to be concerned, not with inserting a "me" into
> language, but with creating an opening where the "me" dis-
> appears while "I" endlessly come and go, as the nature of
> language requires. (30, 35)

For Campos's protagonist, Sabina, the interaction with the other narrative voices is what constitutes her identity as well as serving as an obstacle she must overcome in order to reformulate her self-definition in a free, uncompromised space. What is especially relevant about Minh-ha's theory is the positing of silence as an important strategy for self-expression that strengthens the individual: "Writing, in a way, is listening to the others' language and reading with others' eyes. The more ears I am able to hear with, the farther I see the plurality of meaning and the less I lend myself to the illusion of a single message. I say I write when I leave speech, when I lose my grip on it and let it make its way on its own" (30, 35). Minh-ha's recommendation to "leave speech . . . and let it make its way on its own" is represented, as I discussed earlier, in Sabina by

Campos's exhortations to the protagonist to let silence surround her, assuring her that she is "la promesa de un misterio que culminará en una imagen, . . . sólo si te dejas trabajar tenazmente por el silencio" (Sabina, 44). [the promise of a mystery that will culminate in an image, only if you let yourself be shaped by silence.] Only then can the text that Campos and Sabina want to write be written, the text that reveals and expresses the self-defining moments Sabina wants to capture on film.

According to Cixous female identity can also be articulated through a process she defines as "writing the body." This includes breaking rules, syntax, classes, codes, rhetorics, and reserve in order to establish a discourse that goes beyond the limitations of male discourse. Therefore, according to this theoretic criterion one manifestation of the feminine is in the constant interruption of the female narrative voices (particularly those of Sabina and Campos) by the male narrative voice (in "The Labyrinth"), resulting in a constant destabilization of any one narrator.

This destabilization is also evident in the exchanges between the principal masculine voice and the various female narrative voices. Throughout the text the male narrator expresses a belief in the female, and particularly the female narrative voice's text as an uncentered and irrational example of feminine writing: "The book is diffuse, blurry, lit by twilight, and that alone reveals its feminine origin to us. Dream, care, ecstasy, ephemeral, fleetingness, mystery, hallucination—key words, words which betray that vagueness, that lack of precision which characterizes women when they write" (43). Later in the text the male voice continues his criticism by pointing out to the female voice her "absurd enthusiasm for allowing yourself to slip toward irrationality, of believing in omens, in auguries, in discreet signals from the other world" (*Sabina* 61) while the other narrative voices emphasize the principal voice's desire for independence, to be her own person (87). We then see the principal voice asserting her desires: "I am imagining myself, my very self, as the sea. I am here, in the middle of the afternoon" (64). The use of the first person to express how she imagines herself, communing with the sea, is an important marker of her subjectivity.

The "feminine text" then becomes a continuum, creating spaces and silences in which to make possible the desires that the feminine narrative voices could not realize outside of this fictive environment: "Remember that Paradise is always on the other side of the ocean. But in this novel there is no myth, merely an imaginary gaze that pretends to be a real gaze, although since it is only imaginary it might allude, as it actually does, to all the gazes ever gazed at the ocean" (*Sabina* 131). The "paradise" that the text attempts to create, especially in the case of an example of "feminine writing," is always just beyond reach, engaging the subject in a constant search for fulfillment and empowerment that includes the manipulation of words and of reality by converting it into the imaginary, and by doing so, into what seems impossible. The quote highlights the strategy of not only the text but also, to a certain extent, of the author: by removing themselves from the limiting structure of reality they can more freely explore multiple perspectives. For this reason Sabina's story appears to end but really doesn't: "Although this is not the end but the beginning" (*Sabina* 135). As Campos stated in her interview:

> Sabina's imaginary nature allows me to bring about a coincidence (in her) of realities and fantasies that real life would not have synthesized. In the fictitious realm, what has actually happened does not occur but rather what could have happened, occurs: situations and events finally find their most profound logic by coalescing through the organization of words in a privileged and imaginary space. (85)

This is emphasized in the novel's end, when, despite admitting that the process has not reached a conclusion, the constant attempt at subversion is what is important. In the end, as Bilbija notes, it is not the male narrator, nor the female narrator who ultimately is responsible for her self-definition but Sabina herself: "La Sabina que decide revivir y repensar las historias y reconsiderar sus opciones encuentra su liberación en la creación de un lenguaje nuevo que se presenta como pictórico" (146). [The Sabina that decides to relive and rethink the stories and reconsider her options finds her liberation in the creation of a new language that is presented as pictoric.]

The redefined identity of Sabina is best represented by a text that does not exclude male texts but in reaching for its ideal form is open to new beginnings made up of a multiplicity of voices. As Bilbija states, this opens the door to new opportunities to dialogue with the author and the reader, "señalando así la posibilidad de un verdadero principio nuevo, un principio listo para el diálogo" (146). [thus signaling the possibility of a truly new beginning, a beginning ready for dialogue.]

Up to this point the female voices I have studied have followed two strategies of identity reformulation based on their relationship to historical categories and linguistic constructs of reality. As in Jesus's diary, the hybridity exemplified by the female subjects to this point lies in the multiple discourses (both marginalized and dominant) employed to redefine themselves. Jesus's nonfiction has served as a conduit through which to reformulate a critical sense of self based on race, class, and gender while Campos's self-definition has, although not exclusively, been an ontological and metaphysical exploration of being. Though not mutually exclusive, the nature of the complex process of the reconstruction of identity raises the question of where the two processes can intersect. The autobiography of an African American anthropologist, to be discussed in chapter 7, holds an answer to such a question. Like Campos, Zora Neale Hurston shares the belief in the construction of identity through writing as manipulation—a manipulation of many elements that Campos also explores in *Sabina*: the line between factual and fictional identity, subjectivity, time, and memory. The interaction and at times subversion of these factors leads us to rethink the very structure of the process of self-definition as one not necessarily bound by conventional laws but open to multiple possibilities.

Chapter Seven

The Autobiographical Pact and Hurston's Restructuring of Difference

Autobiography and the Representation of Reality

The representation of identity in Campos's *Tiene los cabellos rojizos y se llama Sabina* was marked by multiplicity, instability, and an overall formulation of self-definition that transcends the strictures of reality, time, and place. This chapter returns to a type of historically positioned self-representation also found in Jesus's diary. In Zora Neale Hurston's autobiography *Dust Tracks on a Road* there is a return to an author very much defined by and defining herself according to sociohistorical categories. However, this does not mean that her identity can be represented according to simple categorizations. Like Lispector and Campos, Hurston's identity is also a complex combination of influences, among them the sociohistorical and the discursive framework in which she operates. While the foundation of Hurston's self-definition is found in the aforementioned historical positioning, her reformulation of the self does not accept unquestioned societal standards of identity, but rather questions them and at times subverts them. While her autobiography can be most closely tied to Jesus's autobiographical diary, it is also part of the continuum of texts (Lispector and Campos) that combine a certain representation of reality with a questioning of it that enters the realm of fictionality.

From the beginning Hurston's autobiographical process of identity reformulation attempts to reconstruct a self that questions the historical positioning in which it is grounded and through writing and the manipulation of the autobiographical structure creates an identity that negotiates truth and artifice. The result is a self-definition that negotiates marginalized and central positions on a social, textual, and linguistic level, while demonstrating levels of dislocation brought about by the subject's various levels of movement. Hurston's process of reformulation begins with her natural birth into a historical position of marginality and her use of language (including education) and the written discourse to bring about a symbolic rebirth that interacts with more central historical and discursive positions. A deeper understanding of this complex process is gained not only through an analysis of Hurston's published manuscript but also by its positioning alongside the original. What is revealed is a structural and thematic difference that ultimately holds important implications for Hurston's written presentation of her identity and our reception of its subject.

Although chronologically the earliest of the texts studied, Hurston's autobiography, published during the period of American modernism, displays certain qualities that make it closer to later, more postmodern works. Delia Caparoso Konzett's analysis of the ethnic modernism in the works of Anzia Yezierska, Jean Rhys, and Zora Neale Hurston provides an important lens through which I reveal the hybridity present in Hurston's autobiographical project:

> All three writers share ... in spite of their diversity, a critical ethnic perspective and avant-garde attitude toward standard-ized notions of cultural identity such as nationality, race and majority consensus. . . . The nonsynchronicity of different cultures existing in various historical temporalities becomes intensified in the modern era ... where a much more significant interaction between various cultures imports nonsynchronicity into the heart of modernity. (10)

Konzett emphasizes that what ties writers like Hurston to the modernist project is a rupture with conventional structures of identification and relation to reality. The nonsynchronicity which forms a cornerstone of her argument is brought about by migration and cultural interactions that is a movement of subjects into different social, historical, and political contexts. One result for these subjects, like Hurston, is an application of Johnson's insider/outsider movement as a navigation of varying states of dislocation and belonging. Konzett observes that:

> Their aesthetics of nonsynchronicity ultimately challenges the ideologies of belonging that can still be found in various modernisms ... in which a modernist suspension of tradition often goes hand in hand with a renewed reinvention of traditions, of collective and subjective identities defined along the boundaries of nation, race, class, or gender. This type of re-

newed closure of a modern present in revision of the past is not possible with . . . Hurston . . . since it contradicts [her] profound experience of dislocation. (11–12)

This nonsynchronicity and instability manifests itself in subjects without fixed identities, representative instead of hybrid conceptualizations of the self: "Their transnationalism informed by the aesthetics of nonsynchronicity, prohibits them from becoming affiliated with any distinct form of social identity . . . since they no longer partake of culturally stabilized communities" (Konzett 12).

In the specific context of the reformulation of a multifaceted identity, "Hurston shows how displacement and race in modern mass culture are not necessarily mutilating forces. . . . [H]er transcultural and transnational ventures challenge commonplace notions of race and ethnic absolutism, demonstrating that identity is not a fixed cognitive or cultural fact" (Konzett 9). The result of what Konzett defines as an ethnic modernism in Hurston's specific autobiography is an identity defined by flux. The challenge this raises for Hurston is how to best use the tools writing affords her to represent her displaced selves. Because of the multiplicity that characterizes this work, a helpful framework through which I will answer this question can be found in a feminist critic writing some forty years after the publication of *Dust Tracks on a Road*. Although one must take into consideration the limits of the historical specificity under which Hurston, an African American writer during the Harlem Renaissance (and after), produces her work, Trinh Minh-ha's (postmodern) strategy for the committed woman writer who uses writing to steal language in order to express what is important to her is relevant to our understanding of Hurston's project. As Minh-ha asks, "[W]here does a committed woman writer go? Finding a voice, searching for words and sentences: say some thing, . . . or no thing. . . . Shake syntax, smash the myths, and if you lose, slide on" (20). Minh-ha stresses the use of writing by women to constantly manipulate and change the discourse in order to find a space in which she can be free to express herself. The dynamic she represents in this quote is between the establishment of meaning and the destabilization of meaning, on one level, and a similar movement between construction and deconstruction on a syntactical level. This strategy is applicable to all the women writers I have studied and will be helpful here in revealing the movement or wandering (for example between voice and silence) that characterizes Hurston's autobiography. The resulting text, as a personal yet public declaration, presents a type of feminine writing that emphasizes its negotiation of the public and private, truth and construction.

Hurston's History: Personal Navigations of Cultural Discourses

A brief history of Hurston's life will serve as a foundation for my discussion of the dynamics of her self-representation. Hurston was an African American anthropologist, folklorist, and novelist born on January 15, 1891, in the farming community of Notasulga, Alabama. While her father was an important presence in her life, it was her mother who shaped her earlier years, giving Hurston and her siblings lessons in grammar and mathematics, and introducing her to the world of reading. In the fifth grade in fact, Hurston so impressed two northern women visiting her school that they later sent her a box of books, a gift that would be the spark for her intellectual growth.

After losing her mother at age nine, and the subsequent remarriage of her father, Hurston was sent to school in Jacksonville, Florida. She travelled with a theatrical group for eighteen months and later enrolled at the Morgan Academy in Baltimore in 1917. She graduated in June 1918, and then studied at Howard Preparatory School for a year before entering Howard University in 1919. Hurston graduated from Howard University in 1920 with an associate's degree, all the while doing odd jobs as a manicurist, waitress, and maid in order to repay her debts. In 1921 she published her first short story, "John Redding Goes to Sea," for the campus literary magazine, the *Stylus*.

In 1925 Hurston received a Barnard scholarship, which allowed her to attend the college from 1925 to 1927. It was there that she studied with the anthropologist Franz Boas and graduated as a social scientist. Hurston stayed in New York for a while and soon became a part of the literary circles that flourished there during the Harlem Renaissance. Her residence in Harlem lasted until 1927, at which time she received a research fellowship from the Columbia University Anthropology Department to travel back to the South, to Eatonville, to record as a social scientist the area she grew up in as a child. Hurston's research in the rural South was later compiled in a collection called *Mules and Men*, published in 1935. This collection was especially noteworthy because it was "the first popular book about Afro-American folklore ever written by a black scholar" (Hemenway 5–6).

In 1927 Hurston met Mrs. Rufus Osgood Mason, a wealthy patron of African American arts who enlisted her aid in creating an opera that would represent Black folk life, dances, and tales. From 1927 to September 1932 Mrs. Mason paid Hurston to collect (and only collect) material on black southern life, drawing up a contract that gave her sole control over the material and not allowing her to publish any of it (Hemenway 104–111). In August 1928, Hurston traveled to New Orleans, where she continued collecting material by immersing herself in the lives of the people she observed. In New Orleans she observed hoodoo ceremonies, presenting herself as someone willing to learn the most basic to the most complex rites. In fact, in one ritual she lay naked and still on a snakeskin for sixty-nine hours straight in order to be able to approach the sacred altar of the legendary spirit Marie Leveau.

Hurston's participation in several rituals and her other experiences were part of what distinguished her from other anthropologists and made *Mules and Men* such a different anthropological text (Hemenway 117–121). While many anthropologists studied their subjects from a distance, objectively attempting to define the Other, Hurston believed that in order to write the Other she had to become it as much as possible. Her participation in religious rituals and various related activities was a way of bridging the gap between herself and her subjects. This approach to anthropological study can be compared with the strategies used by the fictive Rodrigo S. M. to define Macabéa, especially given the fact that the social component of his project gives the text a sociological perspective as well as an obvious literary one. While on the surface the tactics of becoming the Other seem very similar, the execution of their plans is quite different. The activities Rodrigo S. M. participated in to reproduce Macabéa's social marginalization were superficial ones that maintained his privilege, while Hurston's participation endeavored to break down the cultural, linguistic, and class barriers. Nonetheless, both efforts demonstrate the difficulty in comprehending the Other, despite the genuineness of the undertaking.

In 1934 Hurston published an autobiographical novel entitled *Jonah's Gourd Vine*. In the following years she would continue her folklore studies, traveling to Jamaica on a Guggenheim fellowship to study the Obeah practices there and contrast them with the hoodoo rituals she had previously observed. From there Hurston went to Haiti and then returned to New York where she wrote yet another novel, her most famous, *Their Eyes Were Watching God*. After receiving a second fellowship she returned to Haiti and collected enough material to publish *Tell My Horse*, based on the voodoo rites she observed (Hemenway 187–189, 225–229). However, because of financial difficulties she was forced to work as a writer from 1938 to 1939, chronicling Black southern culture and oral traditions (particularly in Florida) for the Federal Writers' Project, a unit of the Works Progress Administration designed to help artists, writers, and others suffering the financial effects of the Great Depression. Because of the stigma of this relief work and the racism which she experienced during this time, Hurston would keep her involvement in this project a secret from her family and from her readers. Despite the effect that this writing experience would have creatively on her future work (as well as on that of other well-known writers who worked for the FWP, like Richard

Wright), Hurston did not speak of this time period in the FWP in *Dust Tracks on a Road*. She would in the following years publish several more novels and short stories, including *Moses Man of the Mountain* (1939), *Dust Tracks on a Road* (1942), and *Seraph on the Suwanee* (1948), her last book. *Dust Tracks on a Road* was especially interesting because it was her autobiography. Nonetheless, as critics like Boyd, Hemenway, Krasner, and Raynaud have pointed out, the reader continuously questions the veracity of the recollections in the book.

At the time that Hurston completed her last novel, *Seraph on the Suwanee*, she was receiving very little income, working as a freelance journalist and substitute teacher to make ends meet. Three months after checking into the Saint Lucie County welfare home in Florida because of failing health and poverty, Hurston died of hypertensive heart disease on January 28, 1960. Although she died alone, donations were made after her death to help in her burial costs, and enough money was gathered to bury her in the Garden of the Heavenly Rest, a segregated cemetery, albeit in an unmarked grave (Hemenway 342–349). As Henry Louis Gates points out in the appendix to his edition of *Dust Tracks on a Road*, it was Alice Walker who later discovered Hurston's grave, marked it, and in 1973 published the article "In Search of Zora Neale Hurston" in *Ms.* magazine, thus beginning the Hurston revival.

Experience and the Structural Revision of the Self

The importance of this autobiographical text for Hurston's reformulation of identity is seen in three areas: (1) the structural revision of autobiography as revision of the self; (2) the specific contrast between the original and the second publications as examples of structurally rewriting the discourse of the self; and (3) the text as a representation of the dialogue between different levels of discourse via its placement in the larger scope of the United States literary tradition.

As the title suggests, what Hurston has written is an autobiography of her life from childhood until the moment of its genesis in textual form. Comprised of sixteen chapters, the text covers important periods in her life, with particular regard to her growing interest in reading and in literature, the struggles with family and with circumstances that for a time prohibited her from receiving the education she wanted, her personal life, and, of course, her early years as a writer traveling both throughout the United States and abroad in order to do research for her novels.

The titles give the reader a sense of each chapter's focus, presenting themes that are usually introduced within the first paragraph and referred to throughout each unit. The titles of these chapters are as follows: My Birthplace; My Folks; I Get Born; The Inside Search; Figure and Fancy; Wandering; Jacksonville and After; Backstage and the Railroad; School Again; Research; Books and Things; My People! My People!; Two Women in Particular; Love; Religion; and Looking Things Over. These chapter divisions refer specifically to the published version of *Dust Tracks*, because there are sections in the original copy that were not included in the final composition of the book, but have been included in later versions of Hurston's text (Gates 211).

While at first glance the more or less chronological arrangement of the chapters seems to be in adherence to the traditional autobiography, Gates notes in his afterword that it is in fact a deviation from that model:

> Hurston's achievement in *Dust Tracks* is twofold. First, she gives us a writer's life, rather than an account, as she says, of "the Negro problem." So many events in this text are figured in terms of Hurston's growing awareness and mastery of books and language, language and linguistic rituals as spoken and written both by masters of the Western tradition and by ordinary members of the black community. (294)

It is this representation of the development of a writer—and specifically of one woman's growing connection to and domination of language—that makes this text important to my analysis. In this respect Sharon Jones's assessment of *Jonah's Gourd Vine* as a combination of a künstlerroman (development of an artist's life) and bildungsroman that meditates on folk, proletarian, and bourgeois aesthetics is also applicable here (70). What *Dust Tracks* represents, as did *Quarto de despejo*, *A hora da estrela*, and *Sabina*, is the use of writing to reestablish a displaced voice, an integral part of an individual's self-definition, through the use and manipulation of a specific textual structure, a structure which in turn, as we have seen in the cases of the aforementioned texts, influences how the author reconstructs her sense of self. As Gates notes, the foundation for Hurston's development is her cultural and literary formation:

> These two "speech communities," as it were, are Hurston's great sources of inspiration not only in her novels but also in her autobiography. The representation of her sources of language seems to be her principal concern, as she constantly shifts back and forth between her "literate" narrator's voice and a highly idiomatic black voice found in wonderful passages of free indirect discourse. (294)

Ultimately, what this process does is to highlight the dynamics between margin and center, insider/outsider present in Hurston's writing. Jones sums up Hurston's life work as an attempt to reconcile the folk, proletarian, and bourgeois aesthetics in her work on a personal and artistic level. Understanding how this dynamic works will on a greater scale also provide important commentary on the relevancy of both thematic and structural components to the possibilities and limitations of the categorization of feminine writing.

Structural Revisions: Autobiography and the Symbolism of the Self

The appropriation of the autobiography's general structure by women of color and specifically Hurston is a starting point for understanding the interaction of the writer to her text. Marcus points out that the autobiographical structure has provided a space for the exploration and representation of questions of presence/absence, unity/alienation and self/text, especially questioning the textual representation of the individual as unified or splintered (multiple), in accordance with postmodern revelations of the self (Marcus 183). While I have used the broader category of self-representational texts where the foundation is the presence of the author in the work, the texts of Jesus, Lispector, and Campos have allowed me to analyze the textual representations of multiplicity in individual identity and the interactive nature of the autobiographical process as defined by de Man. (69–70) He observes, "[T]he autobiographical project may itself produce and determine the life and that whatever the writer does is in fact governed by the technical demands of self-portraiture." Although this theory provides a somewhat unilateral vision of influences, its usefulness lies in highlighting the interaction between the writer and the discursive framework in informing representations of identity (de Man 69). These texts, in addition, can also be said to all represent different types of metafictional projects that blur fiction and nonfiction.

In considering Black women's autobiographies in particular, Elizabeth Fox-Genovese also points out the importance of themes of presence/absence, self/text and unity/alienation in the author's self-representation, but adds that other categories must be considered:

> The classification of black women's autobiography forces careful consideration of extra-textual conditions. . . . The principles of classification must begin with history. . . . The genre of black autobiography contains an important strand that could be subsumed under the general rubric of "report from the war-zone." Brooks uses "report" in her title. Giovanni's *Gemini*

features a rather staccato, journalistic style. Both depict the author's "self" indirectly, obliquely, through reports of actions more than discussions of states of mind. . . . In these ways, many of the autobiographical writings of black women, like those of many black men, do bear witness to a collective experience—to black powers of survival and creativity as well as to white oppression. (165–166)

What Fox-Genovese is emphasizing is the representation of Black autobiographies as part of a collective while at the same time underlining the sociohistorical and political events and oppression that inform their self-definition. This approach is preferred to a concentration on analysis and confession of personal motivations. She astutely points out the importance of external factors (the historical positioning I have spoken of) in understanding Black autobiographies:

Much of the autobiographical writing of black women eschews the confessional mode—the examinations of personal motives, the searchings of the soul—that white women autobiographers so frequently adopt. Black women's autobiographies seem torn between exhibitionism and secrecy, between self-display and self-concealment. The same is true of all autobiographies, but the proportions differ from text to text, perhaps from group to group of autobiographers. (165–166)

The duality of the influence of external factors combined with a tendency toward "exhibitionism and secrecy" is due in part to the historical positioning of the author and in part to the ethnic, and class affiliations of the public that would most likely read their works.

In order to understand Hurston's interaction with the autobiographical model it is important to consider her historical positioning and, in particular, the ways in which it is represented in her text. This is seen just by looking at the titles of the first three chapters: "My Birthplace," "My Folks," and "I Get Born." From the very first chapter Hurston stresses her awareness of her socioeconomic positioning and its importance in her individual growth. In the introductory paragraph she states that her identity has been greatly influenced by external factors: "Like the dead-seeming, cold rocks, I have memories within that came out of the material that went to make me. Time and place have had their say. So you will have to know something about the time and place where I came from, in order that you may interpret the incidents and directions of my life" (*Dust Tracks* 1). Just as Fox-Genovese pointed out, Hurston's emphasis in these first two paragraphs seems to be on events—specifically, time and

place and their part in shaping who she is. She then stresses her dual
awareness of race and class: "I was born in a Negro town. I do not mean
by that the black back-side of an average town. Eatonville, Florida, is,
and was at the time of my birth, a pure Negro town—charter, mayor,
council, town marshal and all (*Dust Tracks* 1). One can see the interde-
pendence of historical positioning and the question of presence and
absence mentioned above. While Hurston was, growing up, *present* in
a Negro town of a specific class, she is at the same time underscoring
her *absence* from another class that the reader might immediately associate her with: the underprivileged class, or as she says, "the black
back-side of an average town." This is even more evident when seen in
light of the facts of Hurston's birth in Notasulga, Alabama, a town she
moved from at the age of two. For Hurston, "being identified with the
all-black town of Eatonville, Florida, rather than with the sharecrop-
ping and tenant-farming plains of rural Alabama was more in keeping
with the image of herself that she was trying to create"(Bordelon "New
Tracks on Dust Tracks" 4). From the very start Hurston is aware of her
difference from the popular perception of Negroes that predominated
and creates specific details of her autobiography as a forum for expressing that difference.

What Hurston's implicit statement of historical positioning reveals in
terms of autobiographical structure is somewhat more complicated. While
there is the emphasis on circumstances and community, Hurston is still
including herself in one group—a more socially centralized group—in order
to separate herself from another, more marginalized community. However,
her ties to that community are never completely severed. This is seen in
her subtle use of oral stories to retell her life. Hazel Carby describes
Hurston's ethnography in general as originating in Eatonville, a tool in her
"creation of [a] discourse of the rural folk that displaces the antagonist
relations of cultural transformation" (qtd. in Pavlovska 78). Hurston's identity was a pure product of Eatonville, no matter how far from it her personal and professional life would take her (Pavlovska 96). When Hurston
writes her autobiography and tells her mother's story for example, she
takes the opportunity to finally express years later the voice that was silenced the afternoon of her death. The paragraph immediately following
Hurston's recognition of her silence serves as an example of this recupera-
tive project: "The Master-Maker in His making had made Old Death. Made
him with big, soft feet and square toes. . . . This was the morning of the day
of the beginning of things" (*Dust Tracks* 65) By relating the story of the
moment her mother dies through metaphors most likely passed on through
oral tradition, Hurston is recuperating a disappearing tradition and show-
casing it in her autobiographical discourse. However, Hurston's reversal of

silence really begins in the introductory paragraph of the chapter when she establishes her mother as subject. Chapter 6, "Wandering," is therefore Hurston's second chance to tell her mother's story (her pain, her desires, her motivations, and her beliefs) after having been denied that privilege on the day she died. In general this chapter represents the influence of Hurston's mother on her identity reformulation, in contrast with the texts of Jesus, Lispector, and Campos, where a strong female influence is absent or not as marked as in *Dust Tracks*.

In these first chapters of *Dust Tracks* the reader is made aware of Hurston's particular use of the autobiographical text to create what some critics have seen as a problematic reformulation of the self. As Lionnet observes, the text can be seen in fact not as autobiography but as *autoethnography*: "Indeed, what I would like to suggest here is that *Dust Tracks* amounts to autoethnography, that is, the defining of one's subjective ethnicity as mediated through language, history, and ethnographical analysis; in short, that the book amounts to a kind of "figural anthropology" of the self" (383). What Lionnet's thesis points out in terms of historical positioning is the complexity of this concept when applied to Hurston and her text. She stresses that Hurston, is aware of but to a certain extent shaped by her socioeconomic position. Hurston reconstructs herself in a way that is not completely dependent on the details of her past:

> In light of the skepticism with which contemporary literary theory has taught us to view any effort of self-representation in language, I would like to propose a different approach to the issue of Hurston's presumed insincerity and untrustworthiness. It may perhaps be more useful to reconsider *Dust Tracks on a Road* not as autobiography but rather as self-portrait, in the sense redefined by Michel Beaujour—"texts which are self-contained rather than being the representation of past actions." (383)

Hurston's self-representation, or what Lionnet calls "autoethnography," is a complex subjective representation of herself that tries to avoid any type of essentialization but rather embraces an objective individualism without completely losing sight of her ethnicity.

Boyd, in a similar assessment, describes *Dust Tracks* as a text in which

> The "truth" that Hurston presents ... is inseparable from the "dream." That is to say, the vision—the selective remembrance—

of what her life *should* have been, even if that remembrance is occasionally contrary to what was. In that regard, *Dust Tracks on a Road* is what readers today might view more as memoir than autobiography. . . . The story of a self-invented woman, *Dust Tracks on a Road* offers a reliable account of a writer's inner life. (355)

Jesus experiences a similar tension between individualism and ethnicity in her adult life. Like Hurston, she distanced herself from one group, the other favelados, because of her education, while still recognizing herself as an Afro-Brazilian woman. Like Hurston, she did not want to be judged solely on the basis of her socioeconomic background and its connotations, choosing instead to actively develop an identity that aspired to membership in one group without completely severing ties with the other. By making these choices regarding their identities, Hurston and Jesus, though separated by time and geography, experience and navigate an aesthetics of dislocation that questions belonging to a specific region or people. Such an evasion of fixed identities exemplifies the characteristics of nonsynchronicity in their relation to group identities and the self (Konzett 72).

Part of Hurston's active self-identification involves her choice of the communities to which she belongs, represented through her molding of experience and the written discourse in which she recounts it. As James Krasner points out, this manipulation of the word in part has its root in African American oral tradition: "But Hurston makes it clear that she is an expert at intentional misrepresentation as well. She is born into a culture in which the people not only interpret their experience by passing "this world and the next on through their mouths," but in which there are "lying sessions" (115). For Hurston, these lying sessions were one part of her cultural heritage that influenced who she was and at the same time was taken with her into other circles far from Eatonville—circles like New York and Barnard College:

No doubt, these tales of God, the Devil, animals and natural elements seemed ordinary enough to most people in the village. But many of them stirred up fancies in me. . . . Life took on a bigger perimeter by expanding on these things. I picked up glints and gleams out of what I heard and stored it away to turn it to my own uses. . . . When I began to make up stories I cannot say. Just from one fancy to another, adding more and more detail until they seemed real. People seldom see themselves changing. (*Dust Tracks* 52, 53)

Several important points can be drawn from this passage that will help understand Hurston's self-definition. First, is the self-reflexive style that is true to the autobiography. On looking back at her life in this forum, Hurston is aware of the influences that shaped her and how she used them to influence others' perceptions of her. However, she also describes an influence on the very text we read. Her recounting of the "lying sessions" is of historical and ethnographical importance but is also a subtle (I believe conscious) warning to the reader to carefully consider what Hurston writes without immediately assessing it as fact. Meisenhelder also describes the influence of the Eatonville community and dynamic on Hurston's negotiation of her identity by pointing to the phrase "hitting a straight lick with a crooked stick": "[S]he repeatedly emphasizes the necessity of this skill for a black woman to survive in a world that conspires to 'squinch [her] spirit' and silence her voice" (147).

This warning to carefully consider the presentation of truth was also Hurston's way of counteracting external constraints (from publishers for example) on her self-presentation. While I will explore in more detail the influence of publishing concerns on Hurston's presentation, her earlier article, "Lying Sessions," is a telling document of the ways in which she was still able to subvert the oppressive dominant autobiographical discourse: "On the verge of becoming discourse (*discourse*), history (*histoire*) is emptied of the "I," another of Hurston's diversionary tactics to subvert the confessional goal of the autobiography" (Raynaud 113). While Raynaud is referring in this case to the textual change from "horizontal chronological progression" to "vertical organization," there is yet another way in which Hurston subverts the expectation of confessional autobiography. Her self-concealment (at times behind the folk stories of the collective, or behind universalist, integrationist political ideologies) can be seen as one way in which she rebels against the expectation that her life is to be opened up submissively before God, or her readers, since this submissive revelation can be seen as a representation of yet another power relationship (Marcus 2).

According to Boi, Hurston's game of disclosure and refusal is a literary weapon "to destructure the dominance of subject terms in the interpretation of human being" (161). She also notes that Hurston subverts the text's questions of truth and consequently subverts the confessional autobiography's demands of truth. As a result *Dust Tracks* becomes an example of what Gates calls "signifying": "To signify means to exert a certain mischievous power over the truth and falsehood of statements. . . . *Dust Tracks* originally derives from a 'matrix of literary discontinuities,' in which the author signifies upon communication as a literary discourse, upon herself as a black writer, and upon autobiography as a literary genre"

(194). For an African American woman seeking success in a predominantly white world, such a skill is a necessity:

> Hurston ultimately emphasizes the necessity of flexibility in a world of "mules and men." Carefully assessing power relations in her own life and charting her varied responses to them, Hurston underscores the importance of black women learning when to fight and when to negotiate or dissemble, when to specify and when to signify, when to be a "tiger" and when to be a trickster. (Meisenhelder 143)

Carla Kaplan also looks to Hurston's folk expressions as revealing strategies of negotiation in society that can be seen not only in close study of her fictional and nonfictional texts but also in her personal correspondence. In particular, the phrase "feather-bed resistance" represents a similar approach to situations of unequal power relations. As Kaplan notes, "Feather-bed resistance is not just play. It is deception necessitated by social inequality. Hurston mastered feather-bed resistance" (21).

When comparing these strategies to Jesus's relationships with Dantas, politicians, and other members of her community, the power dynamics also inherent in those interactions explain the similarity in the strategies she too used. These negotiations, moments of signifying and separations can then be seen as common to Black women of the diaspora in societies where colonial hierarchies of race, class, and gender have left their mark on postcolonial societies.

Creating a "Statue of the Self": Restructuration of Identity through Language

Another point that Hurston's "lying sessions" and signifying reveal is her attitude toward language in general. While Lispector in *A hora da estrela* and Campos in *Sabina* express their mistrust of language on a linguistic level as an inherently flawed transmitter of meaning, Hurston expresses a similar opinion and takes it in a different direction. Although she too distrusts language's ability to represent reality, she still uses it as a tool by emphasizing the complexity and multiplicity of her ideas (and therefore identity) through a combination of contrasting textual elements. As Fox-Genovese observes, "Hurston's statue, like that of her foremothers and successors, was fashioned of disparate materials. Uneasily poised between the discourses through which any writer represents the self and the conditions of gender, class, and race through which any personal experience is articulated, the statue embodies elements of both" (177).

The fashioning of her personal statue out of disparate materials is a process also present in Jesus's text. In bell hooks's theories of multiple identity we have the strategy, used by Jesus and even before by Hurston, that encourages women to take advantage of otherwise negative or debilitating conditions in order to find a site of empowerment. In both Jesus and Hurston there is the valorization of spaces considered marginalized, allowing them to find "a site one stays in, . . . because it nourishes one's capacity to resist . . ." (hooks, Yearning 149–150). In both cases one can see how these women have used the strategy hooks proposes, adapted for their specific historical and geographical moments. When hooks for example speaks of "staying in" a marginalized site, she is not speaking of enclosure in this space and isolation from dominant society, but of a valorization of certain elements of their marginalized condition otherwise seen as inferior, as sites of empowerment. Even with the social restrictions of African American women writers in the 1920s, 1930s and 1940s, or the socioeconomic oppression of poor Black Brazilian women of the 1950s and 1960s, such strategies could be useful.

While Hurston uses her position of marginality as part of her self-expression, she is not afraid to be shaped by other forces that may not necessarily be marginal. As Fox-Genovese states, "But the combining of elements transforms them. Hurston does not simply "tell it like it is," does not write directly out of experience. The discourses through which she works—and presumably expects to be read—shape her presentation of experience even as her specific experience shapes the ways in which she locates herself in discourses" (177). When Fox-Genovese speaks of the influence of the discourses in which Hurston works she is referring to two general categories: the folk tradition that Hurston learned in Eatonville and the dominant discourse she learned in college. The influence of both on Hurston's self-presentation indicates the likelihood of a movement between the marginal sites she was in and a more central discourse without leaving behind the aspects of her background that helped mold her. She was in fact caught between two worlds: part of yet separate from the folk communities of Florida and the bourgeois circles of New York, Baltimore, and Washington (Jones 67). Similarly, Jesus's statue is made of the effects of her historical positioning and the constructive use of marginalized spaces alongside the effects of two years of formal schooling and years of reading—self-education that represents her access to dominant discourse.

One part of Hurston's conscious manipulation of language can be seen in the register in which she voices her opinions. She was aware of the possible audiences for her text: a White readership that would not be familiar with her life in Eatonville, the dynamics of Black southern life or the struggles of an African American woman from the south in the early twentieth century. However, one decision that faced her was what register to choose to best convey information to her reader. The dilemma she faces is one that Minh-ha sees as common to women of color: "Achieve distance, they keep on saying, as much distance from your own voice as possible. Don't direct the reader's attention to yourself, don't fiddle with words just to show off. . . . One must practice to forget oneself, she said" (27–28). Was Hurston to speak of her life and that of other Blacks in Eatonville through the use of the Black dialect or not? If she did, would this call too much attention to her historical positioning and not enough to the value of her material and her worth as a writer? And once her life's narration left Eatonville to the halls of Barnard, was she to keep this dialect or change to a discourse expected of an educated individual? As Minh-ha warns, one of the results of such restrictions is a tendency toward silence, for lack of an empowering solution that does not compromise: "How estranged, deeply estranged, she remains then. Silenced before she even finds the words to name it . . . . But to write well, we must either espouse his cause or transcend our borderlines. . . . We are therefore triply jeopardized: as a writer, as a woman, and as a woman of color" (27–28). The representation of the self is a complex issue that brings together three important elements: (1) the influence of the life recounted on the discourse chosen (and in particular the way in which this discourse is structured); (2) the relation between language and the reconstruction and textual representation of the self; and (3) the influence of the expected reader on the discourse chosen. Fox-Genovese defines these elements as an integral part of Black women's autobiographical discourse, noting that this discourse comes not just from experience (not in an empirical sense, but in terms of the condition of the "interlocking structures of gender, class, and race") but even more from the tension of condition and discourse. This tension is one she describes as stemming "from the changing ways in which black women writers have attempted to represent a personal experience of condition through available discourses and in interaction with imagined readers" (178).

The effect of condition, discourse, and readers creates a tension that must be considered in understanding the subject's reconstruction of the self. As Fox-Genovese continues, "The account of the black woman's self cannot be divorced from the history of that self or the history of the people among whom it took shape. It also cannot be divorced from the language through which it is represented, or from the readers of other classes and races who not only lay claim to it but who have helped to shape it" (198).

Who are the readers (ideal or real) that Hurston believed would be reading her published text? What effect did their presence have on the organization and editing of the manuscript? A consideration of the readers of *Dust Tracks* in part reveals conditions that place Hurston's text in a tradition of Black women's autobiography marked by a White presence, as destined readers or editors. As Stephen Butterfield points out, the readers for the slave narratives were predominantly White, being introduced to these texts at antislavery meetings, lectures, or churches. These readers were targeted by author or editor because they could possibly give money that would help the abolitionist cause or, as in the case of Harriet Jacobs for example, convince northern White women with abler pens to lend their support to the abolitionist movement, all the while being validated by their readers (11–13). Kaplan also sees Hurston's use of secrecy and dissembling as historically determined and common to African American literature since writers of slave narratives had to contend with how to present their lives to readers who included "illiterate African Americans, racist, hostile white southerners and distant, possibly sympathetic northerners ignorant of the harsh realities of slavery" (22). The presence of White readers and editors and their effect on the given text's style and tone (especially considering Black women's slave narratives as the first Black women's autobiographies) are conditions that had become important elements in Black autobiographies, especially around the 1940s, when Hurston wrote (Fox-Genovese 185–186).[1]

As Bordelon has noted, consideration of Hurston's readership must take into account the reasons under which it was born. At a moment in Hurston's life when she was in need of financial help and being urged by her publisher to take advantage of her popularity and write what would be the first of a multivolume work, Hurston consented to write her autobiography for a largely White audience ("New Tracks" 19). For Hurston this created a tension in her text, in terms of language and imagery, that had her struggling to find a point of mediation between the two worlds. As Susan Willis states: "[I]t articulates the contradictory nature of Hurston's project as a black woman writer and intellectual attempting to mediate two deeply polarized worlds, whose terms include: South/North, black/white, rural/urban, folk tradition/intellectual scholarship" (110). While early African American narrative, and particularly the slave narrative I mentioned before, sought to persuade Whites that people of color were human and deserved humane treatment, Hurston's text, while acting as mediator, did not necessarily seek her readers' approval, as her predecessors had done. From the first request by the publishers of Lippincott to tell her life story she expressed her hesitation and her unwillingness to completely cater to her audience: "[I]t is too hard to reveal one's inner self, and there is no use in writing that kind of book unless you do. . . . The white man is always trying to know into somebody else's business. All right, I'll set something outside the door of my

mind for him to play with and handle. He can read my writing but he
sho' can't read my mind" (qtd. in Boyd 356).

As McKay notes, the tension as expressed in Hurston's text turns it
into a transitional work that rejects its predetermined role as a race-
representative document while breaking with the rhetorical patterns of
the slave narrative. The result is a text that opens the doors for more
radical experimentation with form and content (180).

One of the text's later examples of Hurston's relationship with her
reader and its contribution to the multiplicity of her writing on the self-
representational and linguistic level is found at the end of chapter 16, "Looking Things Over." In Hurston's "farewell" to her readers she declares:

> I have no race prejudice of any kind. My kinfolks, and my
> "skinfolks" are dearly loved. My own circumference of every-
> day life is there. . . . So I give you all my right hand of fellow-
> ship and love, and hope for the same from you. In my eyesight,
> you lose nothing by not looking just like me. I will remember
> you all in my good thoughts, and I ask you kindly to do the
> same for me. Not only just me. You, who play the zig-zag
> lightning of power over the world, with the grumbling thun-
> der in your wake, think kindly of those who walk in the dust.
> (231–232)

The contemporary readers note the reference to those who "lose nothing
by not looking just like me," a reference, in all likelihood, to the difference
of skin color between autobiographer and reader. Hemenway notes how
this seeming offering of good will hides contradictions beneath its surface:

> Hurston's comment is most revealing of the stylistic contradic-
> tions, arising out of the confusion of voice, that have been in the
> autobiography from the first. Like a member of the American
> Indian Movement telling whites at a bicentennial celebration
> that he is pleased the American immigrants could visit his coun-
> try as guests for these past 200 years, Hurston assures whites
> that they do not have to feel inferior just because they do not
> look like her. But having delivered that stroke, she immediately
> falls back upon the village voice to characterize the reality of
> white power and loses the cutting edge of her irony in an ide-
> alistic vision of breeding a noble world in a few hundred
> years. . . . Her own language, the optative mood, the vagueness,
> the focus on a time and space beyond the here and now—
> reveals her uneasiness over the position in which she finds
> herself at the end of the book. (286)

This difference, which according to Hurston, ironically (but genuinely?) is not a hindrance to any fellowship between the two, does in fact leave its mark on the whole text. Will this vision of unity ever occur? The space between author and reader is summarized in this last paragraph by the difference in language used. On one hand, Hurston uses the language of Blacks from her Eatonville community when she refers to her community as her kinfolks and "skin folks," stressing the bond she has with them, and continuing by exhorting those with power to consider those without, referring to them as those who "play zig-zag lightning of power over the world." Hurston plays a game of double references: both socially and temporally by using this language to speak to one "community" (or readers who do not look like her) while by its very use keeping her childhood community as a referent.

However, while maintaining a dialogue between the two communities Hemenway notes the uneasiness that Hurston's movement between the voices signals. If we refer back to Minh-ha's statement problematizing the challenges women writers of color face about their language of communication, we see a representation of it here. Hurston wishes to communicate a warning to those in power to show more respect while also indicting their past behavior, yet she shows an uncertainty as to which voice would most effectively relay her point. As Minh-ha observes, with the folk dialect she risks being perceived as too biased, an accusation she tries to counteract by stating her lack of prejudice at the beginning. On the other hand, the other voice threatens to distance her from her audience and her message, thus weakening its intended effect.

The message itself is an interesting study in dueling purposes, both overt and ironic. While on the surface it seems a straightforward extension of the hand of fellowship, underneath is a subtle indictment of those in power. By using the language she does, especially combined with the imagery of the underprivileged as "those who walk in the dust" she is engaging in the movement Boi defines as passing from inside to outside (on the level of the recounting of events) and which Johnson has elaborated on and presented as an overall element of Hurston's work, no matter the content. As Johnson notes, although Hurston could be seen as becoming an outsider to her community of origin, her work "was constantly dramatizing and undercutting just such inside/outside opposition, transforming the plane geometry of physical space into the complex transactions of discursive exchange" (130). This movement between these two poles again demonstrates her cultivation, albeit by circumstance, of the nonsynchronicity of ethnic modernism which allows her to "resist the readopting of organic paradigms of nationhood and blood-related collective definitions of ethnicity" or their mode of expression (Konzett 16).

Inside/Outside Movement and the
Navigation of the Linguistic Register

It is precisely this continuous exchange and subversion of discourses that adds to the impreciseness and nontraditional nature of Hurston's work. The difference of *Dust Tracks* can be described as one of anarchy and antagonism: "It is this apparently antagonistic movement between life and literature, reality and its representation, orality and literacy, which informs the structural coherence of *Dust Tracks*, rather than the simply linear progression through the lived life" (Lionnet 388). Hurston's narration of her mother's death is another example of her use of contrasting language in a manner that distinguishes itself from the linguistic uniformity of the traditional autobiography. This passage shows just such tension and especially emphasizes its existence within the textual framework and outside it, as metatextual antagonist to the model of autobiography constantly trying to completely shape the text and subject. When she describes for her readers the day her mother died and the instructions she, a nine year old girl, was given, there is still a a narrative voice present speaking in a seemingly neutral style. The change, nonetheless, occurs when Hurston laments not being able to fulfill her mother's wishes, her voice and her mother's, suppressed by patriarchy and village customs: "Just then, Death finished his prowling through the house on his padded feet and entered the room. He bowed to Mama in his way, and she made her manners and left us to act out our ceremonies over unimportant things" (65–66). At this moment Hurston linguistically journeys back in time, switching to metaphoric folkloric language to attempt to explain not just the concrete events, but more importantly, the emotions of the moment. As Raynaud observes, "The advantage of this technique is to bring the reader back to the moment of enunciation and, thus, to restore the immediacy of the utterance, while the controlling presence of the narrator is still felt in the verb tenses and the pronouns" (118).

The twofold result of this gesture can be explained by Johnson's theories of inside/outside movement and Konzett's nonsychronicity. While Hurston was unable to be her mother's voice at the time of her death, this autobiography (and particularly the chapter entitled "Wandering") has allowed her to remedy that situation by writing her mother's wishes in a forum where it could no longer be silenced. As an outside movement, the validation of southern Black dialect and beliefs serves as an example of what Minh-ha calls "smashing the myth." By using this linguistic structure and placing it in a position of dominance Hurston is freeing herself and this tradition.

Pressures of Publication: Reader Expectation
and Self-Representation

Hurston's maneuvering through specific structures and linguistic registers to create a multifaceted self is, as I have shown, subject to external and internal factors, among which is the pressure of not only publishers but also the "ideal" readers who will interpret her work. The effects of these pressures on Hurston's identity can be seen if we compare the published version of her text with the original manuscript. Placing these texts side by side shows distinct structural changes (including chapters later omitted) that ultimately reflect a fuller representation of her in four areas: race and questions of Blackness in particular, race politics, gender relations, and sexuality.

A careful examination of Hurston's use of footnotes demonstrates her movement inside/outside of different cultures through changes in linguistic registers and textual structures. As Boyd, Gates, and Hemenway note, Hurston wrote an original manuscript of *Dust Tracks* which was edited and published. What was left behind were several folders containing sections that had been omitted from the published text, in part due to her editors' fears that some of the views expressed originally might be offensive or controversial. In her published text there are three stories where Hurston furnishes footnotes with translations or general explanations for her readers, (other translations occur within the text), further proof that they were most likely expected to be from outside of the southern Black community. In all three, one of which I will discuss here, Hurston uses her footnotes to question or broaden at times accepted definitions of human character and of cultural beliefs in order to include and expand the idea of community or Blackness.

In chapter 3 Hurston relates to us the unique circumstances surrounding her birth, culminating in her delivery not by the expected figure (a Black woman, whether she be a stranger, midwife, or just a friend) but by a White man who through the years visits her and gives her advice on life. In the chapter entitled "The Inside Search" he advises: "Snidlits, don't be a nigger," he would say to me over and over. Niggers lie and lie! Any time you catch folks lying, they are skeered of something. Lying is dodging. People with guts don't lie. They tell the truth and then if they have to, they fight it out. You lay yourself open by lying. Truth is a letter from courage. I want you to grow guts as you go along" (*Dust Tracks* 30–31). Anticipating possible judgment by her reader because of the charged word "nigger," Hurston gives an explanation in a footnote: "The word Nigger used in this sense does not mean race. It means a weak, contemptible person of any race." This footnote is important for two reasons:

its content and structural placement. Hurston's translation of the White man's comments serves as a bridge from those inside the community to those outside (the readers). It is interesting to note that when her White friend cautions her not to be a "nigger" the explanation given is brief and limited. Left out is a more in-depth explanation of the history and development of the word, its use within the Black community, and the implications of its use by a White man. One assumption from the brevity of this definition is that Blacks are knowledgeable about the history of this term. Their knowledge is taken for granted while the White audience must constantly be educated about its meaning and impact (*Dust Tracks* 30).

Susan Meisenhelder sees this episode as indicative once more of Hurston's subtle negotiation of Black-White relations. Her comments do not explicitly address the racism that is part of the White man's comments but implicitly presents them for the reader to judge. She instead chooses to take only the parts of his advice that are useful for her development and "self-determination" (153).

Hurston expands the structures of autobiography by including footnotes, more commonly used in technical documents in science, history, or the social sciences for example but considerably less in literary texts. The result is an emphasis on mixing genres in order to present a product that does not neatly fit categorization.

Careful study of the original manuscript and other articles written by Hurston also reveal a more confrontational racial politics than what we read in the published copy while still expressing views unpopular at the time. Gates's version, for example, includes an appendix that has three chapters either not included in the main text or divided and included in other chapters. They are "My People, My People!," "The Inside Light—Being a Salute to Friendship," and "Seeing the World as It Is."

In the original manuscript of "My People, My People" Hurston not only comments more on educational and class differences among Blacks but also goes so far as to decry the notion of race altogether, prefacing her statement with a folk story about how Blacks accidentally got their skin color because of a misunderstanding of God's commands: "So God hollered at 'em, 'Get back!' Get back!' But they thought He said, 'Git black! so they got black and just kept the thing agoing. So according to that, we are no race. We are just a collection of people who overslept our time and got caught in the draft" (*Dust Tracks* 245–246). The paradoxical use of a folk story, written in southern Black dialect, to illustrate the nonexistence of race is yet another example of Hurston's complex relationship with these issues and with the legacy of her community to her own identity. However, any ideas going against these expectations could be considered dangerous and controversial to the "predominantly white mass-magazine audience" and to her editors, and therefore had to be excluded from the published work. As an example Hemenway cites her more direct essays ("My Most Humiliating Jim Crow Experience" and "Crazy for this Democracy"), published for the *Negro Digest* in 1944 and 1945, as evidence of Hurston's awareness of racial prejudice because of firsthand experience and her criticisms of American social institutions and domestic policy (Hemenway 294).[2] Evidence of Hurston's more aggressive viewpoints is found at the end of the essay on her experience of being examined by a White doctor in an upper-class doctor's office—in the linen closet. Hurston was aware that while she believed strongly in the individual, society still held fast to notions of race, especially as weapons of prejudice and discrimination, weapons that she could be attacked by as much as any other Black American. It is in her article "What White Publishers Won't Print" that she expresses her disappointment and anger at the way this prejudice is manifested in print by an exclusion of certain topics and stereotyping of Blacks.

Comparisons of Hurston's manuscripts also reveal interesting nuances in her relationship with women and the impact they had on her life. In her accounts of relationships with White women in particular, Hurston achieves two purposes. On one hand she shows the commonality and friendship that can exist beyond race, yet on the other (especially in the original manuscript) she shows what Raynaud has called the problematic relation between women of color and White women. In chapter 13 of the published manuscript, entitled "Two Women in Particular," Hurston acknowledges the deep friendship she shared with two special women in her life, Ethel Waters and Fannie Hurst (193). The section describing Hurston's time with Fannie Hurst in particular stresses their ability to find common ground despite racial difference. One important White woman in Hurston's life who must be mentioned is her patron, Mrs. R. Osgood Mason. While on one hand Hurston states that "there was and is a psychic bond between us. . . . She is altogether in sympathy with . . . [Blacks] , because she says truthfully they are utterly sincere in living," [144–145]. Hemenway also points to another side of their relationship, when he speaks of the tension and problematic power relations among the women:

> The situation becomes a power relationship; . . . It is from the vantage of history that Mrs. Mason's kindnesses take on their clearest pattern. . . . Throughout that time [Hurston] chafed under Mrs. Mason's restraints and schemed with Hughes about ways to circumvent them; yet she still revered, even loved, her Godmother. The relations with Mrs. Mason were humanly inconsistent. As Hurston went farther away, the psychic bond deteriorated, and her Godmother became a meddling patron. (107, 109)

Similarly, Raynaud notes that in the appendix of the original manuscript, in the chapter entitled "The Inside Light—Being a Salute to Friendship" Hurston thanks a long list of important people in her life that she believes helped her develop artistically and professionally (39). The omissions of these names from the published texts underscores the difficulties facing Hurston's attempts to question and subtly expose the complicated category of gender and its intersections with race and class in determining the dynamics of female interaction.

These power relations however are not unique to Hurston's situation, but is in fact a legacy of antislavery narratives, particularly of women. Critics like James Olney and Valerie Smith have noted the constraints on ex-slaves' articulation of their experience in the slave narratives because of the assumptions of objectivity by traditional autobiography and the power relations that existed many times between ex-slaves and their patrons or editors. This was for example the case to an extent with Harriet Jacobs and her editor Lydia Maria Childs. As Fox-Genovese points out, these power relationships, not only with specific people but also with the dominant discourse they represent, is one of the links that places *Dust Tracks* in the middle of a literary progression from slave narrative to contemporary African American women's fiction:

> Above all, black women's autobiographies suggest a tension in black women's relation to various dominant discourses. . . . But Hurston also had her eyes on the pinnacles of the prestigious tradition of Western letters, on Shakespeare and his canonized successors. . . . Her difficulty in clearly depicting her own statue resulted at least in part from the deadlock between her commitment to her roots as a black woman in a black community and her commitment to transcending all social and gender roots in her craft. ("My Statue, My Self," 198–199)

Fox-Genovese observes that African American women writers have proven especially susceptible because of their desire to find what she calls "discursive respectability" while not forgetting their heritage.

Lastly, the published version of Dust *Tracks* illustrates the ramifications of structural- and content-based changes on Hurston's identity by excluding her presentation of herself as a sexualized being. Comparisons of her published and original manuscript show that any sexualized aspect of her development is omitted. In the chapter "Figure and Fancy" from the original text Hurston recalls, "There would be, for instance, sly references to the physical condition of women, irregular love affairs, brags on male potency by the parties of the first part, and the like. It did not take me long to know what was meant when a girl was spoken of as 'ruint' or 'bigged' (46). When Hurston, however, asks about one of the sexually explicit stories, her brother slaps her. Due to rules of propriety for women in the 1940s the erotic aspect of Hurston's text could not be included. In the excised passages she shows how as a young girl she was excluded from sexual knowledge, giving the examples of and problematizing the sexist songs and stories she heard. The result of these omissions is to veil her sexual voice:

> A study of the omitted sections emphasizes the complexity of her resistance to the White publishing world, and the ways in which she eventually complied. It stresses how the creation of her fictive self is not solely a self-conscious textual strategy, but also a product of her historical position as a black female writer. It restores from the original text a more accurate, if still extremely puzzling, portrait of Hurston. (Raynaud, "Rubbing a Paragraph" 35)

Nonetheless, Hurston's questioning demonstrates her unwillingness to follow others' definitions of femininity—especially in terms of feminine knowledge as it relates to the sexual. The reality of her defiance however must be contextualized within continuous social pressure in the form of societal mores and publishers' editing against which she was constantly fighting. Such publishing pressure to present a face for a predominantly White readership became a factor in Jesus's presentation of herself in 1950s Brazil. As a poor Black woman who obtained a level of celebrity status through her diary, she was subject to the pressures of such a contrasting representation. Levine notes that her unedited diaries "show her to be more complex than the two-dimensional woman depicted by Dantas's editing of her life story. Dantas knew that Carolina's lack of tact would irritate readers who demanded that lower-class celebrities know their place, as it were" (Levine 65). Hurston interestingly enough perpetuated a rural background so that she would be seen as someone who understood both worlds; for Jesus such duality is seen as one of her greatest flaws. Nonetheless, both are silenced in part because they are women who had a certain place in society—be it North American or Brazilian—and consequently, a certain identity to uphold.

Hurston's Autobiography and Its Literary Contemporaries

Ultimately, the importance of Hurston's literary, political, and social vision and its dialogue with her text can be seen when contrasted with the works of her contemporaries, particularly from the 1940s. Boyd condemns the double standard of the criticism of *Dust Tracks* as opposed to the uncritical acceptance of prominent African-American writers of the time. The critical reception for a male writer's embellishment of the truth is in sharp contrast to the indictment any woman writer receives when replicating the same behavior.

Boyd highlights this double standard and presents Hurston's text as a challenge to the definition of autobiography:

> The story of a self-invented woman, *Dust Tracks on a Road* offers a reliable account of a writer's *inner* life. Unfortunately, Hurston's omissions of some external realities have caused many contemporary critics to dismiss *Dust Tracks* as nothing more than a pack of lies. . . . But readers cannot dismiss *Dust Tracks* unless they also are willing to dismiss Langston Hughes's *The Big Sea* and Richard Wright's *Black Boy*—two other autobiographies published in the 1940s in which black writers engaged in myth-making about their lives. Often, the critical tendency has been to excuse or ignore this "will to adorn" when the perpetrator is a black man, but to vehemently attack Hurston—one of the few black female autobiographers of the first half of the twentieth century—for doing the very same thing. Truth be told, *Dust Tracks on a Road* is an "imaginative autobiography," a term Wright applied to *Black Boy*. And every so-called lie in Hurston's book is an avenue to the truth. (355)

When compared to Hughes and Wright, Hurston's representation of her life is judged as transgressively deceptive, breaking an implicit autobiographical pact of truthfulness. However, critics like Gates also point to "the rhetorical distance that separated Hurston from her contemporaries" that goes beyond stylistic difference (290). Gates observes that during the 1920s and 1930's—from the novel of manners of the Harlem Renaissance to the social realism of the 1930s and the Black Arts movement—the predominant belief was that Black people were mainly reactionary, reduced by racism to a people only reacting to racial oppression, living with an inferior sense of culture that had profound effects on their psychological development.

While some critics believe that the social realism that in part represented these opinions was promoted by male writers like Wright, Ellison, and Brown, Hurston believed in a proactive approach to life and racial oppression, choosing to support an internal freedom based on individual self-determination and not a "defensive reaction to white actions" (Gates 291). This difference in the individual's reaction to oppression is seen in their texts: "If Hurston represents her final moments with her mother in terms of the search for voice, then Wright attributes to a similar experience a certain 'somberness of spirit' " (Gates 290). The result was a general lack of acceptance for Hurston's works because of their opposition to the predominant social beliefs of the time. However, in examining Hurston's autobiography, it is interesting to note the ways in which Gates's assessment is in a sense too general, not accounting for the navigation of Black and White cultures (both socially and literarily, from margin to center and back) that Hurston undertook in her works: a balancing act that did not always leave her on the proactive end.

This theme of navigation and balancing, as I have highlighted, is present in Jesus's diary. It is no coincidence that this theme occurs in both texts given the similar situation they share: that of two women of color trying to establish a literary presence in an environment that considered them marginalized. While Jesus's and Hurston's reasons for fighting for literary recognition were different, the opposition and its manifestation in their textual presentation is similar in some regards. In particular, an examination of Hurston's specific textual representation of the sociocultural and economic factors that impact her reformulated self reveal the nuances of her textual multiplicity as a complement to the structural hybridity we have seen in *Dust Tracks*.

Chapter Eight

Wandering through the Dust: Textual Statues in *Dust Tracks on a Road*

Hybridity and Sociocultural Difference

Hurston's *Dust Tracks on a Road* exemplifies the structural redefinition of a subject whose multiplicity can be found in a manipulation of the autobiographical discourse and the marginalized and dominant discourses that are part of her cultural and literary formation. This chapter will bring the question of multiplicity in autobiography full circle by studying Hurston's textual representation of hybridity. In *Dust Tracks* this is based on her reformulation of a multifaceted self through marginalized and dominant sociocultural experiences that shaped her. While these experiences are external to the text, as part of an autobiographical work they are incorporated into a narrative discourse in order to form a somewhat ordered recounting of Hurston's life. In converting experience to the written word she also brings into question and ultimately subverts the notion of autobiography as full disclosure, choosing instead to assert a subjective self that elides such considerations. It is the sociocultural influence of Eatonville together with the literary and artistic worlds she would circulate among that produce this ambiguity of the text and its subjects (Meisenhelder 143).

From the beginning Hurston recounted the details of her life in a way that emphasized her difference from her birth community and the beginnings of her approach to writing. The result was to create other links with her readers and literary contemporaries of her work. The origins of Hurston's sense of difference can be found early on in her life:

> Mama exhorted her children at every opportunity to "jump at
> de sun." We might not land on the sun, but at least we would
> get off the ground. Papa did not feel so hopeful. Let well
> enough alone. It did not do for Negroes to have too much
> spirit. He was always threatening to break mine or kill me in
> the attempt. My mother was always standing between us. She
> conceded that I was impudent and given to talking back, but
> she didn't want to "squinch my spirit" too much for fear that
> I would turn out to be a mealy-mouthed rag doll by the time
> I got grown. (*Dust Tracks* 13)

This rejection of race and gender limits is similar to Jesus's desires as a
young girl to be a young man, because of the social power it would give
her as well as a sense of belonging and commitment to a national identity. This desire to be part of a Brazilian collective is illustrated by her
confession, "When I was a girl my dream was to be a man to defend
Brazil" (*Child of the Dark* 53).

When framed in a historical context the nuances and seeming contradictions of Hurston's character can be more fully understood. At the time
when she was growing up, Blacks had been free for only a few decades.
Many were still trying to establish their position in a White society and
believed that one way to do so was to be submissive, to continue the
behavior they were forced to adopt as slaves: acknowledge their place and
adjust their aspirations accordingly. When combined with prescribed gender roles (equally as limiting within the Black community of the time) one
can see, as Hurston was told by her father, that her options were limited,
that "The White folks were not going to stand for it" (13). Her reaction
however, was to stress her difference and rebel against those strictures
placed upon her because she was Black and female.

The one strong female influence in Hurston's life that did provide
some of the foundation for the person she would become and present to her
readers in her text was her mother. For her mother, the legacy of slavery did
not mean that her daughter had to set her aspirations only as high as was
allowed. Even if it meant going against the behavior prescribed for her,
Hurston's mother encouraged her to step out and take risks.

Given her influence on her daughter, Hurston's mother's death and
the circumstances surrounding it had a special impact on her development. Although her mother had called her aside and given instructions
as to the last-minute death rituals, Hurston remembers that "that same
day near sun-down, I was called upon to set my will against my father,
the village dames and village custom" (*Dust Tracks* 64, 65). Her father
and elders represent the traditional customs and discourses that she as
a marginalized individual (because of gender and age) is expected to

follow. As Hurston recalls, "My father was with the mores. He had re-strained me physically from outraging the ceremonies established for the dying" (*Dust Tracks* 66). Although there are two women from the village who obligate Hurston to go against her mother's wishes, despite their gender, they are representatives of the patriarchal discourse that the father's demands embody.

When Hurston realizes that she will not be able to carry out her mother's wishes, it is then that the full meaning of their relationship is revealed to her. Her mother relied on her to be her voice in the midst of a tradition that denied her expression. Hurston remembers, "I thought that she looked to me as the head of the bed was reversed. . . . But she looked at me, or so I felt, to speak for her. She depended on me for a voice" (*Dust Tracks* 65).

In the face of the patriarchal traditional rites, Hurston is unable to fulfill her mother's wishes, a failure that would haunt her for the rest of her life, but which would also guide her in a new direction: "Now, I know that I could not have had my way against the world. The world we lived in required those acts. Anything else would have been sacrilege, and no nine-year-old voice was going to thwart them" (*Dust Tracks* 66–7). Hurston's first reaction to this tragedy is a sense of failure at not being able to speak for her mother. At the moment when she is physically restrained from doing what her mother asks (to not remove the pillow from under her head until she dies, and to keep the clock and the looking glass uncovered), both women share a bond of being disempowered and silenced by patriarchy. The legacy of silence that occurs at this moment differs in significant ways from the relationship of oppression that can exist between mother and daughter. While Hurston's mother influenced her by providing a model of a strong Black woman, at the moment of her death each woman's silence becomes the other's in a mutual exchange. This transfer is in sharp contrast to the legacy of silence that is many times passed from mother down to daughter. Although Hurston's mother can not physically speak, her daughter is even more powerless to speak for her and therefore loses her mother's last opportunity to assert her strong voice. The momentary loss of her mother's legacy is an action that alters the formation of Hurston's very character:

> If there is any consciousness after death, I hope that Mama knows that I did my best. She must know how I have suffered for my failure. But life picked me up from the foot of Mama's bed, grief, self-despisement and all, and set my feet in strange ways. That moment was the end of a phase in my life. . . . That hour began my wanderings. Not so much in geography, but in time. Then no so much in time as in spirit. (*Dust Tracks* 66–67)

The silence that so impacts Hurston at this young age is also symbolic of the silencings she would experience as an adult, particularly during her writing career. However, despite this negative silence, the sense of failure, as Hurston emphasizes, is followed by a desire to wander. As Lionnet notes, Hurston's mother's death symbolizes not only "the collective memory of her people's separation from Africa-as-mother and their ineluctable diaspora," but more importantly from a developmental standpoint, a destabilizing force in her life: "In that respect, the death of her mother represents the first moment in a chain of destabilizing experiences that forever undermine her sense of belonging to a specific place" (395–399).

The two facets of Hurston's wanderings help explain her progression through her adult life, particularly as represented in this autobiography. Her lost sense of belonging causes a crisis in her sense of self that seeks resolution in her journeys through time by incorporating the past, especially in terms of her community's heritage, with her present and helping to determine her future. She also seeks to reconstruct a sense of belonging in spirit, in terms of an emotional and psychic progression through the various encounters chronicled in the autobiography and found in accounts of her personal life. The text therefore represents Hurston's constant movement across the country, across class and gender barriers, and between marginal and central discourses. The physical and even more importantly, spiritual wanderings Hurston undertakes exemplify the complex inside/outside dynamics. As part of a reformulation of identity that is continuously wandering and evolving, this process illustrates the modernist nonsynchronicity of Zora's identity. She becomes an actor, "negotiating an essentially displaced and dynamic identity that is always in the process of transforming itself" (Konzett 84).

"Subjective Ethnicity": Identity as a Construct

This journey of the self from the beginning is a reconstruction of identity based on the awareness (in this case) of one's historical positioning and the mediation of factors of language, the subject's positioning, and relevant discursive frameworks. Hurston's active participation in and interpretation of this process is what Lionnet has called "subjective ethnicity." Through specific textual references she acknowledges that her life is a construct. On the first page she explains that the text exists "in order that *you may interpret* the incidents and directions of my life." Her readers have a function to perform with respect to her self-definition: they interpret the information given in order to form their own conclusions. However, as with any interpretation, there is a gap between reality—the author's perception and subsequent representation of that reality—and the reader's interpretation of that reality. While here Hurston welcomingly invites readers to draw their own conclusions, throughout the text she expresses reservations about the way in which others interpret her. Unlike adults who accepted the natural order of the world, Hurston asked why people were categorized in certain ways:

> I was always asking and making myself a crow in a pigeon's nest. It was hard on my family and surroundings, and they in turn were hard on me. I did not know then, as I know now, that people are prone to build a statue of the kind of person that it pleases them to be. And few people want to be forced to ask themselves, "What if there is no me like my statue?" The thing to do is grasp the broom of anger and drive off the beast of fear. (*Dust Tracks* 25, 26)

Despite others' natural attempts to categorize her, Hurston's reaction was always to assert her own sense of self—first, by questioning those categorizations and then by trying to fit where society said she could not (and at times succeeding in that). She converts the anger she would feel at being controlled against the enemy.

Fox-Genovese points out that "Hurston's queries about her identity, her statue, are a frank glance into her inner psyche that ultimately betters our understanding of the autobiography as a whole:

> Hurston should be understood as a woman who was, regarding her self-representation, concerned primarily with a "self" unconstrained by gender in particular and condition in general. . . . [S]he wrestled—not always gracefully or successfully—with the expectations of those around her. (173)

This sense of resistance is another point of comparison with Jesus. Both women lived as marginalized beings because of their gender and socioeconomic status and yet continually fought against those restrictions. Jesus's refusal of marriage proposals was her fight against the expectations of domesticity that society imposed on her, just as Hurston fights against the societal limitations of the American South (*Child of the Dark* 1, 44). Although Campos comments on a metaphysical construction of identity while Hurston and Jesus focus on the socioeconomically grounded meaning of identity construction Hurston's reformulated statue is also constructed on a linguistic level. Her concern is not only how to avoid being categorized by the more centralized discourse of society and its embodiment in her family, but also how to represent in writing the identity she desires.

It is the love of language and books that allows Hurston to take back her identity and cultivate a sense of uniqueness: "In a way this early reading gave me great anguish through all my childhood and adolescence. My soul was with the gods and my body in the village. People just would not act like gods" (*Dust Tracks* 41). Reading was not just about traveling to another place outside of her circumstances, but also traveling within herself. As occurred at many other times in her life, and many other sections in her autobiography, Hurston recognizes her difference: wanting to be with the gods (and the qualities of enlightenment, self-knowledge, and education that they represent) while seeing around her only reminders of the village (representing qualities of mundanity, ignorance, blindness, normalcy, and conformity). One result of this difference, and more importantly, of her awareness of it, was a sense of anguish at the constant tension. However, it is this crossing of seemingly opposite approaches to knowledge that not only causes a sense of uneasiness but is part of the text's and author's hybridity.

On a thematic level Jesus also asserts her difference for her readers. Her various assurances to her reader of her upstanding moral behavior emphasize the distance from this lifestyle and attitude that her formal education and love of learning has provided her (*Child of the Dark* 68). For example, in the opening paragraph of *Dust Tracks* when Hurston gives the special history of her town, one can see how she and Jesus constantly assert their difference for their readers.

Historical Positioning and the Tensions of Identity

Hurston's declaration of her difference was also part of a tenuous balancing act between inclusivity and separation from particular communities. Part of this inclusion was a consequence of her belonging to specific racial, gendered, and class communities. Her life moved in and out of these categorizations, at times using them as markers while at other times rejecting their limitations. Ultimately Hurston's text shows her awareness of historical positioning and the tension her talent created between the community she came from and the community she spoke to in her writing. The resulting friction is a representation of a hybridized identity that subverts the racial, gendered, and class designations. This hybridity can in part be found in Hurston's continuous reinvention of herself in *Dust Tracks*, refusing in her own way to be neatly categorized. Jesus's views on race, and in particular the concepts of race pride and racial solidarity, are one example of her reformulation of the sociohistorical categories frequently used to define her. Lionnet recognizes the complex relationship Hurston has to race when she observes:

The resulting text/performance thus transcends pedestrian notions of referentiality, for the staging of the event is part of the process of "passing on," of elaborating cultural forms, which are not static and inviolable, but dynamically involved in the creation of culture itself. It is thus not surprising that Hurston should view the self, and especially the "racial self," as a fluid and changing concept, an arbitrary signifier with which she had better dispense if it is meant to inhibit (as any kind of reductive labeling might) the inherent plasticity of individuals. (386–387)

While growing up Hurston looked at others in her community to help her gain important knowledge about herself. However, the most disturbing problem she encountered was reconciling at times conflicting ideas on race relations. Her observations on the contradictory, at times hypocritical, feelings Blacks had about themselves, combined with examples of intraracial tension she found within the Black community, led her to conclude that the best way for her as an individual not to get trapped in these contradictions was to assert her individuality and not her racial identity: "Light came to me when I realized that I did not have to consider any racial group as a whole. . . . I learned that skins were no measure of what was inside people" (*Dust Tracks* 190–191).

Although on the outside she is marked by a skin color that includes her in a community that is important to her (the southern Black community of Eatonville, whose drive, self-enterprising spirit, and stories influenced who she would become), on the inside (both character and ideology) she finds difference that refuses to defer to racial limitations: "So none of the Race clichés meant anything any more. . . . I saw no curse in being black, nor no extra flavor by being white. . . . There is no *The Negro* here. Our lives are so diversified, internal attitudes so varied, appearances and capabilities so different, that there is no possible classification so catholic that it will cover us all, except My people! My people!" (*Dust Tracks* 191–192). The result is a careful balancing act, where her Blackness as a link to the Eatonville community is never abandoned while her Blackness as the basis for an ideological link to the Blacks of her time is critically questioned. The multiple relationality of Blackness proves to Hurston that it is "a complicated cultural construction rife with contradictions and multiplicities. It can be negotiated, strategically advanced and/or retracted" (Konzett 84). Ultimately, as a fictional creation, its identity lies not in consistent historical, biological, and social ties between individuals but in "dislocation and difference" (Konzett 85).

Hurston does not just declare her individuality (and therefore, in a sense, universality) but also exposes the flaws she sees in the political racial ideas of her time. For example, concepts such as "race solidarity" for her are nonexistent and artificial impositions because of the variety that exists within the Black community: "It is freely admitted that it does not exist among Negroes. . . . Our interests are too varied. Personal benefits run counter to race lines too often for it to hold" (*Dust Tracks* 179). These criticisms serve as Hurston's declaration of the "fluid self" by telling her reader that she refuses to have others dictate her political views and behavior.

As McKay points out, the at times almost integrationist nonconfrontational racial politics was Hurston's way of not accepting the oppression of Blacks as a defining element, nor writing a text that could be categorized as race literature (188). These nonconfrontational politics brought Hurston much criticism by members of the Harlem literati of the 1940s and widened the gap between herself and her Black audience while narrowing the gap with her White readers (181–182). This complex relation with race is a tension Hurston shares with Frantz Fanon, who recognized the inadequacy of binary terms of Black-White relationships in resolving these tensions: "Unlike Fanon, Hurston did not develop the visionary perspective into a revolutionary one, but her mystical desire to be one with the universe stems from a similar utopian need for a "waking dream" of the possible that might inspire us to see beyond the constraints of the here and now to the idealized vision of a perfect future (Lionnet 392–393).[1] Just as Hurston distinguishes between different race politics, so too does Jesus divide Black Brazilians into separate categories based on class affiliation and a sense of personal worth (*Child of the Dark* 51). Jesus uses supposed classifications from Africa and the example of a young Black Brazilian boy's moral decay to demonstrate for her readers the need to judge each person separately.The question then arises as to which Negro Jesus can be classified as: the regular "Negro tu," the refined "Negro Yes Sir," or the worthless "Negro turututu." Hurston, for example, constantly emphasizes her inclusion in two worlds: Eatonville's southern folk circle and Barnard's educated circles. Similarly, Jesus's movement between her role as a poet of the poor and identification as favelada contrasted with references to her moral character and educational formation lead one to believe that she would be classified as "Negro Yes Sir" (or in her case "Yes Madam")—a bridge between Black Brazilians who have been able to find a place in high society and the marginalized poor Black Brazilians.

Gendered Community: Multiple Feminine Identities

The complexity of Hurston's self-identification can especially be seen when we consider not only her racial allegiances but also the relation to issues of gender. In one statement about her first realization that she was Colored, Hurston links gender and race: "Jacksonville made me know that I was a little colored girl. Things were all about the town to point this out to me," while in the chapter "My People! My People!" she declares, "I maintain that I have been a Negro three times—a Negro baby, a Negro girl and a Negro woman," only to end the chapter by asserting that there is no "The Negro"(*Dust Tracks* 70, 192).

As a response provoked by these examples Fox-Genovese asks, "If the Negro does not exist, and the only times that she has been a Negro included the times at which she was a girl and a woman, then what? The reader is left to complete the syllogism" (195). The implication is that if gender is so closely linked to a nonexistent concept of race, then does that not suggest that gender too is nonexistent?

The answer can be found by further examining Hurston's opinions about gender and about the women with whom she has come into contact. As with Jesus, Hurston knew as a child that she did not want to fit the proscribed gender roles to which society and particularly the legacy of slavery had assigned and limited her. She expresses her difference by questioning the limits on her behavior and the conflicts she has with her grandmother over a woman's role: "My grandmother worried about my forward ways a great deal. She had known slavery and to her my brazenness was unthinkable" (*Dust Tracks* 34). This conflict highlights Hurston's struggle to formulate a sense of herself as a woman outside of the prescribed norms, including the limitations imposed by slavery, particularly on Black women. Just as she fought to leave slavery's impact on her racial identity behind, she sought to do the same concerning its impact on gender and her development as a woman.

Hurston in fact valued gender more than some of her statements suggest. As Raynaud highlights, the strong Black women in Hurston's community served as her models:

> The link privileged, be it friendship or hatred, is that between women. . . . Ultimately, the unifying motif of female friendship and rivalry, of female strength and courage, is much more powerful as a structuring device than the superimposed twelve prophetic visions. Hurston sees herself as a female warrior with a sword and a poet with a harp. . . . She sees her life and her gender, the process of growing up Black and female, as having marked her more than her race alone. Such a vision accounts no doubt, for the powerful female figures of her text, for her feminism avant la lettre, [before the letter/ahead of its time] to which contemporary Black female novelists have been so sensitive. (Raynaud "Autobiography as a Lying Session" 127–128, 131)

Her mother is just one important example of the strong women in
Eatonville who despite the threat and use at times of physical violence
maintained the upper hand in their relationships with their spouses.
Another important example is Big Sweet, a woman Hurston met and
befriended during her research in Polk County, Florida. When Hurston
first arrives in Polk she is immediately impressed by Big Sweet's direct-
ness: "She was really giving the particulars. She was giving a 'reading,'
a word borrowed from the fortune-tellers" (136). Big Sweet is important
because she represents with spoken word the strength Hurston has with
the written word, ". . . the unique privilege of using poetry as a swinging
blade " (Boi 200). In addition, as Meisenhelder notes, she represents the
model of the active, strong Black women that contrasts to the undesired
passive White women that Hurston met in her lifetime. (156)

Navigations of Class: Crossing Communities

As with any individual development of identity, race and gender are not
the sole factors influencing the subject's formation. Hurston first establishes that class difference within the Black community is an important
category to consider in the very first chapter when she describes her
birthplace, the beginning of Eatonville. She makes it clear that the town
in which she would eventually grow up was created by enterprising
Blacks who would form a community like any White town, in no way
inferior or representative of a stereotypical Black Southern town: "It was
not the first Negro community in America, but it was the first to be
incorporated, the first attempt at organized self-government on the part
of Negroes in America" (Dust Tracks 1). One important result of this
enterprising spirit was the election of Hurston's father as mayor for three
consecutive terms. As with some of her character traits expressed later
(for example her wandering spirit), Hurston presents this description of
her town as a way of showing part of the origin of her enterprising
spirit—formed by a community of Blacks that did not fit the typical
image Hurston most likely felt her readers would envision. However, it
is in the chapter entitled "My People! My People!" that Hurston expresses her belief in the existence of different classes within the Black
community and the important differences that exist between them: "My
people! My people! From the earliest rocking of my cradle days, I have
heard this cry go up from Negro lips. It is forced outward by pity, scorn
and hopeless resignation. It is called forth by the observation of one class
of Negro on the doings of another branch of the brother in black" (Dust
Tracks 177–78). What Hurston is describing for her readers is a mutual

antagonism between Blacks of different classes because of conflicting views of what their relationship should be to dominant discourses (like language and, as part of that, education) and dominant social systems:

> It is like this: the well bred Negro has looked around and seen America with his eyes. . . . Therefore, after straining every nerve to get an education, maintain an attractive home, dress decently, and otherwise conform, he is dismayed at the sight of other Negroes tearing down what he is trying to build up. . . . What that educated Negro knows further is that he can do very little towards imposing his own viewpoint on the lowlier members of his race. Class and culture stand between. (*Dust Tracks* 177–178)

While educated Blacks see their role as conformist, Blacks of lower socioeconomic classes, according to Hurston, feel no such obligation, instead choosing to behave as they see fit: "The humble Negro has a built-up antagonism to the Big Nigger. . . . [H]e does not resent a white man looking down on him. But he resents any lines between himself and the wealthy and educated of his own race" (*Dust Tracks* 178). Hurston does later point out that even the phrase "Big Nigger" is open to double meaning, also referring to the pride that Blacks may feel when witnessing the mischievous but harmless actions of other Blacks (Meisenhelder 145).

Based on Hurston's description, does she, an educated Black woman from Howard and Barnard, consider herself a conformist like the other educated Blacks she has just described? Given her viewpoints on other important issues (like politics), it is difficult to believe that she would completely subscribe to such a relationship with society. However, given the complexity of character we have seen to this point, especially regarding her desire to be a literary mediator between two cultures, it is most likely that Hurston in fact held to a middle ground between complete conformism or assimilation and total independence from socially prescribed behavior.

Hurston's views contradict commonly held stereotypes that group all Blacks together in one homogeneous racial grouping, disregarding any source of difference. Her reference to "the humble Negro" and the "Big Nigger" further clarify this difference among Blacks (be it because of class, culture, or another category) by placing it in the historical context of slavery. By referring to these categories Hurston is showing yet another legacy of slavery originating in colonial times and continuing in the modern, postcolonial capitalist society: the difference in working condition and social position of house slaves versus field slaves.

As further proof of Hurston's intermediary position I point to the conflict between her ideas and those of the black thinkers of the time in two important areas. On one hand we see the clash of Hurston's political beliefs on racial solidarity, race pride, and American policy (domestic and foreign) with those of other conservative blacks. On the other hand Hurston's personal politics, particularly her interest and participation in Voodoo rites, was frequently at odds with conservative blacks. Her differences drew criticism from the black sector and further complicated their attempts to label her as "conservative" or "radical" (Hemenway 283).

Part of Hurston's dismay and confusion, especially divisions of class and the ways in which people define and unite themselves within class through particular political beliefs, comes from the conflicting ideas she suggests that Blacks seem to have about themselves. She gives as an example the conflicting stories, criticisms, and praises Blacks would offer about themselves, on one hand praising their unique contributions to society yet at the same declaring examples of ignorance or stupidity by a Black person as typical of "my people" (*Dust Tracks* 180–181). We can better understand Hurston's confusion and dismay if we look at her opinions about the dynamics of racism in the United States. In her article "What White Publishers Won't Print" Hurston laments the general public's lack of interest in blacks in social classes higher than servants. This is exacerbated by White publishers' tendency to present their readers with very one-dimensional stereotypical representations of blackness. Instead they present invented portraits of upper class blacks "exploiting the race problem."

Hurston's resistance to racial and political categorization, especially as it regards class affiliation, is another important link between Hurston and Jesus. Because of her outspoken nature and her personal contact with some of the leading national and regional politicians of the day, once she achieved national and international success, Jesus was called upon by many to be a political spokeswoman of sorts for the disenfranchised. Both leftist and conservative groups sought to gain her allegiance, possibly in hopes of gaining through her a wider political base. However, referring back to the observations that Levine notes in his biography, Jesus's beliefs and actions were too "contradictory" in the minds of either political party to enable them to manipulate her to their benefit. For the politicians she did not prove the theories of the ever battling underclass or the conscious victim of marginalization. For others Jesus seemed racist and conservative (Levine and Meihy 20).

Hurston's emphasis on class differences among Blacks serves not just to highlight unfortunate difference but also to raise the issue of the existence of difference, a fact that racism prevented the majority public from acknowledging. The result for publishers was the continued propagation of these beliefs by ignoring images of Blacks that directly challenged these stereotypes. Lionnet notes how the presentation of difference within a given community serves an important role in deconstructing hegemonic notions of identity:

> I would thus argue that [Hurston's] unstated aim is identical to Fanon's later formulation to destroy the white stereotype of blacks in culture not by privileging "blackness" as an oppositional category to "whiteness" in culture but by unequivocally showing the vitality and diversity of nonwhite cultures around the Caribbean and the coastal areas of the South, thereby dispensing completely with "white" as a concept and a point of reference. (389)

Although Hurston recognized the importance of folk culture, as exhibited in the numerous books and articles written about her Eatonville community, as an educated Black woman who was able to move into another social position because of these opportunities, she was personally aware of the variety that existed in Black culture.

By bringing this diversity to the foreground and highlighting how it intersected issues of race, gender and class Hurston was revealing that "Black culture" was not constructed to oppose "White culture" but had an identity of its own. However, there was a second purpose behind her statements. By encouraging Whites to look past stereotypes and see the complexities of group identity, she hoped they would turn that critical gaze inward. The hope was that such an exposure of the "cracks" (or complex facets) in dominant identity combined with a recognition of the complexity of non-White peoples would lead to disarming the power of reductive stereotypes.

Jesus also felt it important to speak of her community, which was not always limited to Afro-Brazilians, but many times encompassed all races uniting under the category of class. One such example was her poetic observation of the protests of the poor against their unsatisfactory working conditions. The juxtaposition of informal and formal not only demonstrates a certain class sympathy but also illustrates the two worlds she mediated. Like Hurston, this tension was not an easy one to equate, precisely because of the implications and standards of each community. Like Hurston, Jesus attempted to separate herself from her neighbors—at times according to ethnic background, at times according to geographical origins. For example, while Hurston continuously questioned the solidarity felt among Blacks, Jesus questions the solidarity expected among the poor. As she states on one occasion, "I don't know why it is that the *favelados* are so destructive. It's not enough that they don't have any good qualities, but bad characters show up around here to make things worse" (*Child of the Dark* 67). The result is similar to Hurston's criticisms of race politics. Just as Hurston wanted to avoid the labeling of her autobiography as "race literature," neither did Jesus want her diary to be reduced to a manifesto of poverty written by a woman defined in specific limiting terms.

The varied political beliefs both women held is also indicative of attempts to reflect their identities in processes that were not exclusively linked to their awareness of their historical positioning and therefore, not leading them to feel obligated by their social conditions to subscribe to one political agenda over another. Instead, their political beliefs were determined by a variety of factors, which included their historical positioning, education, and believed (and desired) relationship to dominant social discourses.

Reformulation of Identity and the Woman Writer of Color

In the end significant parallels in the effects of dislocation and difference can be made between Zora Neale Hurston's life and that of the Brazilian writer Carolina Maria de Jesus. Both women started from fairly humble positions and were able to achieve success through their literary talents, which in part drew on their beginnings for inspiration and as part of their artistic vision. However, neither woman's success was able to maintain itself and insure a secure end to their lives. Both women died in relative poverty, and both were subsequently forgotten for a time in the literary circles of their respective countries until there was a revived interest in their works and contributions. This raises important questions about the pressures on women authors, especially in a field still dominated by men, and about the lack of support for them once they have reached a certain level of success. Even during their success, their pressures to present an image in their published works that did not coincide with what is later revealed in their original manuscripts shows the ability of publishers and White society in general to mutilate the cosmic self claimed in the autobiography (Meisenhelder 172). This attempt to silence the autobiographical voice is just as relevant for Jesus. In the context of affirmation of power for women in general, a similar dynamic takes place with Macabéa's relationship with Rodrigo S. M. and Campos's protagonist looking out to sea. These questions of power and representation are also complicated by issues specific to women writers of color, in this case of African descent, whose very educational and social formation as well as their literary production deal with the confrontations between marginalized and dominant discourses of self-articulation.

Identity beyond Historical Positioning:
Reconfigurations of Time and Memory

Hurston's transgression of boundaries includes not just socioeconomic categories but also time and memory. As we have seen with the table of contents of her text, past, present, and future are not categories to which she must strictly adhere. As Boi states, "Her 'self-portraying' is not an event, but an appropriation of the event. She destructures the domination of time and opens a way of telling that is not controlled by past events" (195).

One example is found in chapter 7, "Jacksonville and After," when Hurston relates her confrontation with her stepmother after years of seeing her manipulate her father. When she recounts that her father finally divorced this woman, Hurston writes, "And that is all that woman rated. But, you understand, this was six years after I went up to Jacksonville. I put it in right here because I was thinking so hard" (*Dust Tracks* 78).

Like Jesus, Hurston uses these narratives to move in and out of positions of marginality and interactions with central discourses while continuously acknowledging that where her journey, and consequently identity reformulation, ends is unknown to her. This is evidenced by the constant references to the act of wandering. From her early childhood, Hurston recalls always moving: "[I]t seems that I just took to walking and kept the thing a'going. The strangest thing about it was that once I found the use of my feet, they took to wandering. I always wanted to go" (*Dust Tracks* 22). Raynaud notes that the title *Dust Tracks on a Road* exemplifies "the temporariness of the traces left on a road, the fleetingness of dust announce the silences and the voluntary omissions" (113). These shifting traces can also be combined with the constantly shifting declarations (and important communal traits) that Hurston makes about herself in the text to underscore her reformulation of identity. What it also demonstrates is how she uses her autobiography to represent this process in such a way that, while suffering to an extent the impositions of dominant discourse, she is able to find and create empowering ways of subverting these power structures to benefit herself and her community. Her particular metafictional references to her process of writing, the ethos of mobility that informs her creative act, and her temporal manipulations exemplify the intersection of a hybrid discourse and modernist nonsynchronicity.

Like Jesus, Hurston's textual and personal journey explores the ways, as Feal and Hall note, that identities are given based on one's position in relation to past and present narratives. Hurston's textual movements back and forth in structure, tone, chronology, and content are also similar to

Campos's *Sabina*. She, like Campos, creates a work that cannot be easily categorized, like their respective authors, but is instead rooted in geographical and ethnic dislocation. Both use a displacement of time and memory, not as forces that dominate them but rather as elements that they manipulate and subvert in order to examine and reinvent themselves, to create an empowering sense of difference.

Hurston's manipulation of time have three important effects. First, it helps to affirm that life is not a chronological recounting of dates but rather the experiences and emotions that these events represent. Second, it helps to destabilize the aforementioned categories that possess specific meanings dependant on the time periods in which they occur. Last, by affirming meaning in experience and emotions, it is yet another way in which she transgresses the traditional structure of the autobiography.

Silence as Voice: Hurston's Link to Jesus, Campos, and Lispector

However, Hurston also finds meaning in the spaces where words cannot express her reality. The theme of silence in her defense of an independent identity and her right to reconstruct it as she desires links her once more with Jesus, Lispector, and Campos. For all four women, Minh-ha's belief in the empowerment silence can give holds true. As she states, "Silence as a refusal to partake in the story does sometimes provide us with a means to gain a hearing. It is voice, a mode of uttering, and a response in its own right" (83). For all women silence is a moment of truth, a space in which their identity can be revealed, as they would have it, without the interference of external forces that would distort it. Hurston's and Jesus's manipulation of silence (differentiating these moments from the imposition of silence by dominant social and historic structures) gives moments of greater clarity, similar to Macabéa's brief moment of purpose revealed in the silence of her death. Similarly, Campos's protagonist looking out to sea is in a constant struggle to find that truth in the midst of forces that fight to silence her while imposing their own voice onto (her) story.

The strongest parallel nonetheless in the reasons for silence can be found between Hurston and Jesus. While Hurston had to fight against editors who censored her ideas in order to best appeal to a massive, most likely predominantly White audience, Jesus, as I have discussed, had to fight with one editor in particular, Audálio Dantas. The reasons for her censorship went beyond the need to correct grammatical and structural mistakes in her diary caused by a lack of sufficient educational training, and the need to correct esthetic mistakes (repetition of daily events) in order to make it easier for the reader to follow. As her *Unedited Diaries* show, Jesus's text also underwent the suppression of ideas that might possibly generate controversy.

Multiplicity as Creativity: A Writer's Control of Identity

The result of Hurston's multiple identity was to assert her identity as a writer "First, she gives us a *writer's* life, rather than an account, as she says, of the Negro problem." So many events in this text are figured in terms of Hurston's growing awareness and mastery of books and language, language and linguistic rituals as spoken and written by masters of the Western tradition and by ordinary members of the Black community" (Gates 264). I would amend this statement by adding that what Hurston portrays is a *reader's* life as well as a writer's, showing how the two are inextricably linked. What she reads becomes part of the material from which her writing style and content are derived. In her experiences with language and the process of literacy and the feelings they inspire, Hurston demonstrates how her ideas of what constituted her constant reformulation as a writer crossed 'the historically posited categories of race, gender, and class. One incident that demonstrates Hurston's defiance as a Black woman writer is her rejection of a marriage proposal by a Black graduate student with whom she is involved (identified only as A. W. P): "I really wanted to do anything he wanted me to do, but that one thing I could not do. It was not just my contract with my publishers, it was that I had things clawing inside of me that must be said. I could not see that my work should make any difference in marriage. . . . One did not conflict with the other in my mind" (*Dust Tracks* 208). Once again Hurston finds herself dealing with societal norms—this time regarding gender—that dictated that her individual interests and career not conflict with the role she was expected to play as wife, that love and professional calling do not mix in a woman's world. She was more than willing to accept the institution of marriage, but not at the expense of the personal space and opportunity for reinvention, self-exploration, and engagement with the community. Although almost twenty years and a continent away (given the specific historical, social, and political contexts), Jesus would face a similar choice in her life. Neither Hurston (as she explicitly confirmed) nor possibly Jesus seemed to reject the institution of marriage per se nor the other gender expectations that accompanied it, but both did reject the limitations that expressly excluded any reformulation of identity outside of the family framework.

Hurston's multiple voices and identities and her recognition of similar multiplicity in the Black collective are key elements of her complex self-definition. While Gates compares her divided voice to that of DuBois, both he and Konzett also emphasize a strong parallel between Hurston and the "psychological fragmentation" and nonsynchrony of a modernist esthetic of displacement and instability that fight categorization.

The implication of modernism for concepts and categories of self-definition is the exposure of the shifting, complex nature of these points of reference, calling into question any term—such as "blackness" or "whiteness"—that posits a central positioning as homogeneous concepts. As we will see later with postmodernity, these shifts and instability would be broadened in scope—referring to the identity of the self in general, as an impossible unified subject. While all the female subjects are ironically rooted in some displacement, there is a difference between a subject like Hurston, who viewed herself as a complete self with multiple facets of her character and beliefs, and a subject like Campos's Sabina, who found the idea of a unified subject close to impossible.

Expansions of "Feminine Writing": Hurston's Reformulations of Her "Statue"

The result of Hurston's representations of her multifaceted identity is a text that defines itself by being writing not completely dependent on or governed by any one dominant discourse (of genre or historical positioning). Instead her work navigates both dominant and marginalized discourses. One question that therefore arises is whether, on any level, her project of self-definition reflects a type of "feminine writing." As Boi notes, Hurston uses signifying, the lying contest, and similes and metaphors as weapons in order to exercise feminine and literary power (199). While critics like Raynaud see Hurston's use as writer and autobiographer of metaphors, colorful language, and similes as evidence of displacement, suggesting a reactionary position, these images are also a proactive mask: purposefully concealing and replacing reader expectations, societal norms as represented in the text, and structural elements. All these actions are Hurston's way of controlling the "statue" she presents and undermining the discourses (of language, literature, politics, and economics) that would establish strict boundaries within which she could operate (113).

She declares, "Life poses questions and that two-headed spirit that rules the beginning and end of things called Death, has all the answers. And even if I did know all, I am supposed to have some private business to myself. Whatever I do know, I have no intention of putting but so much in the public ears" (*Dust Tracks* 211). Here she is expressing her continued uneasiness with the autobiographical process and the implications of full disclosure that I spoke of earlier, and claiming a space—where she can control the dissemination of information, representation of her life, and, consequently, reformulation of her identity. This is an example of a feminized space because of two important factors: first, her emphasis on strong female relationships in her life and her community and their impact on her self-identity, and second, her transgressions of boundaries of gender, race, class, and autobiographical discourse.

When we consider Hurston's emphasis on strong Black women combined with the structural tension within the text and an overall manipulation of traditional male autobiography, *Dust Tracks* becomes a vehicle for more than the expression of all the different facets of feminine expression. Through her statements on the limitations of words to verbalize her hunger for spiritual growth and her propensity toward stories (about her life and others' experiences), we see a woman who knows language is flawed, as did Lispector and Campos, and thus is not always able to express the complexities of identity that she wants to communicate. Consequently, as they also realized, what accompanies this awareness is a recognition of one of the possibilities of language: the possibility of manipulation in order to reconstruct whatever identity one would like, for whatever purpose. From these statements and Hurston's earlier expression of youthful anguish at her recognition of gender roles, one can see that her "feminine writing" is a form of manipulation and subversion. On one hand her violations of the dominant codes of identity are a sign of her unease with the discourse and her place in it. However, as Bernd notes, the text presents opportunities to recover and assert a lost voice from childhood that exemplify feminine writing because they represent Hurston's rejection of categorization by society and literary norms, a willingness to embrace her displacement from it, and her recuperation of a place suppressed by dominant societal discourses through an assertion of difference.

Hurston's Wanderings: Movements Inside and Outside Discourse

In the end even Hurston's physical dislocation symbolizes her movement between discourses. When contextualized as a specific action, Hurston's "wandering" is one moment of empowerment that can be seen as a direct response to a specific moment of silencing. However, as is the case for writing in general, and the autobiographical act in particular, the whole text is the assertion of a voice that was silenced not just on the day of her mother's death, but rather, as her personal recollections reveal, at many other times throughout her life. A study of Hurston's travels shows the appropriateness of the use of "wanderings" as an important leitmotif throughout her text and life.

Hurston best summarizes her self-definition through the writing of her text and its subsequent effect on her identity when she exhorts her readers in powerful positions to remember "those who walk in the dust" (*Dust Tracks* 232). Like those who walk in humble places, Hurston is one of those who walks in the dust, constantly wandering, leaving temporary traces. The result is a process of negotiation and self-invention, constantly replacing the tracks of the previous self.

Conclusion

As Michael Dash observes in *The Other America: Caribbean Literature in a New World Context,* the migrations and intersections of social, political, and historical factors that affect identity can especially be examined in the literature of the "heteroglossic" Americas, a region uniting sometimes complementary, sometimes originally antagonistic forces. However, this definition can be extended to the larger region of the Americas, encompassing everything from Benítez-Rojo's repetitious islands and the multiplicity of Brazilian society to the United States' ever-evolving "multicultural society." While the reformulation of identity in this region is a complex process that can involve many different discourses, my book has focused on the use of self-representational writing by four women of the Americas to redefine both how they see themselves and how society views them. The common factor that unites Jesus, Lispector, Campos, and Hurston is not simply an originary position of sociocultural, racial, and gendered dislocation but a subversion of this origin and difference to a position of agency through varying strategies of hybridity that dialogue with and counter dominant discourses. The displacement of a specific racial and gendered insider/outsider across the boundaries of societal norms and literary discourses that is central to my original positioning of Hurston is the model in which all four subjects operate. It is the fulcrum that connects the dislocated favelada who incorporates classic Brazilian poetry into the story of her life and aspirations, the Jewish Ukranian Brazilian whose gender-crossings tell the story of the northeasterner in Rio, the Cuban émigré to Mexico whose multiple textual voices engage in the battle for one woman's control of her subjectivity, and the African American writer and anthropologist who physically, linguistically, and textually moves between rural Alabama and the elite circle of artists in cities like New York and Washington. It is the link that drives this displaced African American/Caribbean literary critic to take the journey with them.

As Trinh Minh-ha states "You who understand the dehumanization of forced removal-relocation-reeducation-redefinition, the humiliation of having to falsify your own reality, your voice—you know. And often cannot *say* it. You try and keep on trying to unsay it, for if you don't, they will not fail to fill in the blanks on your behalf, and you will be said" (80). Directing her comments at those women who have experienced physical and emotional domination, Minh-ha emphasizes the necessity to speak before being spoken for. Her strategy, rooted in a postcolonial context, can be applied to these four postcolonial subjects—Jesus, Lispector, Campos, and Hurston—despite their specific historical positionings. For the four writers in this study, this is one of the principal reasons they have chosen to write their lives and critical approach to identity. As a process of redefinition of the self, the marginality that serves as the starting point is not the final point of revelation. By the application of the theories of Vieira, Johnson, and Fox-Genovese regarding insider-outsider movement—or displacement of the subject—on an individual level to similar sociocultural, political, and economic frameworks, what their writing has demonstrated is that the interaction of the extratextual and textual subjects with the discursive framework leads to a reformulation of each writer's self-definition in a constant movement between marginal and central positions. The result is a commentary on and expansion of feminine writing as a hybrid action on several levels: structurally, socially, culturally, and in terms of gender.

For Jesus the years of marginalization as a favelada silenced her behind societal prejudices that defined how she would live and how much she could achieve. Through the diary structure she was able to create a forum in which her voice could at last express itself, socially and politically. The account of daily rituals of survival, the commentary on the struggles of those in the *quarto de despejo* (or garbage dump), and political observations combined with poetry that was the voice of the individual and disenfranchised community at the same time resulted in an expansion of the diary's limits. An equally important result was the genesis of a text that by its thematic and structural contrasts represented Jesus's creation of radical spaces of marginality while engaging in a constant dialogue with the dominant social and political powers of the time in an attempt to create an identity not limited to the favela but indicative of her complexity. Due to the overwhelming success of the diary, Jesus was able to turn a marginalized historical positioning into one that had access to central positions of power and representation through the distribution of her text. As the editor Audálio Dantas notes in his introduction to the second edition of *Quarto de Despejo,* Jesus's candor influenced students to found the Movimento Universitário de Desfavelamento (the University Movement of Removal from the Favela) and prompted the Câmara Municipal of São Paulo to confer on her the official title of citizen. This last title in particular is an example of the movement from marginality to centrality that characterized her life and writing. Becoming an official citizen was a statement of acceptance and belonging that society had previously denied her, yet she did not leave behind the key aspects of her identity that developed because of such difference.

This sense of belonging, however, was short lived. Jesus's position in society was a navigation of sites of alienation and acceptance which ended in a distancing once more from society. As Levine and Meihy note, this marginalization was in part due to disenfranchisement experienced in the beginning of her life:

> Carolina was weighed down by the scorn heaped upon her by society. Even though she shielded herself and her children from the squalid aspects of slum life, these conditions took their toll. By the time she was liberated from the favela by a stroke of fate, it was too late. She was exhausted, too beaten down to learn middle-class manners, to censor her thoughts, to remove the layers of suffering from her psyche, or to prescribe solutions for society's ills. (143)

Like Jesus, Hurston's marginalization was due in large part to societal devalorization based on race and class. As a poor Black woman from the South her self-definition was constantly under the influence of discourses that relegated her to the periphery. As was the case with Jesus, this distancing was not just of the individual but of the community and traditions she represented. However, Hurston was able through education to gain access to the upper-class literati of the Harlem Renaissance and of White American literary circles. Through her autobiography she was able to explore, problematize, and redefine what it meant to be a bridge between two worlds. The autobiography thus provides a space where structurally she is able to represent the movement between marginal and central positions of language and theme. As Raynaud notes, Hurston's manipulation of the autobiographical text is a form of resistance and the reestablishment of her narrative power:

> It might be precisely because autobiography, growing out of the confessional mode still places the individual in a relationship of subservience that Hurston must at all moments fake the autobiography without adhering to it. To fulfill the autobiography contract could mean to condone the power relationship, inscribed within the history of the genre, between the individual and God (or any of His worldly representatives),—here intensified by the relationship between Black

female writer and White reader. Hurston's ease in the persona
of the folklorist proves that the anthropological and the White
reader is always safer, and potentially more subversive. ("Autobiography as a Lying Session" 131)

Consequently, Hurston is able in the end to expand the boundaries of the
discourse itself by challenging how identity is articulated. In an expan-
sionist modernist application of this project Hurston takes a literary language that has been manipulated and "mutilated through experiences of
migration and disruption" to turn it into something "aesthetically productive in verbalizing dislocation and for imagining a new aesthetic of
nonsynchronicity" (Konzett 10). Nonetheless, as with Jesus, the constant
pressure by society and lack of support once she reached a level of success made it almost impossible to maintain a positive interaction with
central social, political, and literary structures. Her death in relative anonymity and poverty was only redeemed years later with renewed interest in her life and work by Alice Walker and the many readers who
would later read Walker's chronicle of this "discovery."
     As Minh-ha observes:

"I" is, therefore, not a unified subject, a fixed identity. . . ."I" is,
itself, *infinite layers*. . . . Whether I accept it or not, the natures
of *I*, i, *you, s/he, We, we, they,* and *wo/man* constantly overlap.
They all display a necessary ambivalence, for the line dividing
I and *Not-I, us* and *them,* or *him* and *her* is not (cannot) always
(be) as clear as we would like it to be. (94)

For Campos and Lispector their navigation between margin and center is
represented by texts that demonstrate this close link between the processes
of self-representation and representation of the Other. However, the challenge of the process is the impossibility of completely achieving an understanding of the Other. This reformulation of the self is represented by their
incorporation into the text through the interaction of various intertwining
narrative voices. What these two texts demonstrate structurally is not only
the decentralization and displacement of the narrative voice but also the
manipulation of textual order. In Lispector's *A hora da estrela* there is a
structural decentering through additions to the main body of the text that
question not only narrative authorial power but also the reader's interpretations of the perspectives present in the text. In Campos's text there is a
decentralization of time that is accomplished by intertwining the past and
the present in such a way that the present, and therefore the identities
constructed in the present, are continuously questioned.

However, these subjects are not just connected by what they say or write but as much by what they do not. In the context of the insider/outsider paradigm the movement between speech or revelation and silence or concealment is a significant defining element for all four women. As original excerpts of her diary attest, Jesus was at times silenced by editors, or silenced herself, in order to tailor her text to a specific readership. The result is a text marked by revelations contrasted with moments of silence. What is presented to us is, consequently, a voice that is unstable—revealing and hiding meaning and identity within a struggle for resistance and empowerment. In a parallel reading, Lispector's text presents a female protagonist who also moves from moments of silence to speech. However, it is between the lines, within the silence, that some of the most significant moments of self-revelation are found.

While Campos's narrative voices are never completely silenced, it is her protagonist Sabina who fights against being silenced by the other narrative voices. Similarly, the question, "Can my story be my own?" is posed not only by Campos's protagonist and Lispector's Macabéa, but almost fourteen years earlier by Jesus and thirty years earlier by Zora Neale Hurston. Studies of Hurston's original manuscripts show a silencing of controversial opinions and, more significantly, the complex multifaceted self that is present in Jesus's work. The difficulty for the displaced Black woman to posit difference as strength is no more evident than in these two women's lives and written works. The challenge for the displaced woman to engage in a similar project is what links Jesus and Hurston to Campos and Lispector.

When we see feminine writing as "the desire to make up for successive losses and displacements created by the insertion of the woman into a universe which has not invited her to participate in its organization" (Didier, qtd. in Bernd 26), these four texts display aspects of just such a project by using the diary, autobiography, and novel to reestablish an agency and subjectivity previously denied them. It is not on this level alone, however, that these texts display characteristics of feminine writing. While Campos's and Lispector's texts most explicitly demonstrate the constant interruption of the patriarchal discourse that is characteristic of "l'écriture feminine," Jesus's appropriation of predominantly male literary models is a similar retaliatory action. Given the hybridity of the texts themselves, a critical assessment of their place is also marked by destabilization. Their projects are not simply linguistic feminine subversions or sociocultural resistance. These theories cannot be strictly applied to the four texts without a consideration of the cultural differences in Latin America, the Caribbean, and the United States, nor can they be reduced to simplified relationships of a temporally, geographically, and historically bound subject.

One area in which the reconstruction of feminine identity can be further explored is in the movement between public and private spaces. While this book deals primarily with the interaction between the literary self and the autobiographical self that influences it, a fuller understanding of American (in the regional sense) women's self-representation can benefit greatly from an expansion of their identity formulation to the development of nationhood and of political identities. For example, with Jesus and Lispector it would be interesting to study their movement in and out of Brazilian conceptions of national identity. The work in that area can be amplified by exploring further their possible political activities, as well as the attitude of political powers toward them as women and writers.

Similarly, the question of marginality as a site of radical resistance, as explained by hooks, is particularly relevant in all four contexts. When placed in the Brazilian context, one can see similarities with the concept of Quilombismo, based on the *quilombos* (communities) of runaway Brazilian slaves (as well as other ethnic groups) that separated themselves from the oppressive institution of slavery to create self-sufficient communities. In Black Brazilian history and literature, the idea of renegotiating the center and the concept of reterritorialization are very linked to Quilombismo's social ideals. An important question to be asked therefore, is how one can use Jesus's text as a springboard for exploring growing emphasis in Afro-Brazilian literature on the idea of valorizing marginality to recenter representations of identity and distributions of power. Similarly, Lispector's text, when placed in the context of the Jewish presence in Brazil, exhibits movements of reterritorialization and reconceptualization of nationhohood. Campos's displaced text, when placed alongside the author's geographical multiplicity, also serves as a challenge to the question of diaspora—in this case, Cuban—and the widening of its personal and literary borders.

The concept of feminine writing, particularly in a postmodern context and beyond, is one that is still open and in flux, like the subjects whose expressions it constitutes. The constant interaction of peripheral and dominant discourses is a dynamic to be further analyzed, specifically as it relates to the continuous challenge to configurations of the masculine and the feminine, their intersection with categories like race, class, and nationality, and the displaced historical subject.

Notes

Introduction

1. For further reflections on the origin of the subject see also Philippe Lejeune, in *On Autobiography*. Laura Marcus, *Auto/biographical Discourses: Theory, Criticism, Practice* (New York: Manchester University Press, 1994), is another important classic text in understanding the development of autobiography as well as the ambiguity included in it.

2. I will be referring to these works with their original titles in Spanish or Portuguese. However, all textual references and citations are taken from the English language editions.

3. As Levine and Meihy note, the 1950s were characterized by attempts by President Getúlio Vargas to give Brazil the economic boost it needed (as problematic as his policies turned out to be) by proposing internal changes and encouraging monitored foreign investment in the country. The truth of these promises however was isolation of the poor from government "benefits," causing an increase in poverty in these cities. For further discussion of Brazil's social and economic situation at this time see Thomas Skidmore and Peter Smith, *Modern Latin America* (Oxford: Oxford University Press, 1989), 170–182. Edmar L. Bacha and Herber S. Klein, eds., *Social Change in Brazil, 1945–1985: The Incomplete Transition* (Albuquerque: University of New Mexico Press, 1989) also give a detailed look at this period in Brazil's history from Vargas's presidency through its authoritarian regimes to democracy.

4. In Levine and Meihy (37–42) there is a brief account of Jesus's life in the favela. The English equivalent of a favela is a shantytown—an area of residents living in depressed socioeconomic conditions. At the time when Jesus moved into the favela in Canindé these shantytowns were well established in Rio de Janeiro but new to São Paulo. These favelas existed and still exist throughout Brazil, but are concentrated in metropolitan areas where the poor migrate in search of better economic opportunities. The problem arises when they are unable to find jobs and have no way and little desire to return home to their original hardship and oppression. Thus, they establish communities in their respective cities using the materials available.

One other important explanation for the rise of shantytowns was the effect of São Paulo's postwar economic boom. Because of the sudden prosperity, developers started constructing luxury apartments on land inhabited by old tenements. The previous inhabitants were evicted in order to make land available for these projects, forcing these families to move to the low-cost housing on the city's periphery. These slums were the most affordable places that migrants and evicted families could live.

For further information see Nabil G. Bonduki, "The Housing Crisis in the Postwar Years," in Lúcio Kowarick, ed., *Social Struggles and the City: The Case of São Paulo* (New York: Monthly Review Press, 1994), 94–120.

1. The Radicalization of Marginality in Jesus's *Quarto de despejo: Diário de uma favelada*

1. Unless otherwise stated, all translations are mine.

2. One interesting example of her political development is represented in her account of her trip to the police station:

> I went to the police station and talked to the lieutenant. . . . The lieutenant was interested in my boys' education. He said the favelas have an unhealthy atmosphere where the people have more chance to go wrong than to become useful to state and country. I thought: if he knows this why doesn't he make a report and send it to the politicians? . . . Now he tells me this, I a poor garbage collector. I can't even solve my own problems. (*Child of the Dark* 33).

In this account Jesus seems to have internalized and accepted the very division of roles and empowerment that society has promoted. The lieutenant with whom she speaks is the authority figure with the power and access to the politicians. Here, Jesus gives her voice, power, and agency to him, expressing her desire to have him express the injustices she faces to the politicians. As a poor garbage collector she feels that she has no access to power and those who control it; her daily struggles leave little time to seek out those in power, and her problems are enough to resolve without trying to solve the problems of an entire community. Although she believes the person who can make the most change in Brazil is someone like her, that specific person is not her.

The most salient feature of this quote is the line Jesus's attitude draws between politics and her daily life (the personal). Although the two areas do intersect in times of crisis there is always a mediator—never direct access—and consequently never any true possibility of active, effective participation.

Nonetheless, this attitude is one Jesus seemingly modified as she wrote her diary and considered its potential for reaching a broader audience.

2. Jesus's *Diário* and the Hybrid Forms of Textual Agency

1. Jesus's larger collection of poetry, entitled *Antologia Pessoal*, presents the reader with previously unpublished poems written while she wrote her diary and further emphasizes two important points about Jesus's poetic production: 1) the volume of poetry produced attests to the fact that poetry was an important

defining force in her conception of her identity; and 2) Jesus's poetry was not just grouped by themes but also by style, further evidence of the variety she exhibited in her pieces.

According to João Pacheco in his introduction to the collection *Poemas de Casimiro de Abreu*, one quality of the young poet (he died in 1860 at the age of twenty-one) was his ability to touch both cultured and more common readers:

> [This common base identifies him with any sensibility. . . . One finds in him the ability to join together all the same even the educated and the average man, the simple sensibilities and the complex sensibilities; he brings them closer, unites them.]

> Esse fundo comum a identifica a qualquer sensibilidade. . . . Nêle se acha a sua capacidade de irmanar no mesmo até o letrado e o homem médio, a sensibilidade simples e a sensibilidade complexa; aproxima-as, une-as. (10–11)

Also following the path of other Romantic poets, De Abreu's themes included a certain banality in the themes chosen, naiveté with regards to the emotions stirred up by the surrounding reality, the articulation of associated ideas more by emotive ties than by intellectual ones, and a sentimentality that valorized a sentimental perception of the world above all (12–13). It is very possibly de Abreu's ability to write poetry that served as a bridge between the cultured and uncultured that attracted Jesus. It is a quality that her poetry reflects in that her intention when writing much of it was most likely to present it to a readership (probably very similar to the readership she expected for her diary) unfamiliar with some of the themes expressed and expose them to other opinions, interpretations, and realities.

2. As both José Garbuglio and João Pacheco reveal in their respective introductions to the anthologies of Gonçalves Dias and Casimiro de Abreu, both poets had poems entitled "Canção do Exílio" (Song of Exile) where they chronicled the common Romantic theme of a poet's longing for his native land and the loves left behind. While neither poet was a victim of political exile, both spent time in Europe, mostly in Portugal, studying various subjects (in Gonçalves Dias's case) and writing poetry expressing their longing for Brazil.

Jesus's "O Exilado," (The Exiled One) nonetheless, is just one of the various references to the poet that we find throughout her *Antologia pessoal*. Another poem where the references seem to indicate that the voice speaking, at least at that moment, is Jesus's, is "Quadros":

Quero-lhe propor um negócio	I want to propose a transaction
De sociedade contigo,	Of companionship with you,
Eu soube que tu tens dinheiro	I found out that you have money
Por que não te casas comigo?	Why don't you marry me?
Eu disse: o meu sonho é escrever!	I said: my dream is to write!

Responde o branco: ela é louca.	The White man responds: she is crazy.
O que as negras devem fazer . . .	What Black women should do . . .
É ir pro tanque lavar roupa.	Is go to the tank to wash.
. . . Os poetas que passaram	. . . The poets that passed on
Construiram castelos no ar	Built castles in the air
E quase todos idealizaram	And almost all dreamed
Somente os sonhos para sonhar . . .	Only dreams to dream . . .
Eu sempre fui vaidosa	I was always vain
Mas o destino comigo foi cruel	But fate was cruel to me
Obrigando-me a andar andrajoso	Forcing me to walk ragged
Pelas ruas catando papel . . .	Through the streets collecting paper . . .
Ninguém amou a poesia	No one loved poetry
Certamente mais do que eu	Certainly more than me
Nem mesmo Gonçalves Dias	Not even Gonçalves Dias
Nem Casimiro de Abreu . . .	Nor Casimiro de Abreu . . .
Minha existencia sombria	My somber existence
Vivo tão só neste mundo	I live so alone in this world
Minha amiga a poesia	My friend poetry
Que não me deixa um segundo	That doesn't leave me for a second.
(201, 205–206, 211–212)	

The first two stanzas seem to be based loosely on a situation in Jesus's own life, recounted in *Quarto de despejo,* where she turns down a marriage proposal by Don Manuel because of the importance of writing in her life. (See the entry for June 2, 1958, for Jesus's account of this proposal and her reaction.)

In the fourth stanza the narrative voice, like Jesus, laments that her life has been and will most likely continue to be one of suffering and a seemingly permanent sense of wandering. This sense of displacement and the crisis of identity it provokes is only muted by her poetry. This literary production is in the end her only companion, the only stable, defining force in her life.

3. One negative aspect of the collective side of any representation of Jesus's identity is that her triumphs were at times credited more to others than to her, constantly burdening her with stereotypes of favelados. Such was the case with Jesus's grammar. Critics, as I mentioned, debated Dantas's editorial control over *Quarto de despejo* while the improvements of later works were attributed to other important people in her life. Her increased grammatical capabilities and technical management of the language were two areas seen to be greatly improved because of her daughter Vera Eunice's input:

> Brazilian reviewers commenting on her writing disparaged Carolina's talents to the end of her life. Before she died, some of them commented on the fact that her grammar was improving, but they attributed this to her daughter Vera's help. One reporter complained that Carolina's improved "erudition . . . manifests itself [in] a certain mental confusion [that] perhaps robs her of the authenticity she showed in the favela .(Levine and Meihy 89)

3. Authorial Intervention in *A hora da estrela:*
Metatextual and Structural Multiplicity

1. In his introduction Vieira cites several critical reasons for the difference felt by Jews in Brazil, among them the existence of an at times subtle racism that cannot be reduced to an either/or, Black or White equation. Instead, this discrimination includes attitudes and behavior that foster apprehension, distance, and at times visible prejudice. Vieira notes that these at times subtle attitudes demonstrate what sociologist Roberto da Matta would define as the Brazilian dilemma: the contradictory relation between hierarchy and equality. One result Vieira cites is an interiorization that consequently fosters an already existent sense of difference by way of selective inhibition.

> In other words, the Jewish practice of selective inhibition becomes synonymous with alterity, providing a sense of interiority, a sense of an alternate self, by internalizing the external. As Starobinski aptly states, selective inhibition is "what we become by virtue of our ever changing relationships with the other, of our relationship with the outside, with that which we have never been, or with that which we have ceased to be." (16)

Because of the perspective of Hebraic culture and theodicy combined with access to writing, debating, and a questioning spirit, Brazilian Jews have been able to continue expressing their Otherness through literature by incorporating traits such as a tendency toward metafictional and prophetic prose; writings that resist facticity, rigid genres, or authoritarian history; and an emphasis on prophetic thinking.

2. As Barbosa notes, "Language, more than characterization, theme, or social relevancy, plays an outstanding role in Lispector's fiction. At the same time that she is concerned with language as a means to attempt to communicate, she examines the failure of language in its fullest implications" ("Reinforced Affirmative Reply" 234).

Sá points out the effect of this incapacity of language on any representation of the tangible:

> O que ela considera perigoso não é simplesmente a linguagem conotativa. É o próprio ato de escrever, enquanto ato de nomear. . . . O que ela questiona é a possibilidade subjetiva da linguagem e, portanto, a possibilidade do "eu" exprimir "a coisa". . . . [P]ara Clarice, a palavra é incapaz de atingir o inexpressivo. O indizível não é o inefável, mas o inexpressivo. (153)

> [What she considers dangerous is not simply a connotative language. It is the very act of writing, even the act of naming. . . . What she questions is the subjective possibility of language and, as such, the

possibility of the "I" to express "the thing". . . . [F]or Clarice, the
word is unable to reach the unexpressed. The unsaid is not the inef-
fable, but the unexpressed. (translation mine)]

3. If we return to Vieira's analysis of the characteristics of Jewish herme-
neutics that is found in Lispector's writing, we find an interesting connection
with Figueiredo's observation about the unattainable future represented in the
phrase "Quanto ao futuro" [As for the Future]. As Vieira notes:

> The Jewish cultural element of social justice and the plight of being
> affected many aspects of Lispector's life and writing even though her
> heritage was never a conscious central force. Nevertheless, we cannot
> discount the presence of Jewish culture in her work. Her spiritual
> quest reflects the plight of the modern wanderer—groping in the
> existential exile of human imperfection yet striving for the freedom
> that is just out of reach. (130)

In the last moments of Macabéa's death, when both the protagonist and the
narrator are trying to understand the relevance of that moment to the fulfillment
of her life (be it as a woman, or as the individual who has attained a state of
grace), she utters the words that reflect the hope in a future that would bring a
realization not found while alive. Macabéa therefore is an embodiment of the
imperfect, displaced wanderer searching for answers even until the end.

By contrast, in his article "Clarice Lispector and the Question of the Nation" Paulo de Medeiros sees *A hora da estrela* as a revision, and even subversion,
of the founding fictions of Brazilian nationhood presented in works like José de
Alencar's *Iracema*. In this context, the phrase "quanto ao futuro" is not a declaration of hope but the opposite:

> This denial of any specificity of an individual destiny can also be read
> as a denial of any collective destiny and thus as an erasure of the
> teleological conception of the nation. . . . [I]f one defining characteristic
> of any future is its openness, its unpredictable possibilities, by enclos-
> ing the phrase between full stops the text is effectively denying such
> openness and thus denying the possibility of the future at all. Macabéa's
> death is . . . the death of (a certain idea of) the nation too. (157)

4. One literary text that can help us understand the importance of rhapsody in *A hora da estrela* is "Prefácio Interessantíssimo," Mario de Andrade's introduction to his modernist poetry and explanation of the tenets of just such a
literary and musical endeavor. He writes that one of the goals of modernist
poetry is to spacialize time. Just as harmony in musical terminology represents
a superposition of notes, resulting in a simultaneity of sound, so also did modernist poetry seek to represent simultaneity and thus show the rapid pace of
modern times and thought.

5. The text contains many manifestations of violence articulated with gender and narrative: "There is, first, a mimetic violence: the representation of dominating or aggressive interactions between men and women, often set in the family or placed within larger systems of social and even racial oppression. . . . [I]n larger terms, she writes about the multiple violences unavoidably present in biologic, psychic, and social life" (Peixoto xiii).

Thus, as a victim on many levels of biological, psychological, and social violence Macabéa frequently experiences feelings of loss. However, the recognition of these feelings is only possible when she acknowledges the violence surrounding her. More often than not she engages in a negation of reality stemming from a lack of comprehension of her rights and therefore, a lack of awareness of her inequality (both socially and economically). In the beginning of the text for example, Macabéa rarely admits to any feelings of loss. In fact, as she tells Olímpico, she does not even really remember her life with her parents. As Rodrigo tells us, Macabéa "didn't know how to embellish reality. For her, reality was too enormous to grasp. Besides, the word reality meant nothing to her" (Lispector, *Hour of the Star* 33). Macabéa knows she is poor but has never understood what it means, in part because she grew up expecting nothing from life. Nevertheless, the reader gradually sees changes in this philosophy particularly during (and after) her relationship with Olímpico.

One evidence of this is her reaction on the days when she does not go to work and instead chooses to take part in other activities. The first day she describes the surprising freedom that she feels, being alone and able to experience a "happiness" that her daily life has never allowed her. The third time we see Macabéa not going to work is when she decides to visit the psychic Madame Carlota. After receiving the "good news" about the new life that awaits her, Macabéa expresses—through the narrator—her newfound joy: "Only now did she realize that her life had been miserable. She felt like weeping as she perceived the other side. For as I've already stated, until this moment Macabéa had thought of herself as being happy. . . . If she was no longer herself, this signified a loss that counted as a gain" (Lispector, *Hour of the Star* 78–79). This realization is near the end of Macabéa's gradual awareness of the complexity of her humanity, a humanity that she has always had difficulty acknowledging. Up to this point and as a result of her underdeveloped sense of identity and lack of belonging to a group, we have seen a Macabéa who kept this sense of loss with her, not attempting to construct an identity. However, through the course of the text this cycle is one she does slowly break.

6. The events of Macabéa's life and the narration of her experiences in Rio de Janeiro result in a text with multiple tones reflecting the different phases in the protagonist's experience as well as the conflicting emphases of the author, Clarice Lispector, and narrator, Rodrigo S. M. The two titles "Registro dos fatos antecedentes" and "História lacrimogênica de Cordel" serve as proof of this. On their own, each is presented as an all-encompassing summary of the text's narrative tone and focus but, as with the other titles, is immediately questioned by the use of the preposition *ou* (or), which presents the following title as an equally viable alternative to the first one, thus emphasizing the multiplicity of interpretation and voice in *A hora da estrela*.

7. See also Vieira's application of Levinas's theories of the advantages of pluralism when relating to the Other:

> In *Totality and Infinity* the French phenomenological thinker Emmanuel Levinas claims that pluralism informs the notion that totalitarian thinking may not only jeopardize or limit the individuality of the other but may also limit's one's own individuality: "Pluralism implies a radical alterity of the other whom I do not simply *conceive* by relation to myself, but *confront* out of my egoism." Levinas sees the effectiveness of pluralism via alterity as recurring "out of my egoism"—that is, beyond and outside. (17)

4. Textual Cross-Gendering of the Self and the Other in Lispector's *A hora da estrela*

1. To understand this subversion and its purpose it is necessary to comprehend the story that will be, as Rodrigo states, composed of seven characters and a traditionally structured, chronological narrative development. The progression of the text, nonetheless, will reveal yet another misrepresentation in the narrator's structurization of Macabéa's story. *Hour of the Star* is in fact composed of eleven characters, including death, which turns out to have as vital a role in the story's progression as the narrator. Part of the rationale behind the seven characters has to do with the origin of Macabéa's name.

2. In the "Foreword" of *Pedagogy of the Oppressed* Richard Schaull notes that Paulo Freire emphasizes the empowering objective all individuals share:

> Freire . . . operates on one basic assumption: that man's ontological vocation (as he calls it) is to be a Subject who acts upon and transforms his world, and in so doing moves toward ever new possibilities of fuller and richer life individually and collectively. . . . Provided with the proper tools for such encounter, he can gradually perceive his personal and social reality as well as the contradictions in it, become conscious of his own perception of that reality, and deal critically with it. (12–13)

Although Macabéa never realizes the full social and political transformation that Freire espouses, her attempts to fulfill this ontological vocation center on an identification of her subjectivity combined with an increasing perception of the social reality that oppresses her. Despite continuous textual relegation to silence Macabéa becomes increasingly able to turn it into a critical, reflective act.

3. According to Lacan, there are three stages in the development of the subject. The first is the imaginary/mirror stage where the subject engages in the search for identification with others, particularly the maternal figure, and the integration of his "alienated image" through the use of fantasy and imagination.

The second stage is referred to as the symbolic and is marked by a separation from the mother and acceptance of the father. Therefore, there are two different writings that emerge: the father's, which is linear in nature, and the mother's, which is fragmented and disjointed. Finally, Lacan's stages end with the subject's access to the real (Agüera 532).

4. *A hora da estrela* contains many other spaces that Macabéa finds or creates in order to reformulate her sense of self into something that is not devalued in society's standards. One important example is her relationship with Radio Relógio : "Every morning . . . she invariably tuned into Radio Clock, a channel that broadcast the correct time and educational programmes. . . . Do you know the best thing I've learned? They said on Radio Clock that we should be glad to be alive. And I am." (Lispector, *Hour of the Star* 36, 50).

According to Elódia Xavier Macabéa's use of this radio program is proof of her linguistic inabilities:

Entre o esforço de falar e o resultado do esforço há um choque porque há falência da linguagem verbal: Macabéa encontra apenas um clichê, representado pela comunicação impessoal e distante de uma Rádio Relógio. (137)

[Between the effort to speak and the result of the effort there is a clash because there is a lack of verbal language: Macabéa scarcely finds a cliché, represented by the impersonal and distant communication of a Radio Clock.]

However, although to Xavier they would seem to be superficial, distant categories, for Macabéa these reminders of beliefs and cultural tastes are important actions, especially when contrasted with Rodrigo's assessment of her lack of self-reflection. For Rodrigo, Macabéa's daily existence depended on others: "Except that she needed others in order to believe in herself, otherwise she would become lost in the continuous spiraling vacuum inside her" (Lispecter *Hour of the Star*, 37–38).

Rodrigo's emphasis on her need for another individual reinforces his importance in and control of her life while underscoring his own independence from her. However, Macabéa's use of Rádio Relógio counteracts this characterization, presenting a woman who utilizes this medium to give her a sense of her identity (however flawed and limited her understanding) and who attempts to actively frame herself as a participant in a discourse, and not remain an outsider unaware of the discourse's existence. It becomes a means of leaving the marginality of ignorance for the acquisition of knowledge that brings her closer to the centrality of assimilation.

5. The writer and critic Ihab Hassan also sees silence as a key characteristic of postmodern literature of the 1960s and 1970s. The literature of this time period is characterized by characters who speak continually, without communicating anything significant, resulting therefore in a state of silence. (Hassan qtd. in Fitz "Discourse of Silence" 421).

For Lispector silence does have a component that is in part a negative metaphor for the lack of communication and the failure of language (Fitz "Discourse of Silence" 422), while in "Receiving the Other: The Feminine Economy of Clarice Lispector's *The Hour of the Star*," Archer emphasizes the ambivalent relation it shares with the feminine: "The problem is to assume the proper distance, to be close enough in proximity to speak for the other, while maintaining enough distance so as not to possess or incorporate the other . . . to leave the other intact in all its otherness while still allowing its voice. For one of the first definitions of the other is silence—just like the feminine" (257).

Archer defines silence as a possible danger that can result from the appropriation of the Other and denial of the Other's right to self-articulation. Thus she sees Lispector's feminine mode of expression as an ambivalence resulting from a sensitivity to the possession of other that counteracts the negative definition of feminine that equates it with silence.

One problematic aspect of Archer's argument that does stand out however is the assertion that speaking for the Other is a viable option when seeking the Other's empowerment without any problematization of this approach as contributing to silence.

5. Campos's *Tiene los cabellos rojizos y se llama Sabina:* The Multivocality of Identity

1. First narrative voice:

What do you think of the Latin American novels of the "Boom"? . . . If our novels are interesting for Europe, you know, it is because of the fatigue of Occidental culture, which like Narcissus is worn out from looking at itself in the mirror . . . Our world swarms with characters who are wildly excessive and bent toward myth, and our novelists will have to find them if they want to be great (Campos *Sabina* 13).

Second voice:

As far as my book goes, no, it has nothing to do with any antecedent, nor with the rest of the novels that could or should be written in Latin America. No, it does not pretend to name things, nor to discover the great myths that have the capacity of fleshing out our past, our present, and our future. I am more modest, you know, and besides I hardly believe in the present (Campos *Sabina* 14).

As she states at a later point in the text, "Remember that Paradise is always on the other side of the ocean. But in this novel there is no myth, merely an imaginary gaze that pretends to be a real gaze. . . . (Campos *Sabina* 131)

2. According to Eco in "The Open Work":

We have, therefore, seen that (i) "open" works, insofar as they are in movement, are characterized by the invitation to make the work together with the author and that (ii) on a wider level (as a subgenus in the species "work in movement") there exist works which, though organically completed, are "open" to a continuous generation of internal relations which the addressee must uncover and select in his act of perceiving the totality of incoming stimuli. (Eco 1989)

3. The fusion of Sabina and her lover is particularly evident in his many declarations of love to her: "I become you, and you become me. . . . I borrowed your visibility and it was through you I made my imprint on the world. I praised my own flame in you" (Nin 184–186).

4. The original can be found in the 1974 edition, p. 169. See Bruce-Novoa's assessment of the characteristics of Campos's earlier prose (43–45). He notes that one special feature of *Muerte por agua* is its combination of qualities of Woolf's, Sarraute's and Robbe-Grillet's prose in terms of the periodic use of third-person narrative, anonymous dialogue, and objective, detailed descriptions. Also of interest is Fabienne Bradu's interpretation of Campos's ouevre in "Julieta Campos: La cartografía del deseo y de la muerte." Bradu emphasizes the importance of symbols of death in Campos' work. In particular, he points to the constant tension between the fear of death and fascination with death that runs throughout Campos' oeuvre. (42)

6. Telling My Story: Compos's Rewriting of the Feminine Voice in *Sabina*

1. In her interview with Garfield, Campos explains the role of the news article in her text:

Yes, I took the announcement verbatim from the newspaper. It was never clear as to whether or not it was a suicide or murder. But it was a man, not a woman who died. When I was about to complete Sabina, in the last days, I saw the newspaper article. It seemed very curious that while I was writing the novel, all of a sudden I ran across that very news item about a man who died in Acapulco under similar circumstances. From the start I had already chosen that ending. (Garfield 89)

2. This fluid sense of socioeconomic position can be seen in the different class and economic categories attributed to the narrative voices. One example is when the narrator recalls his departure from Naples, when he left behind his friend Gabriela and the memory of a young boy and his father killed by the

police on the patio of an orphanage. While the young boy seemed to be from the lowest socioeconomic stratus or, no higher than the middle class, the narrator relates his friendship (apparently of equals) with a seemingly well-off woman named Gabriela who lived in a villa in Naples. A few sentences later he has transported himself back in time twenty-two years to his memory as a young boy in a small town victimized by murders: "I am on another shore, twenty-two years ago, and never have I read a novel. . . . I was around eight or nine then. The band played on Sundays but they went out shooting on the other nights of the week" (Campos, *Sabina* 98–99).

The narrative voice is later presented as an intellectual, and therefore, most likely belonging again to at the very least, the middle class. This is especially true if we consider that writing in Latin America was often a luxury that only a few could afford. In this section the narrative voice comments, "Writers have good memories. You do not consider yourself a writer, much less an intellectual? . . . [W]hatever you say may be used against you. It is a privilege of whoever exercises the holy office of informing others" (100).

3. The reference to Salvador Elizondo is to his text *El hipogeo secreto*, which the narrator refers to by name in the text: "Julieta Campos, the one who I am and am not, has written an essay on a novel titled *The Secret Vault . . .* " (107) (143). Nonetheless, as Bruce-Novoa points out, there is a very important difference between Campos's text and Elizondo's:

> Though *Sabina* is as highly intellectualized as *El hipogeo secreto*, and even resembles it somewhat in the dynamics of performance and witness to the act of writing, Campos avoids Elizondo's more sensational elements of eroticism and his penchant for the esoteric and hermetic. Moreover, while Elizondo places his female characters in traditionally passive roles . . . Campos privileges women as active agents: the narrators, creators, and recreators of their fictions and self-images, albeit within a world dominated by males. (46)

4. Laura Beard analyzes the representation of a fractured, disjointed self in Campos's text in her recent article, "Discordant Identities and Disjunctive Authority in a Perverse Narrative: Julieta Campos' *Tiene los cabellos rojizos y se llama Sabina.*"

7. The Autobiographical Pact and Hurston's Restructuring of Difference

1. In her article "Zora Neale Hurston's Autobiographie Fictive," Boi makes the interesting point that, contrary to most studies of Hurston's autobiography, Hurston's audience may in fact not be White: "More probably she is questioning 'the better thinking Negro,' the refined and cultivated negro intellectuals, the 'Race Champions,' who wanted nothing to do with anything frankly Negroid, . . . who drew color lines within the race (198)." I believe that this theory cannot be entirely

disregarded, but that references to the prominent Race Politics theories of the day, when contrasted with Hurston's explanation—for example, of different folk tales—lead to the possible presence of both audiences as her readers.

2. See Alice Walker's *I Love Myself When I am Laughing: A Zora Neale Hurston Reader* for copies of both articles.

In *Wrapped in Rainbows: The Life of Zora Neale Hurston,* Boyd describes the impact of the attack on Pearl Harbor on Hurston's autobiography. After the bombing, when the United States declared war on Japan, Hurston's publisher at Lipincott chose to pull from *Dust Tracks* her critical comments about the U.S. foreign policy, its role as a "beacon of justice," and her criticism of President Roosevelt that he "could extend his four freedoms to some people right here in America before he takes it all abroad, and, no doubt, he would do it too, if it would bring in the same amount of glory" (348–349).

8. Wandering through the Dust:
Textual Statues in *Dust Tracks on a Road*

1. Like Hurston, Fanon recognized racial prejudice: "What? While I was forgetting, forgiving, and wanting only to love, my message was flung back in my face like a slap. . . . I was expected to behave like a black man—or at least like a nigger. I shouted a greeting to the world and the world slashed away my joy. I was told to stay within bounds, to go back where I belonged" (114–115).

However, like Hurston, this is counterpoised against a desire to transcend these limitations: "Do I have to be limited to the justification of a facial conformation? . . . I find myself suddenly in the world and I recognize that I have one right alone: That of demanding human behavior from the other. . . . In the world through which I travel, I am endlessly creating myself. I am a part of Being to the degree that I go beyond it" (Fanon 228–229). Note that Fanon's admissions that he is constantly creating himself are similar to Hurston's subtle hints that she too partakes in "lying" sessions, constantly creating her "statue."

Works Cited

Abreu, Jose Marques Casimiro de. *Poemas de Casimiro de Abreu*. Ed. João Pacheco. São Paulo: Editôria Cultrix, 1971.

Agüera, Victorio. "El discurso de lo imaginario en *Tiene los cabellos rojizos y se llama Sabina*, de Julieta Campos." *Revista Iberoamericana* 51 (1985): 132–133, 531–537.

Anderson, Benedict. *Imagined communities: reflections on the origin and spread of nationalism*. London: Verso, 1983.

Archer, Deborah J. "Receiving the Other: The Feminine Economy of Clarice Lispector's *The Hour of the Star*." *Anxious Power: Reading, Writing, and Ambivalence in Narrative Women*, Ed. Carol J. Singley and Susan Elizabeth Sweeney. Albany: State University of New York Press, 1992. 253–257.

Arrington, Melvin S., Jr. "From the Garbage Dump to the Brick House: The Diaries of Carolina Maria de Jesus." *South Eastern Latin Americanist* 36.4 (Spring 1993): 1–13.

Aschcroft, Bill, Gareth Griffiths, and Helen Tiffin. *The Empire Writes Back: Theory and Practice in Post-colonial Literataure*. London: Routledge, 1989.

Barbosa, Maria Jose Somerlate. "*A hora da estrela*: A Reinforced Affirmative Reply." *Romance Notes* 29.3 (Spring 1989): 233–239.

———. "*A hora da estrela* and *Um sopro de vida*: Parodies of Narrative Power." *Chasqui: Revista de Literatura Latinoamericana*, 20.2 (Nov. 1991): 116–121.

Barthes, Roland. *Writing Degree Zero*. Trans. Annette Lavers and Colin Smith. New York: Hill and Wang, 1968.

Beard, Laura J. "Discordant Identities and Disjunctive Authority in a Perverse Narrative: Julieta Campos' *Tiene los cabellos rojizos y se llama Sabina*." *Narrativa femenina en América Latina: Prácticas y perspectivas teóricas*. Madrid: Vervuert, 2003.

———. "Navigating the Metafictional Text: Julieta Campos' *Tiene los cabellos rojizos y se llama Sabina*." *Hispanófila* 129 (May 2000): 45–58.

Behar, Ruth. "Foreword." *Cubana: Contemporary Fiction by Cuban Women*. Ed. Ruth Behar. Boston: Beacon Press, 1998. vii–xix.

Berenguer, Carmen, et al. Compiladoras. *Escribir en los bordes: Congreso internacional de literatura femenina latinoamericana*. Santiago de Chile: Editorial Cuarto Propio, 1990.

Bernd, Zilá. "The Construction of Femininity and Black Consciousness in Brazilian Literature." *Journal of Afro-Latin Studies and Literature*. Knoxville: New Paradigm Press, 1988.

Bilbija, Ksenja. "*Tiene los cabellos rojizos y se llama Sabina* de Julieta Campos: ¿Es Sabina lista para el diálogo?" *La Palabra y el Hombre: Revista de la Universidad Veracruzana* (Oct–Dec 1992):137–146.

Bloom, Harold. *A Map of Misreading*. New York: Oxford University Press, 1975.

Boi, Paola. "Zora Neale Hurston's Autobiographie Fictive: Dark Tracks on the Canon of a Female Writer." *The Black Columbiad: Defining Moments in African American Literature and Culture*. Ed. Werner Sollors. Cambridge: Harvard University Press, 1994. 191–200.

Bordelon, Pamela. "New Tracks on *Dust Tracks*: Toward a Reassessment of the Life of Zora Neale Hurston." *African American Review* 3.1 (Spring 1997): 5–21.

———. "Zora Neale Hurston: A Biographical Essay." *Go Gator and Muddy the Water: Writings by Zora Neale Hurston from the Federal Writers' Project*. Ed. Pamela Bordelon. New York: W. W. Norton, 1999.

Boyd, Valerie. *Wrapped in Rainbows: The Life of Zora Neale Hurston*. New York: Scribner, 2003.

Bradu, Fabienne. "Julieta Campos: La cartografia del deseo y de la muerte." *Vuelta* 11 (1987): 42–46, 128.

Bruce-Novoa, Juan. "Julieta Campos' *Sabina*: In the Labyrinth of Intertextuality." *Third Woman* 2.2 (1984): 43–63.

Bueno, Eva Paulino. "Carolina Maria de Jesus in the Context of Testimonios: Race, Sexuality, and Exclusion." *Criticism* 41.2 (Spring 1999): 257–284.

Bunkers, Suzanne. "Diaries: Public and Private Records of Women's Lives." *Legacy* 7.2 (Fall 1990): 17–27.

Burns, E. Bradford. *A History of Brazil*. New York: Columbia University Press, 1993.

Butterfield, Stephen. *Black Autobiography in America*. Amherst: University of Massachusettes Press, 1974.

Campos, Julia. *Celina o los gatos*. México: Siglo Vientiuno Editores, 1987.

———. *La herencia obstinada: análisis de cuentos nahuas*. México: Fondo de Cultura Económica, 1982.

———. *El miedo de perder a Eurídice*. México, D. F.: Joaquín Mortiz, 1979.

———. *Función de la novela*. México: Editorial Joaquín Mortiz, 1973.

———. *La imagen en el espejo*. México: Universidad Nacional Aútónoma de México, 1965.

———. "Julieta Campos." By Evelyn Picon Garfield. *Women's Voices from Latin America: Interviews with Six Contemporary Authors*. Detroit: Wayne State University Press, 1985, 73–96.

———. *Muerte por agua*. México: Fondo de cultura económica, 1965.

———. *Oficio de leer*. México: Fondo de cultura económica, 1971.

———. *She Has Reddish Hair and Her Name is Sabina*. Trans. Leland Chambers. Athens: University of Georgia Press, 1993.

———. *Tiene los cabellos rojizos y se llama Sabina*. Mexico City: Joaquín Mortiz, 1974.

Castillo, Debra. *Talking Back: Toward a Latin American Feminist Literary Criticism*. Ithaca: Cornell University Press, 1992.

Childers, Joseph, and Gary Hentzi, eds. *The Columbia Dictionary of Modern Literary and Cultural Criticism.* New York: Columbia University Press, 1995.

Cixous, Hélène. "The Laugh of the Medusa." *Critical Theory Since 1965.* Ed. Hazard Adams and Leroy Searle. Tallahassee: Florida State University Press, 1986. 308–321.

Conley, Verena. *Hélène Cixous.* Toronto: University of Toronto Press, 1992.

Cortazar, Julio. *Rayuela.* Buenos Aires: Editorial Sudamericana, 1961.

Crespo, Angel, ed. *Antologia de la poesía brasileña: Desde el romanticismo a la generación del Cuarenta y Cinco.* Barcelona: Seix Barral, 1973.

Damasceno, Leslie. "Narrative Distancing: The Male Narrator and the Female Camera in Susana Amaral's *The Hour of the Star.*" Princeton: Department of Romance Languages, Princeton University.

Dash, J. Michael. *The Other America: Caribbean Literature in a New World Context.* Charlottesville: University Press of Virginia, 1998.

Davies, Carole Boyce. *Black Women, Writing and Identity: Migrations of the Subject.* New York: Routledge, 1994.

de Man, Paul. "Autobiography as De-Facement." *The Rhetoric of Romanticism.* New York: Columbia University Press, 1984. 67–81.

de Medeiros, Paulo. "Clarice Lispector and the Question of the Nation." In *Closer to the Wild Heart: Essays on Clarice Lispector.* Oxford: Legenda (European Humanities Research Centre of the University of Oxford), 2002. 142–162.

de Sousa, Mendes. "Mother, Body, Writing: The Origins and Identity of Literature in Clarice Lispector." *Closer to the Wild Heart: Essays on Clarice Lispector.* Oxford: Legenda (European Humanities Research Centre of the University of Oxford), 2002. 9–27.

Dias, Antonio Gonçalves. *Os melhores poemas de Gonçalves Dias.* Seleção de José Carlos Garbuglio. Rio de Janeiro: Global Editora, 1991.

Dias, Gomes. *O pagador de promessas.* Rio de Janeiro: Civilização Brasileira, 1967.

DuBois, W. E. B. *The Souls of Black Folk.* New York: Bantam Books, 1989.

Eco, Umberto. *The Open Work.* Trans. Anna Cancogni. Cambridge, Mass.: Harvard University Press, 1989.

———. "The Poetics of the Open Work." *The Role of the Reader: Explorations in the Semiotics of Texts.* Bloomington: Indiana University Press, 1979. 47–66.

Elizondo, Salvador. *El hipogeo secreto.* México: Editorial J. Mortiz, 1968.

Fanon, Frantz. *Black Skin, White Masks.* Trans. Charles Markmann. New York: Grove Press, 1967.

Feal, Rosemary Geisdorfer. "Reflections on the Obsidian Mirror: The Poetics of Afro-Hispanic Identity and the Gendered Body." *Afro-Hispanic Review* 14.1 (Spring 1989): 26–32.

Figueiredo, Maria Cristina Vianna. "A personagem feminina na literatura de Clarice Lispector." *Minas-Gerais, Suplemento Literário, Belo Horizonte* 21.1021 (May 1986): 2–3.

Fitz, Earl. *Clarice Lispector.* Boston: Twayne Publishers, 1985.

———. "Discourse of Silence: The Postmodernism of Clarice Lispector." *Contemporary Literature* 28.4 (Winter 1987): 420–436.

————. "Point of View in Clarice Lispector's *A hora da estrela.*" *Luso-Brazilian Review* 19.2 (Winter 1987): 195–208.

————. *Sexuality and Being in the Poststructuralist Universe of Clarice Lispector: The Difference of Desire.* Austin: University of Texas Press, 2001.

Fox-Genovese, Elizabeth. "My Statue, My Self: Autobiographical Writings of Afro-American Women." *Reading Black, Reading Feminist: A Critical Anthology.* Ed. Henry Louis Gates Jr. New York: Meridian, 1990. 176–204.

Francescato, Martha. "Un desafío a la crítica literaria: *Tiene los cabellos rojizos y se llama Sabina.*" *Revista de Crítica Literaria Latinoamericana* 7.13 (1981): 121–125.

Freire, Paulo. *Pedagogía do Oprimido.* Trans. Myra Bergman Ramos. New York: Continuum, 1990.

Friedman, Susan. "Women's Autobiographical Selves: Theory and Practice." *The Private Self: Theory and Practice of Women's Autobiographical Writings.* Ed. Shari Benstock. Chapel Hill: University of North Carolina Press, 1988. 34–62.

Fukelman, Clarisse. "Apresentação. Escrever estrelas (ora direis)." *A hora da estrela.* By Clarice Lispector. Rio de Janeiro: Francisco Alves, 1977. 5–22.

Galvez-Breton, Mara. "Post-Feminist Discourse in Clarice Lispector's *The Hour of the Star." Splintering Darkness: Latin American Women Writers in Search of Themselves,* ed. Lucia Guerra Cunningham. Pittsburgh: Latin American Literature Review, 1990. 63–78

Garcia, Carlos. *O que é Nordeste Brasileiro?* São Paulo: Editora Brasiliense, 1986.

Gates, Henry Louis Jr. Afterword. *Dust Track on a Road.* By Zora Neale Hurston. New York: HarperPerennial, 1995. 287–297.

Gilbert, Sandra. "Literary Paternity." *Critical Theory Since 1965.* Ed. Hazard Adams and Leroy Searle. Tallahassee: Florida State University Press, 1986. 486–496.

Gilkin, Durie Jo. "Fierce with reality." *A Women's Diaries: Miscellany.* Ed. Jane DuPree Begos. Weston: Magic Circle Press, 1989. 3–8.

Gotlib, Nádia Battella. *Clarice: Uma vida que se conta.* São Paulo: Editora Ática, 1995.

Hall, Stuart. "Cultural Identity and Diaspora." *Colonial Discourse and Post-colonial Theory: A Reader.* Ed. Patrick Williams and Laura Chrisman. New York: Columbia University Press, 1994. 392–403.

Hansen, João Adolfo. Lecture of Literaturas Brasileiras I Class. 11 Apr. 1996. São Paulo: Universidade de São Paulo.

Hemenway, Robert E. *Zora Neale Hurston: A Literary Biography.* Chicago: University of Illinois Press, 1980.

hooks, bell. *Feminist Theory from Margin to Center.* Boston: South End Press, 1984.

————. "Postmodern Blackness." *Colonial Discourse and Post-colonial Theory: A Reader.* Ed. Patrick Williams and Laura Chrisman. New York: Columbia University Press, 1994. 421–427.

————. *Yearning: Race, Gender, and Cultural Politics.* Boston: South End Press, 1990.

Humm, Maggie. *Feminist Criticism: Women as Contemporary Critics.* Sussex: Harvester Press, 1986.

Hunsaker, Stephen. *Autobiography and National Identity in the Americas.* Charlottesville: University Press of Virginia, 1999.

Hurston, Zora Neale. *Dust Tracks on a Road: An Autobiography* Ed. Henry Louis Gates Jr. New York: HarperPerennial, 1995.

―――. *I Love Myself When I am Laughing . . . and Then Again When I am Looking Mean and Impressive: A Zora Neale Hurston Reader.* Ed. Alice Walker. New York: Feminist Press, 1979.

―――. *Jonah's Gourd Vine.* Philadelphia: J. B. Lippincott Co., 1934.

―――. *Mules and Men.* Philadelphia: J. B. Lipincott Co., 1935.

―――. *Tell my Horse.* Philadelphia: J. B. Lippincott Co., 1938.

―――. *Their Eyes Were Watching God: a novel.* Philadelphia: J. B. Lippincott Co., 1937.

―――. "Historiographic metafiction." *Metafiction.* Ed. Mark Currie. New York: Longman. 71–91.

Hutcheon, Linda. *Narcissistic Narrative: The Metafictional Paradox.* Waterloo: Wilfrid Laurier University Press, 1980.

Jesus, Carolina María de. *Antologia Pessoal.* Ed. José Carlos Sebe Meihy. Rio de Janeiro: Editora UFRJ, 1996.

―――. *Bitita's Diary: The Childhood Memories of Carolina Maria de Jesus.* Trans. Emannuelle Oliveira and Beth Joan Vinkler. London: M.E. Sharpe, Inc., 1998.

―――. *Casa de alvenaria: diário de uma ex-favelada.* Rio de Janeiro: Editôra P. de Azevedo, 1961.

―――. *Child of the Dark: The Diary of Carolina María de Jesus.* Trans. David St. Clair. New York: Mentor Books, 1962

―――. *Diário de Bitita.* Rio de Janeiro: Editora Nova Fronteira, 1986.

―――. *I'm Going to Have a Little House: The Second Diary of Carolina Maria de Jesus.* Trans. Melvin S. Arrington Jr. and Robert M. Levine. Lincoln: University of Nebraska Press, 1997.

―――. *Meu estranho diário.* Organização José Carlos Sebe Bom Meihy and Robert Levine. São Paulo: Xamã Editora, 1996.

―――. *Pedaços da fome.* São Paulo: Editôra Aquila, 1963.

―――. *Provérbios.* São Paulo: Luzes [Gráfica Editôra Ltda.], 1965.

―――. *Quarto de despejo: diário de uma favelada.* São Paulo: Livraria F. Alves, 1960.

―――. *The Unedited Diaries of Carolina Maria de Jesus.* Ed. Robert M. Levine and José Sebe Bom Meihy. Trans. Nancy P.S. Naro and Cristina Mehrtens. New Brunswick, NJ: Rutgers University Press, 1999.

Johnson, Barbara. "Thresholds of Difference: Structures of Address in Zora Neale Hurston." *Zora Neale Hurston: Critical Perspectives Past and Present.* Ed. Henry Louis Gates Jr. and Kwame Anthony Appiah. New York: Amistad Press, 1993. 130–139.

Jones, Sharon. *Rereading the Harlem Renaissance: Race, Class, and Gender in the Fiction of Jessie Fauset, Zora Neale Hurston, and Dorothy West.* Westport: Greenwood Press, 2002.

Kaplan, Carla. Introduction. *Zora Neale Hurston: A Life in Letters.* By Kaplan. New York: Doubleday, 2002.

Klobucka, Anna. "Clarice Lispector by Clarice Lispector." *Closer to the Wild Heart: Essays on Clarice Lispector.* Oxford: Legenda (European Humanities Research Centre), 2002. 28–39.

Konzett, Delia Caparoso. *Ethnic Modernisms: Anzia Yezierska, Zora Neale Hurston, Jean Rhys, and the Aesthetics of Dislocation.* England: Palgrave Macmillan, 2002.

Krasner, James. "The Life of Women: Zora Neale Hurston and Female Autobiography." *Black American Literature Forum* 23.1 (Spring 1989): 113–126.

Kristeva, Julia. "Woman's Time." *Critical Theory Since 1965.* Ed. Hazard Adams and Leroy Searle. Tallahassee: Florida State University Press, 1986. 471–485

Lajolo, Marisa. "A leitora no quarto dos fundos." *Leitura, teoria & pratica: Revista semestral da Associação de Leitrua do Brasil* 14.25 (June 1995): 10–18.

Lejeune, Philippe. *On Autobiography.* Ed. Paul John Eakin. Trans. Katherine Leary. Minneapolis: University of Minnesota Press, 1989.

Levine, Robert. "The cautionary tale of Carolina Maria de Jesus." *Research Review* 29.1 (1994): 55–83.

———. "Different Carolinas." *Luso-Brazilian Review* 38.2 (2001): 64–73.

Levine, Robert, and José Carlos Sebe Bom Meihy. *The Life and Death of Carolina Maria de Jesus.* Albuquerque: University of New Mexico Press, 1995.

Lionnet, Françoise. "Autoethnography: The An-Archic Style of *Dust Tracks on a Road*." *Reading Black, Reading Feminist: A Critical Anthology.* Ed. Henry Louis Gates Jr. New York: Meridian, 1990. 382–415.

———. *A Descoberta do Mundo.* Rio de Janeiro Editorial Rocco, 1999.

Lispector, Clarice. *Agua viva.* Rio de Janeiro: Francisco Alves, 1990.

———. *A hora da estrela.* Rio de Janeiro: Libraria Francisco Alves Editora, 1990.

———. *A maça no escuro.* Rio de Janeiro: J. Alvaro, 1965.

———. *A paixão Segundo G. H: romance.* Rio de Janeiro: Editôra do Autor, 1964.

———. *Discovering the World.* Trans. Giovanni Pontiero. Manchester: Carcanet Press, 1992.

Lispector, Clarice. *The Hour of the Star.* Trans. Giovanni Pontiero. Exeter: Carcanet Press, 1986.

———. "In search of the Other." *Discovering the World.* Trans. Giovanni Pontiero. Manchester: Carcanet, 1992. 158.

———. *Um sopro de vida: pulsações.* Rio de Janeiro: Editora Nova Fronteira, 1978.

Lugones, Maria. "Purity, Impurity, and Separation." *Signs* 19.2 (Winter 1994): 458–479.

Marcus, Laura. *Auto/Biographical Discourses: Theory, Criticism, Practice.* New York: Manchester University Press, 1994.

Martin, Diane E., ed. *Women Writers of Spanish America: An Annotated Bio-Bibiliographical Guide.* New York: Greenwood Press, 1987.

Martinez, Martha. "Julieta Campos o la interiorización de lo cubano." *Revista Iberoamericana* 51 (1985): 132–133, 793–797.

McKay, Nellie. "Race, Gender, and Cultural Context in Zora Neale Hurstons' *Dust Tracks on a Road*." *Life/Lines: Theorizing Women's Autobiography.* Ed. Bella Brodzki and Celeste Schenck. Ithaca: Cornell University Press, 1988. 175–188.

Meihy, José Carlos Sebe Bom, and Robert Levine. *Cinderela Negra: A Saga de Carolina Maria de Jesus.* Rio de Janeiro: Editora UFRJ, 1994.

———. "O Inventário de uma certa poetisa." *Antologia pessoal.* Organização José Carlos Sebe Bom Meihy. Rio de Janeiro: Editora UFRJ, 1966. 7–36.

Meisenhelder, Susan Edwards. *Hitting a Straight Lick with a Crooked Stick: Race and Gender in the Work of Zora Neale Hurston.* Tuscaloosa: University of Alabama Press, 1999.

Minh-ha, Trinh. *Woman, Native, Other: Writing Postcoloniality and Feminism.* Bloomington: Indiana University Press, 1989.

Mishra, Vijay, and Bob Hodge. "What is Post-colonialism?" *Colonial Discourse and Post-colonial Theory: A Reader.* Ed. Patrick Williams and Laura Chrisman. New York: Columbia University Press, 1994. 276–290.

Nance, Kimberly A. "From *Quarto de Despejo* to a Little House: Domesticity as Personal and Political Testimony in the Diaries of Carolina Maria de Jesus." *PALARA* 5 (Fall 2001): 32–41.

Neuman, Shirley. "Autobiography: From Different Poetics to a Poetics of Differences." *Essays on Life Writing: From Genre to Critical Practice.* Ed. Marlene Kadar. Toronto: University of Toronto Press, 1992. 213–226.

Nin, Anäis. *Winter of Artifica and House of Incest.* London: Peter Owen, 1974.

Olney, James. " 'I was born': Slave Narratives, Their Status as Autobiography and as Literature." *The Slave's Narrative.* Ed. Charles T. Davis and Henry Louis Gates Jr. New York, 148–175.

Pavlovska, Susan. *Modern Primitives: Race and Language in Gertrude Stein, Ernest Hemingway, and Zora Neale Hurston.* New York: Garland Publishing, 2000.

Peixoto, Marta. *Passionate Fictions: Gender, Narrative and Violence in Clarice Lispector.* Minneapolis: University of Minnesota Press, 1994.

Piedra, José. "Literary Whiteness and the Afro-Hispanic Difference." *New Literary History: A Journal of Theory and Interpretation.* 18 (Winter 1987): 303–332.

Poovey, Mary. "Feminism and Deconstruction: Feminist Studies." *Feminist Literary Theory: A Reader.* Ed. Mary Eagleton. 2nd ed. Oxford: Blackwell, 1996. 262–267.

Ramos, Graciliano. *Vidas Secas.* São Paulo: Martins, 1968.

Raoul, Valerie. "Women and Diaries: Gender and Genre." *Mosaic* 22.3 (Summer 1989): 56–65.

Raynaud, Claudine. "Autobiography as a 'Lying Session': Zora Neale Hurston's *Dust Tracks on a Road.*" *Black Feminist Criticism and Critical Theory.* ed. Joe Weixlmann and Houston A. Baker Jr.Greenwood: Penkevill, 1988. 111–138.

———. "Rubbing a Paragraph with a Soft Cloth? Muted Voices and Editorial Constraints in *Dust Tracks On a Road.*" *De/Colonizing the Subject: The Politics of Gender in Women's Autobiography.* Ed. Sidonie Smith and Julia Watson. Minneapolis: University of Minnesota Press, 1992. 34–65.

Rivera-Potter, Alicia. "La creación literaria en Julieta Campos: *Tiene los cabellos rojizos y se llama Sabina.*" *Revista Iberoamericana* 51 (1985): 132–133, 899–907.

Rivera-Potter, Alicia. "The Role of the Reader in Julieta Campos' *Tiene los cabellos rojizos y se llama Sabina.*" *Hispania: A Journal Devoted to the Portuguese* 73.3 (1990): 633–640.

Robbe-Grillet, Alain. *La jalousie.* Paris: Éditions de Minuit, 1957.

Sá, Olga de. *A escritura de Clarice Lispector.* Rio de Janeiro: Editora Vozes, 1979.

Sarraute, Nathalie. *Martereau: roman.* Paris: Gallimard, 1953.

Simons, Judy. *Diaries and Journals of Literary Women from Fanny Burney to Virginia Woolf.* Iowa City: University of Iowa Press, 1990.

Skidmore, Thomas E., and Peter Smith. *Modern Latin America.* 2nd ed. Oxford: Oxford University Press, 1989.

Smith, Sidonie. *A Poetics of Women's Autobiography: Marginality and the Fictions of Self-Representation.* Bloomington: Indiana University Press, 1987.

Smith, Valerie. *Self-discovery and Authority in Afro-American Narrative.* Cambridge: Harvard University Press, 1987.

Spivak, Gayatri Chakravorty. "Three Women's Texts and a Critique of Imperialism." *The Feminist Reader: Essays in Gender and the Politics of Literary Criticism.* Ed. Catherine Belsey and Jane Moore. Malden: Blackwell Publishers, 1997. 148–163.

Surfiction: fiction now—and tomorrow. Ed. Raymond Federman. Chicago: Swallow Press, 1981.

Sturrock, John. *The French New Novel: Claude Simon, Michel Butor, Alain Robbe-Grillet.* London: Oxford University Press, 1969.

Vieira, Else Ribeiro Pires. "Can Another Subaltern Speak/Write?" *Renaissance and Modern Studies* 38 (1995): 96–125.

Vieira, Nelson H. *Jewish Voices in Brazilian Literature: A Prophetic Discourse of Alterity.* Gainesville: University Press of Florida, 1995.

Vogt, Carlos. "Trabalho, pobreza e trabalho intelectual (*O Quarto de despejo*, de Carolina Maria de Jesus)." *Os pobres na literatura Brasileira.* Ed. Roberto Schwarz. São Paulo: Editora Brasilience, 1983. 204–213.

Walker, Alice. "In search of Zora Neale Hurston." *Ms.* (March 1975): 74–90.

Walker, David H. "Formal Experiment and Innovation." *The Cambridge Companion to the French New Novel: From 1800 to the Present.* Ed. Timothy Unwin. Cambridge: Cambridge University Press, 1997 126–143.

Waugh, Patricia. *Metafiction: The Theory and Practice of Self-Conscious Fiction.* New York: Methuen, 1984.

Willis, Susan. "Wandering: Hurston's Search for Self and Method." In *Zora Neale Hurston: Critical Perspectives Past and Present.* Ed. Henry Louis Gates Jr. and Kwame Anthony Appiah. New York: Amistad, 1993. 110–121.

Woolf, Virginia. *A Room of One's Own.* San Diego: Harcourt, Brace, Jovanovich, 1957.

Xavier, Elódia. *Tudo no femenino: A mulher e a narrativa brasileira contemporánea.* Rio de Janeiro: Francisco Alves Editora, 1991.

Index

231